W9-BZY-463

DATE DUE

FEB 2 5 '0?

NAFTA and Labor
in North America

NAFTA and Labor in North America

NORMAN CAULFIELD

UNIVERSITY OF ILLINOIS PRESS

Urbana and Chicago

Library of Congress Cataloging-in-Publication Data
Caulfield, Norman.
NAFTA and labor in North America / Norman Caulfield.
p.   cm.
Includes bibliographical references and index.
ISBN 978-0-252-03492-3 (cloth : alk. paper)
ISBN 978-0-252-07670-1 (pbk. : alk. paper)
1. Industrial relations—North America.
2. Labor—North America.
3. Canada. Treaties, etc. 1992 Oct. 7.
I. Title.
HD8045.C325   2009
331.88097—dc22   2009009429

For Maria Elena and Margarita

Contents

Acknowledgments

My interests in writing this book go back at least ten years. While making revisions on my first book, *Mexican Workers and the State: From the Porfiriato to NAFTA,* in preparation for publication, the late Tracy Row, then editor for Texas Christian University Press, suggested that I include a final chapter that updated materials on developments in the Mexican labor movement since the 1960s. It was then when I began to think seriously about why the fortunes of workers and organized labor in Mexico and the United States had taken a turn for the worse in recent times. I resolved then to make my next project a study on why and how labor's fortunes had been reversed.

In 2002, my endeavors in this area landed me in Washington, DC, where for three years I researched labor issues in North America at the Secretariat of the Commission for Labor Cooperation, created as part of the NAFTA labor side agreement. While in Washington, I attended countless meetings on labor-related issues. I met and spoke often for long periods with a variety of individuals who worked in government, nongovernmental organizations, and private think tanks. Of course, I spent even more of my time interacting and socializing with my colleagues at the Secretariat, who as labor lawyers, labor economists, and industrial-relations specialists from the three NAFTA countries helped shape my understanding of labor in North America.

As a result, I am indebted to many people too numerous to mention. I do, however, want to express my sincere thanks to Tony Giles, now the Director General of Strategic Policy, Analysis and Workplace at Human Resources and Skills Development Canada. As a colleague at the Secretariat, Tony was very generous with his time, sharing with me his in-depth knowledge of the world of labor, especially as it relates to Canada. I also express my gratitude to Enrique de la Garza Toledo, one of Mexico's best and brightest authorities on labor. When I travel to Mexico, Enrique's warm hospitality is unmatched.

Fort Hays State University deserves much credit for providing me with financial assistance and large chunks of leave time to pursue the research and writing of this book.

I also wish to thank the readers of an earlier version of this book. As referees for the University of Illinois Press, they made comments on how to make improvements on that earlier version. I am indebted especially to David Montgomery, who as series editor for the press made suggestions that were insightful and a challenge to implement. The staff at the University of Illinois Press needs thanks for the work in getting this book to the reading public. I sincerely appreciate the support of Laurie Matheson, who as series acquisition editor believed in this project from the very start.

Finally, I express gratitude to my immediate family, who with their unflagging patience, support, and sacrifice of their time always make the unlikely a reality, including publication of this book.

NAFTA and Labor
in North America

Introduction

On January 31, 2008, in Mexico City's huge Zocálo plaza, tens of thousands of peasants and farmers converged from all over Mexico in convoys of tractors, motorcades, and other vehicles. Joined by labor activists from independent unions, the worker-peasant-farmer unity witnessed on that day delivered a powerful message to the Mexican government. The activists demanded the repeal of the North American Free Trade Agreement (NAFTA) entered into by the United States, Canada, and Mexico in 1994. In a manifesto, protestors declared that NAFTA had caused unemployment, the destruction of agriculture, the deterioration of purchasing power and wages, and extreme poverty to increase at alarming rates.[1]

In Chicago, home to the second largest urban concentration of Mexicans living in the United States, hundreds protested the visit of Mexican President Felipe Calderón by calling for the "renegotiation" of NAFTA.[2] At the same time, a leadership delegation of copper miners from Cananea, Mexico, visited Capitol Hill in Washington, DC. Backed by U.S. and Canadian franchises of the United Steelworkers Union (USW), Mexican miners petitioned members of the U.S. Congress to withhold a $1.4 billion funding package for the country's security forces proposed by the Bush administration.

The miners and their USW allies asked that Congress hold public hearings to investigate the use of the Mexican police and military to violently crush a six-month-old strike over unsafe conditions at the huge Grupo México mining complex located along the U.S.-Mexican border. In 2005–2006, the USW had conducted its own strike against Grupo México in Arizona on the grounds that the company had bargained with the union in bad faith. In the midst of these disputes, the USW filed a complaint under the NAFTA labor side agreement, the North American Agreement on Labor Cooperation (NAALC), alleging that the Mexican government had violated its terms by unilaterally removing Napoleon Gómez Urrutia as president of the Mexican mineworkers' union.[3]

NAFTA has been a target of worker protest since its inception because it is a visible representative of larger developments that have taken place in the global economy since the 1970s. While those developments have adversely affected labor, perhaps most important they also have paralleled the relative decline of the United States as the world's preeminent economic power. In 2009, this relative decline is projected to accelerate when China replaces America as the world's leading manufacturing nation, a position held by the United States for more than a century.[4] Accordingly, NAFTA is more than just a free-trade agreement among neighboring countries; it is part of much broader, historical context.

The rise of the United States as the world's leader in manufacturing depended greatly on its access to Canada and Mexico for sources of raw materials, labor power, and outlets for capital investment. Although Canada and Mexico did manage to develop a margin of economic independence as this process unfolded, by the time the United States achieved undisputed global hegemony after World War II, American domination over its North American neighbors had been firmly established. The postwar economic boom provided handsome profits for businesses, higher wages for workers, and the enactment of social reforms, all of which resulted in better living standards for workers in all of North America. Beginning in the 1970s, however, when Japan and Europe emerged to challenge U.S. economic hegemony, the postwar boom in North America faded, the rate of profit began to fall, especially in manufacturing, and with it labor's fortunes started to change.

Stagnating wages, rising unemployment, and soaring inflation combined with the building up of competitive pressures in the global economy not only posed greater challenges to U.S. hegemony abroad but also unsettled social relations at home. As domestic political pressures mounted from rising labor unrest protesting these economic developments, the U.S. government responded, at least in part, by enacting a series of legislative measures designed to protect a host of basic industries against foreign competition. But this punitive strategy that targeted nation-states like Japan had too many negative repercussions for United States–based corporations trying to do business in an increasingly competitive and integrated global economy.

As a result, the U.S. government then attempted a more ambitious, multilateral gambit of rewriting the General Agreement on Tariffs and Trade (GATT), established by the United States at the close of World War to set the rules of world trade under its direction and domination. But the upstart Europeans along with leading developing countries like Brazil and India balked at accepting changes to the global trade regime. Still determined to advance its free-trade agenda as a means to reverse its economic decline, the United States initiated bilateral trade negotiations with some countries as a strategy to gain its objectives. In doing so, the United States had hoped that bilateral agreements would establish precedents and thereby exert pressure on recalcitrant nation-states to concede to American demands in the writing of new rules to govern the global economy.

Although Israel was the first to sign a bilateral agreement with the United States, the 1989 Canada-United States Free Trade Agreement (CUFTA) was much more significant. The agreement represented the first stage in a process that sought to restore Washington's economic clout internationally by strengthening its traditional domination of its continental neighbors. In 1994, Washington's bilateral strategy extended CUFTA to include Mexico, giving birth to NAFTA. The power of this continental trade block and its potential impact on Europe's economic fortunes effectively forced the European Union to join with the United States in creating the World Trade Organization (WTO) in 1995.

But getting agreement on new trade rules under WTO auspices proved difficult because many developing countries banded together and held out for more favorable terms. Thus the United States, along with other developed countries, began using bilateral trade agreements to win concessions they were unable to obtain through the WTO. In so doing, the goal of the United States was to extend NAFTA to the rest of the Western Hemisphere through the Free Trade Area of the Americas (FTAA).

The FTAA, however, encountered fierce resistance from organized labor and from other nation-states in the Western Hemisphere such as Brazil, Argentina, Venezuela, and Bolivia that balked at entering the agreement without significant concessions from the United States.[5] While these countries opposed the extension of NAFTA on the basis of protecting their national economies and industries from American domination, workers and unions in North America have done so because they believe NAFTA has enhanced the power of transnational corporations and in so doing has adversely affected the fortunes of labor.

Unlike the foreign outposts of multinational enterprises that in the past manufactured for the national markets in which they were located, the transnational corporation produces for the global market by organizing commodity production across national and continental divides. Aided by new technologies that have sharply reduced the cost of communication and transportation that in the past had divided markets, previously unified production processes are now disaggregated and dispersed as components for a range of commodities, from computers to cars, are manufactured and assembled in any number of countries. Consequently, the globalization of production not only has resulted in the transnationals dominating world markets but also, even more important, has enhanced their ability to determine participation in the international division of labor, rather than arms-length transactions.[6]

These qualitative changes in the structure of world capitalism are what separate today's global economy from earlier periods. There is virtually no commodity or economic process that does not involve in some way the integration of productive systems and labor from far-reaching corners of the globe. The production of energy, extraction of raw materials, food production, manufacturing, and communications are all subject to this process. In the current period, even firms that generate a high percentage of revenues from their national markets have their costs, efficiency, productivity of labor, and rate of profit determined on an international scale. Firms everywhere are forced to interface with a global cost structure even when goods and services are only produced and sold within a particular national market.[7] On average, the world's largest companies have affiliates in forty different countries, and an estimated 10 percent of world gross domestic product (GDP) is now produced within the global production systems of individual transnational corporations.[8]

Complementing the global domination of transnationals in the area of production is the deregulation of financial markets. Since the early 1970s when the U.S. dollar began to float against other nations' currencies, the global economy has witnessed an ever-increasing and continuous movement of finance capital, consisting of shareholders' funds. These funds of all classes scour the globe in search of the best rate of return, obliging corporations and businesses to continuously develop their production methods and adjust cost structures to secure a competitive rate of return.[9] Firms failing to maximize their profits on an international scale find that their share price declines while funds look elsewhere for higher rates of return.[10] When companies fail to meet the expectations demanded by global financial capital, they are forced to pay a higher premium on capital to attract funds or higher interest rates to the banks. Firms also become subject to takeovers or mergers or are forced out of business altogether by their more profitable rivals.[11]

Most who study these developments in the global economy refer to this phenomenon as globalization.[12] Nobel Prize–winning economist Joseph Stiglitz describes globalization as "the closer integration of the countries and peoples of the world which has been brought about by the enormous reduction of costs of transportation and communication, and the breaking down of artificial barriers to the flows of goods, services, capital, knowledge, and (to a lesser extent) people across borders."[13]

In North America, globalization has been characterized by two dominant trends that have gained serious momentum since the advent of NAFTA. The first is the turning away from manufacturing in Canada and the United States. Claiming that wages are too high and that benefits of the job such as medical insurance and guaranteed pensions are no longer affordable in a competitive global economy, the transnationals have moved more than a million jobs to Mexico in search of lower costs.

In factories called maquiladoras, the transnationals not only pay employees wages that are substantially lower than those earned by workers in the United States and Canada, they also deny them their internationally recognized rights on a wholesale basis. At the same time, employers in the United States rely more on Mexican labor to fill jobs in myriad economic sectors and industries. These workers, who now number in the millions, constitute a vast labor pool with few legal rights that give employers a decided advantage in determining their wages and other conditions of employment.

This new international division of labor has tilted power in the workplace heavily toward the transnationals as they pit workers against one another based on locale, region, industry, and nationality. The implementation of this strategy not only has benefited transnationals, it also has given capital leverage against labor everywhere. Its impact has been felt the most in collective bargaining as employers engaged in this process are increasingly successful in rolling back the hard-won gains made by workers in earlier periods. The consequences of this development are evident in labor's shrinking share of national income in the NAFTA countries.[14] Meanwhile, the NAALC, created by NAFTA to enhance and protect workers' rights as a means to ensure that increased economic integration would raise the living standards of working people instead of lowering them, has failed to stop this trend.

The ineffectiveness of institutions like the NAALC has reinforced the long-standing fears held by North American trade unions that extending free trade to other low-wage countries will accelerate the transformation of what once were living-wage jobs into dangerous, starvation-wage, sweatshop jobs. Yet as these transformational pressures build and gain momentum, the strategy of the unions in trying to halt these trends has been one of retreat from struggle and a sharp move toward conciliation that is principally characterized by their pursuit of what they call partnership with employers. This strategy is based on the idea that successful national economies and industries will keep jobs within the national borders of the countries in which the unions are based.

The nationalist outlook of the trade unions that overarches this strategy is not the product of bad or misguided leadership. Rather, it is rooted in the bargaining outcomes following World War II when workers organized in unions were able to win certain concessions from employers and from the state in the form of higher wages and benefits. The occurred, however, under conditions when nationally regulated economies guided general global economic expansion.

Today, the globalization of production and the dismantling of industry, particularly in the United States, have undermined the ability of the unions to pressure capital for concessions in the national labor market. As corporations have shifted production around the world in search of cheap labor, the unions have retained their allegiances to the national state and the corporate structure into which they have been steadily integrated. The campaigns to defend "American," "Canadian," or "Mexican" jobs have been invariably combined with the acceptance of major concessions and wage cuts for North American workers. The role of the trade unions in North America has been transformed from pressuring the employers and the state for concessions to the worker, to pressuring the workers for concessions to the employers so as to attract capital.

The implementation of this strategy occurs primarily through deploying the twin tactics of no-strike pledges and concessionary bargaining. Seeking to help employers gain a competitive advantage in the global economy, concessionary bargaining by unions usually involves cuts in pay and benefits for their membership along with changes in work rules designed to boost worker productivity. Although unions have pursued partnership in every economic sector and in myriad businesses, it has been most notable in the auto industry, North America's most integrated industry. But the partnership strategy has failed in its objectives in all sectors and industries. Jobs have been destroyed rather than saved. At the same time, the unions have experienced a protracted decline in membership.

While the dynamic of contemporary union-management relations in North America and other themes discussed previously are analyzed in greater detail in later chapters, a complete understanding of them first requires an overview of labor and economy in North America in the earlier periods.

Doing so not only provides a basis for comparison with what is presented later in the book, it also shows how North American integration has been a protracted historical process in which commodities, investment capital, workers, and unions crossed borders long before NAFTA. Most important, a look into labor and economy in the earlier periods will show that globalization and its North American template, NAFTA, have ushered in a new era for labor, one that significantly departs from those it has experienced in the past.

1

Labor and Global Capitalism
in North America, 1850–1970

When the 1848 revolutions of Western Europe removed the remaining feudal roadblocks to economic expansion, Britain, through the use of its military and naval might, not only knocked down barriers to its expansion, but in so doing provided the basis for the expansion of capitalism in other nations. As the world's preeminent capitalist power, Britain advocated free trade and the freeing up of labor everywhere. In North America, British investment in railroads and other capital ventures provided important traction for the growth of capitalism on the continent and with it the expansion of national and regional labor markets based on the principle of free-wage labor.[1]

In the United States, the Civil War had a profound impact on these developments, and following the North's victory, the nation experienced an unprecedented economic expansion. With slavery and the political challenges of the southern aristocracy swept away, northern industrial and financial elites used their control of the state machinery to carry out measures to promote industrial expansion by subsidizing the construction of railroads and other internal improvements. At the same time, they enacted protective tariffs and established a national banking system.[2]

In 1873 when this rapid economic expansion halted and turned downward, a series of financial crises erupted that affected the entire capitalist world. In response to enormous downward pressure on profits, capitalists the world over looked for ways to restore profitability by developing new production methods through innovation, longer working hours, and the acquisition of new labor markets. In the United States especially, while all of these factors came into play, it was the development of new forms of industrial organization and technologies resulting in innovative production methods that proved most important. These changes boosted labor productivity to unprecedented heights. The 1913 opening of Henry Ford's Highland Park, Michigan, assembly-line car plant represented the culmination of this process.[3]

Among the European countries, the downward pressure on profits precipitated a renewed scramble for colonies among the great powers, a process reflected by the carving up of Africa and China in a twenty-year period. This weakened the relative position of Britain internationally and marked the beginning of the decline of British global hegemony. Although the success of the American economy took place within tariff walls, the United States entered the competitive world stage in this period under the banner of the "open door." In contrast to European efforts to obtain colonies, open-door policy reflected the emerging industrial and economic superiority of the United States over its rivals, just as Britain's free-trade agenda in the nineteenth century expressed the domination of British industry.[4]

Another major factor driving this economic dynamism was that regions of the world were pulled into the capitalist orbit of production, made possible by new forms of transport and communications. Minerals and raw materials, such as rubber, copper, lead, iron ore, and zinc were all transported in bulk to be processed in factories. In North America, the construction of extensive railroad networks allowed for the opening up of the mineral-rich Canadian west and northern Mexico. By 1895, the ability to secure quantities of these commodities at lower costs had helped generate another round of global capitalist expansion that lasted until the outbreak of World War I. Output per capita for the advanced industrial countries doubled between 1895 and 1913 from what it had been during the previous fourteen years. At the same time, the United States emerged as the world's leading manufacturer, surpassing its leading rivals, England, Germany, and France.[5]

Rising rates of profit resulting from this economic output led to significant growth of foreign investment abroad by U.S. industrialists and bankers. Much of that investment found its way to Canada. The country possessed material power in the form of industry-serving minerals and power-generating rivers, a factor that helped Canada become the recipient of around 33 percent of U.S. direct investment.[6] Also attracting investment was the national policy implemented during Canada's transition to Dominion status within the emerging British Commonwealth system. Its key components were the launching of an import substitution-industrialization strategy with railway construction to connect eastern and central Canada with the western provinces, immigration aimed to attract labor to work in industries, and tariffs to induce foreigners to develop a manufacturing economy in Canada.[7] The result was that American corporations like General Electric, Westinghouse, and National Cash Register set up Canadian operations. These multi-entity corporations exercised head-office control over their subsidiary operations (both factories and mines) without giving up their ownership rights. Consequently, American investors retained control while they increased their share of Canada's burgeoning manufacturing and resource economy. By 1900, Canada had become the world's first branch-plant economy.[8]

This early domination of Canada's industrial base benefited the American economy in several ways. While Canada gradually detached itself from the British Empire, the United States discouraged the nation's capacity to compete with American firms through tariff walls against its manufactured exports. Functioning like an appendage of the American economy, Canada would supply resources, help integrate U.S. capital markets, and offer a consumer market for American firms to gain economies of scale.[9]

These economic changes also created the beginnings of a North American labor market. While the process began drawing many of Canada's marginal farmers and fisherman into wage labor for the first time, the increased integration of the Canadian and American economies began generating continental labor mobility. English- and French-speaking Canadians migrated to work in Detroit and in the textile and shoe factories of New England. Montreal acted as a temporary passageway for many European-born workers headed to the United States, especially to New York.[10] The accelerated economic development of the United States also began drawing Mexicans to the western and southwestern regions of the United States to work on the railroads, in the mines, and on farms.[11]

While some of these new arrivals and their native-born American counterparts improved their standard of living in this period, periods of unemployment caused by shifting seasonal demands, boom-and-bust cycles, and depressions often offset the gains.[12] Economic insecurity and unsafe conditions on the job combined to generate a wave of labor unrest marked by great, dramatic, and often bloody and violent strikes such as Homestead (1892) and Pullman (1894). As employers backed by the state's armed intervention crushed these struggles, sharp ideological conflict and divisions emerged within the U.S. workers' movement.

In the late 1880s and early 1890s, the two competing ideological tendencies were represented by the Knights of Labor and the American Federation of Labor (AFL). Beginning in Philadelphia in 1869, the Knights drew on craft traditions and organization but sought to unite workers regardless of trade, skill level, or social background. Recognizing that factories often employed large numbers of both skilled and unskilled labor, women as well as men, and workers of many ethnic backgrounds, the Knights attempted to span the traditional divisions based on skill, gender, ethnicity, and region by recruiting wage earners of all kinds. By the late 1880s, the Knights had a membership of 730,000. Many anarchist and other workers' groups shared this same outlook, and they, like the Knights, were swept up in the repressive environment directed against labor radicals of all tendencies that followed the 1886 Haymarket affair. The repression, combined with internal factionalism, crippled the Knights, and by the mid-1890s they had ceased to exist in the United States.[13]

In contrast to the Knights, the AFL and its president, Samuel Gompers, sought accommodation with capitalism, believing that employers would tolerate unionism if it was limited to the skilled trades, rejected militancy, and was reasonable in its demands. Unlike the Knights, the AFL was implacably hostile to blacks, immigrants, female labor, and many other oppressed sections of the working class.[14] But the AFL's promotion of what became known as business unionism, which favored pursuit of workers' immediate demands like better working conditions, wages, and control over jobs, appealed to industrial unions as well. The United Mine Workers (UMWA), International Ladies' Garment Workers' Union, and the United Brewery Workers made up the bulk of AFL membership. As a result, from 1897 to 1904, union membership in the United States climbed from 447,000 to 2,072,700. In the same period, the number of international unions affiliated with the AFL rose from 58 to 120.[15]

Although the AFL emerged as the predominant labor organization in the United States, many groups of workers had become disenchanted with its outlook. In a June 1905 convention held in Chicago, two hundred socialists, anarchists, and radical trade unionists from all over the United States formed the Industrial Workers of the World (IWW). The IWW opposed the AFL union model and its exclusionary policies that included the refusal to organize many unskilled immigrants. Unlike the AFL, the IWW refused to sign contracts, which it claimed restricted the only real leverage workers possessed: the power to strike.[16]

While promoting industrial actions and sympathy strikes to affect immediate changes in the workplace, the IWW envisioned the eventual carrying out of a general strike as the means by which the wage system would be overthrown. The new order would resemble a type of collective commonwealth run by workers from syndicates organized on the workshop floor. This idea was called revolutionary syndicalism, and the IWW goal was to spread it worldwide. Although the IWW eventually extended itself into all of North America, the AFL was the first to establish itself as an international union in the region.

When U.S. firms began moving into Canada, many workers looked to American-based international unions for support. In the 1880s, many Canadian workers linked up with the Knights of Labor, who by organizing almost every conceivable craft eventually established central organizations at both local and national levels. In 1886, these organizations formed the Trades and Labor Congress (TLC). In 1901, the TLC had nearly 88 percent of all Canadian union locals in its ranks, many of which were affiliated with the AFL.[17] In 1902, when the TLC expelled all organizations that it considered rival or "dual unions," the Knights faded into oblivion.[18]

Even though the TLC also expelled some unions linked organizationally to the AFL, the U.S.-based Federation continued to have a strong influence in Canada, especially among skilled workers. In 1902, membership in Canadian unions affiliated with the AFL included carpenters, bricklayers, printers, shoe workers, iron molders, and mine workers. All of these international unions were headquartered in the United States, along with their AFL parent affiliate. Traveling cards provided by the internationals allowed Canadian workers belonging to 1,000 local unions to cross the border back and forth in search of jobs, contributing to the growth and development of a North American labor market.[19]

This expanding labor market also led to the emergence of autonomous unions. From 1890 to 1914 in the far western provinces of Canada, where many workers from the United States arrived, miners organized local unions affiliated with the IWW. Although the IWW succeeded in organizing dozens of locals and waging a number of important strikes, especially among immigrant workers in the construction camps of the Canadian Northern Railway, its ideological and organizational influence in Canada remained much weaker in comparison to that of the AFL. Limiting the influence of both the IWW and the AFL was the growth of a different form of unionism in Quebec. There, autonomous unions influenced by papal encyclicals and nationalism sprang up under the fostering care of the Catholic Church hierarchy. In 1921, these unions formed the Confédération des Travailleurs Catholiques du Canada/Canadian and Catholic Confederation of Labor (CCCL).[20]

As union membership grew, labor leaders and workers became more assertive during disputes with employers. As the eruption of strikes became more common, some provincial government officials searched for ways to prevent work stoppages and promote peaceful industrial relations. In 1905, the Alberta provincial government brought in a series of reforms, including the eight-hour workday. In 1907, the federal government, at the instigation of Mackenzie King, the deputy minister of labor, sought to discourage strikes in industries deemed of national importance, such as coal mining. The result was the passage of the Industrial Disputes Investigation Act, which recognized the rights of both sides in labor disputes and established a mandatory period of conciliation and negotiation before a legal strike could start.[21]

War, Revolution, and Labor in North America

Mexico's entrance into the geopolitical and economic orbit of its northern neighbor began in the 1850s, after war with the United States resulted in the loss of more than half of its territory. What followed that conflict was civil war in Mexico over attempts by liberals to break up ecclesiastical property holdings and the communal lands of Indians. Their eventual victory in that struggle effectively dispossessed peasants from their lands. This created a new pool of labor for capitalists, both domestic and foreign, setting the stage for an unbridled capitalist expansion.

This expansion accelerated when Porfirio Díaz reigned over Mexico as dictator from 1876 to 1911. During what is called the Porfiriato, American industrialists and financiers played a dominant role in the modernization of the country's economy, making the nation ever more dependent on American capital. Through the granting of territorial concessions, the lowering and removing of tariffs and other financial barriers, the Mexican government opened the floodgates for U.S. business. American capital provided numerous U.S.-owned firms with funds to build railroads, excavate mines, exploit oil fields, establish factories, and develop commercial agriculture.[22]

By 1910, American investors controlled a substantial portion of the Mexican economy and foreign concerns owned more than half of the nation's wealth. According to then–U.S. Consul General Andrew D. Barlow, more than 1,100 U.S.-based companies and individuals had invested more than $500 million in Mexico. Firmly integrating Mexico with the development of American capitalism were businesses like Standard Oil and International Harvester and wealthy individuals such as William Randolph Hearst. During the first decade of the twentieth century, almost 40 percent of all foreign investment from the United States went into Mexico.[23]

But the American enterprises that penetrated Mexico were mere foreign enclaves nailed into an economic system in which precapitalist social relations still prevailed. Notwithstanding, the onslaught of American capital disrupted these social relations in vast areas of the nation. The result was a tearing apart of the precapitalist social fabric that produced mass removal of peasants from lands, the ruin of artisans, rising unemployment, and the emergence of a migratory surplus population.[24] This migratory population first moved from rural to urban areas within central Mexico, but thereafter many followed higher pay by pushing into the northern Mexican states, and some even began crossing the border to work in the United States.[25]

Many of those who crossed into the United States had worked in the mines and on the railroads inside Mexico. After arriving in the United States, some came into contact with radical unions like the Western Federation of Miners (WFM) and later the IWW. As documented by labor historian Emilio Zamora, in Texas alone roughly 50 to 75 percent of migrants returned to Mexico every year.[26] Many workers involved in this cross-border flow also had been influenced by the exiled anarchist opponents of the Díaz government, Ricardo and Enrique Flores Magón, members of the Partido Liberal Mexicano/Mexican Liberal Party (PLM). For Mexican workers, the PLM provided the initial linkages both ideologically and organizationally on both sides of the border for taking up the fight against the abusive management practices of multinational enterprises.

Founded in 1901, the PLM opposed the Díaz dictatorship on the grounds that it effectively violated the 1857 Mexican constitution. Accordingly, the PLM called for the suppression of the Catholic Church, the restoration of economic competition, and political liberties. Threatened by this challenge, the Díaz dictatorship repressed the PLM by jailing its leaders, including the Flores Magón brothers. Radicalized by these events, the Flores Magóns went into self-imposed exile in the United States, where they organized Mexican workers to oppose both the Díaz regime and capitalism through their Spanish-language newspaper, *Regeneración*.[27]

Inside Mexico, the country's rapid industrialization under the aegis of increasing foreign ownership of production and economic infrastructure in combination with miserable wages and conditions helped radicalize the nation's working class. Because of constitutional restraints that prevented agitating in the workplace for improving conditions on the job or from forming independent political parties, the revolutionary syndicalism advocated by the PLM, the IWW, and other groups gained traction among Mexican workers.

In 1906, miners influenced by these organizational currents walked off their jobs at the American-owned copper complex in Cananea, Sonora. They protested management abuses such as the practice of wage discrimination against Mexican nationals who had been paid more in the United States for doing the same work they performed in their native land. In 1907, textile workers influenced by the PLM struck foreign-owned mills across central Mexico in protest of abusive management practices. The result was that Mexican syndicalism, unlike the brand found in the United States or Canada, took on a nationalist coloration. Although the Mexican army and Arizona Rangers brutally crushed these uprisings, the events acted as a catalyst in forging a nationalistic multiclass alliance that in 1911 brought down the Díaz government.[28]

But Díaz's fall from power did not usher in a government controlled by workers. Leading the fight against Díaz were northern landowners and elites who initially backed Francisco Madero, the first president of the revolution. Madero attracted support through his initial backing of the PLM and its liberal program. That liberal program had evolved during the struggle against Díaz, and it increasingly mixed with Mexican nationalism and efforts to prevent the mortgaging of the Mexican economy to the United States.[29] Because Madero made land reform a rallying cry for overturning the Díaz dictatorship, at first he drew support from sections of the peasantry in the central region of Mexico, where a struggle over land had long been simmering. But this was an uneasy alliance. By 1913, Emiliano Zapata, the leader of the rural rebellion, already had denounced the northern forces for betraying the peasantry through his Plan of Ayala. Zapata's plan called for an unconditional return of all lands usurped by the oligarchy and their foreign allies.[30]

After Madero's assassination in 1913, political and social instability characterized by intense and bloody fighting rocked Mexico. Victory in the revolution eventually came to the Constitutionalist Army of the northern elite leader Venustiano Carranza. In order to win, Carranza took advantage of Zapata's lack of a program and his followers' religiosity. In so doing, Carranza appealed to the workers of Mexico City, who were led by the fiercely anticlerical anarcho-syndicalist Casa del Obrero Mundial. Convincing Casa leaders to form Red battalions made up of workers, these armed forces helped Carranza defeat the peasant armies and establish his regime. Once in power, however, Carranza crushed workers' general strikes, dissolved the Red battalions, and persecuted their leaders.[31] By effectively keeping workers and peasants divided, Carranza subordinated them to the interests of the propertied elites, making the Constitutionalist Army the arbiter among the contending social classes.[32]

When the major fighting in the revolution ended in 1917, Mexico ushered in a new constitution. The document addressed many of the long-standing grievances held by all of the nation's social classes. Article 27 declared state ownership of subsoil resources such as oil and other minerals. It satisfied the nationalist aspirations that served to unify all social classes around the revolutionary slogan "Mexico for the Mexicans." For the masses of peasants and laboring people, the 1917 constitution promised land reform and workers' rights. More important, the document guaranteed the ownership of private property and profits while forming the legal basis for the establishment of capitalist social relations.[33]

The framework for workers' rights and the regulation of labor activity in postrevolutionary Mexico was Article 123, which among other things gave workers the right to strike and form unions. Although acknowledged as the most advanced labor code in the world at the time, state power was at the core of Article 123. The goal of the "revolutionary" government in the enforcement of Article 123 was effective control over labor and the creation of a stable environment in which capital could operate, both foreign and domestic.

Although the basis for the formation of the revolutionary government was Mexican nationalism, it had to operate and maneuver within the context of growing rivalries and antagonisms among the major world powers.[34] These struggles centered on conflicts over economic resources, strategic spheres of influence, and colonial empires, which over time emerged more bitter and intractable. While the earlier period of capitalist growth took place under the aegis of a dominant power, Great Britain, whose economic might worked to ensure the expansion of the capitalist economy as a whole, the economic upswing that took place in the years preceding World War I occurred when competing interests in key areas of the globe had led to complex diplomatic maneuvering and shifting alliances.

In other words, the economic growth and dynamism between 1870 and 1914 failed to reestablish a balance of power and equilibrium of the earlier period dominated by Britain. Instead, these conditions led to a crisis in international relations and a series of upheavals that went on for decades.[35] As the advanced capitalist countries maneuvered to reconfigure the world's political and economic map, not only did a world war erupt as a result, but explosive social convulsions in the developing world also occurred, marked by revolutions not only in Mexico, but also in Russia, China, and Iran.[36]

The revolution in Mexico, like others around the globe, became victim to forms of meddling and direct intervention by the advanced capitalist nations.[37] In Mexico, all of the vying revolutionary factions (save the provincial, religious, and inward-looking Zapatistas of Morelos) fought for varying degrees of economic independence from the United States. Most important, through these struggles they sought protection of the nation's national resources and economic infrastructure. Even when the procapitalist northern elite Carranza emerged as the revolution's "first chief," American President Woodrow Wilson and his close circle of advisers still viewed the revolutionary nationalism on its own border as a threat to U.S. economic interests.[38]

When the United States directly intervened with military force on two occasions to influence the revolution's outcome, policy makers in Washington also searched for other ways to moderate the revolution, and it included enlisting the support of Samuel Gompers and the AFL.[39] But labor radicalism had taken up strong roots in Mexico, much more so than in the United States. By espousing a stridently anticlerical and nationalistic program that advocated the seizure of foreign-owned enterprises under workers' control, Mexican syndicalism constituted an important ideological wing of the revolution. Although Carranza had successfully repressed the Casa del Obrero Mundial in Mexico City, Mexican syndicalism continued to attract worker support throughout the country, so much that other currents such as Catholic unions never got off the ground organizationally.[40] When the AFL entered Mexico to spread its organizational model of business unionism, it faced an enormous challenge.

AFL motivation for involvement in the revolution reflected both its opposition to syndicalism and a shift away from its earlier opposition to the expansionist policies of the American government. In 1898, AFL President Samuel Gompers had spoken openly of the dangers involved with the United States annexing lands populated by "servile races" and "a semi-barbaric population." Gompers opposed American expansionism at the time because he feared that as capital moved to less-developed countries and established colonies, labor there could produce goods cheaper and thereby undercut wages and jobs in the United States.[41]

According to Gompers, the only way living standards would go up for workers was through manufacturing goods at home for consumption by "civilized" men and women paid union wages.[42] But as illustrated in the case of Canada, when American business expanded beyond U.S. borders, the AFL followed. With union membership in the United States on the rise, the AFL increasingly looked to America's burgeoning foreign trade as a means to expand its ranks even further. In a span of less than two decades, the AFL's nationalist and isolationist foreign policy had turned into a policy of supporting American expansionism and imperialism.

Although the U.S. railway brotherhoods had organized skilled workers in Mexico, they were American and British employees because English was the working language of Mexico's railways until 1907 when the Diaz dictatorship "Mexicanized" the system. Mexicans working on the rails in their native land had been formally excluded from the skilled railway brotherhoods and relegated to the less-skilled jobs.[43] While the AFL never had any international affiliates like it did in Canada, as historian David Montgomery suggests, actions taken by AFL leaders in Mexico were in large part motivated by their fight against the IWW and syndicalism at home. This converged with the Wilson administration's growing efforts to marginalize labor radicals and build an alliance with the AFL to gain the support of working-class voters at the polls. The appointment of William B. Wilson of the United Mine Workers of America as secretary of labor reflected these developments. As war preparedness escalated in late 1916, the AFL executive council worked even more closely with the Wilson administration after Gompers's appointment to the Council of National Defense.[44]

When the United States entered World War I in 1917, the AFL worked to establish and administer the American Alliance for Labor and Democracy. The organization collaborated with the government-created Committee on Public Information (CPI) and its head, George Creel. The CPI and the Alliance jointly produced propaganda materials and organized rallies in support of the war. In 1918, they conducted a one-week nationwide "labor loyalty" program, specifically designed to drum up support for the war in the workplace.[45]

Complementing its political work in support of the war, the AFL and its affiliates sought to blunt labor unrest and marginalize IWW influence in key war-related industries. Expanding labor markets resulting from wartime full employment gave bargaining leverage to workers in many industries. In 1917, the number of strikes reached an all-time high of 4,450.[46] Important to war-related production were strikes in mining. In the strikes that occurred in the Arizona towns of Clifton-Morenci, Jerome, and Miami, Mexicans belonging to the IWW played leading roles as agitators.[47] The War Labor Board intervened to mediate and resolve major disputes, especially in mining, where many were settled in labor's favor. In the sixteen months it functioned, the War Labor Board disposed of more than 1,100 cases.[48] This intervention combined with police and vigilante action to drive the IWW out of many mines, and it involved the arrest and persecution of Mexican IWW leaders. Complementing these actions, AFL unions signed agreements with employers that pledged around-the-clock production and no strikes.[49]

In Canada, government officials moved to undermine labor radicalism using the same strategy and employing many of the some tactics. As in the United States, full employment resulted in a wave of strikes by Canadian workers. The number of work stoppages in 1919 reached 428, involving the participation of 149,309 workers. The government took quick and decisive action in many of these conflicts, such as in the 1919 Winnipeg general strike when police violently attacked striking workers and arrested their leaders. At the same time, the federal government sought to undermine support for the IWW (now called the One Big Union in Canada) by encouraging workers to back more moderate unions. Local unions affiliated with the Canadian Federation of Labor (CFL), like their AFL counterparts in the United States, signed agreements with employers that guaranteed uninterrupted production in the war years.[50]

In Mexico, the AFL promoted moderate unionism by allying with the Carranza government-backed Confederación Regional Obrera Mexicana (CROM). Founded in 1918, the CROM and its principal leader, Luis Morones, embraced the AFL model of business unionism. Gompers firmly believed that the AFL model would provide many Mexican workers opportunities to make wage gains and thus give them the purchasing power to consume goods manufactured by union members in the United States. And because most Mexican workers at the time were involved in the production of raw materials and foodstuffs, their organization did not threaten manufacturing jobs in the United States. At the same time, both Gompers and Morones believed that the spread of the AFL model would provide workers an organizational alternative to syndicalism.[51] As Gregg Andrews writes in his study of the AFL and the Mexican Revolution, management in the American-owned mining industry already was willing to pay higher wages if Mexican unions would change their ideological orientation and follow company dictates.[52]

The AFL and CROM initiatives represented a continuing effort on behalf of successive Mexican governments to control labor and working-class organization. During the rule of Porfirio Díaz, the government directly sponsored labor organizations that promoted mutualism as a way to shield workers from radicalism. This same strategy emerged in a more sophisticated fashion during the brief tenure of Madero's presidency, when his government created a labor department to hear workers' grievances and resolve disputes. The Madero government also sponsored a workers' council, called the Gran Liga, in an attempt to counter the growing influence of the Casa del Obrero Mundial. Although the 1917 Mexican constitution called for "Mexico for the Mexicans," the revolutionary government had no reservations allowing foreign meddling in its internal affairs for the purposes of taming the country's radicalized working class and its organizations. The persistence in the government's efforts to do so was testimony to the continuing and enduring organizational strength of Mexican syndicalism.[53]

Labor and Political Economy in the 1920s

Despite support it received from the AFL, the Mexican government, and sections of business and industry, the CROM struggled in its early years to win workers over to business unionism. Mexican syndicalism fed on the federal and state governments' failure to enforce most of the provisions of Article 123, especially as they applied to foreign employers. In the early to mid-1920s, unions that organized around Mexican syndicalism like those belonging to the Confederación General de Trabajadores/Confederation of General Workers (CGT) gained members and waged fierce battles against the government and the CROM. While these unions agitated around immediate goals such as higher wages and conditions, they also continued to demand the nationalization and workers' self-management of foreign-owned enterprises. This organizational current based on these demands endured even while state governors established labor boards that included the participation of the politically connected CROM, giving it great influence in the negotiation of labor-management conflicts.[54]

Major testing grounds for implementing this labor relations model occurred in the foreign-dominated textile and mining industries and in the Tampico oil fields operated by the emerging giants of the U.S. and British petroleum industries. Some oil workers already had joined the IWW as a result of contact made with seafarers from the U.S. port of Philadelphia. These workers not only waged militant strikes to demand higher wages and better conditions, they also advocated organizational autonomy and workers' self-management.[55]

By using violent force to crush the IWW and other radical groups in Tampico, the government cleared the way for the CROM to negotiate an industry-wide contract in textiles. One of the most important provisions included in the 1927 industry-wide contract was the exclusion clause that required workers to belong to the union as a condition to secure employment. The exclusion clause also authorized union officials to expel members for antiunion activity, which for workers also meant the loss of employment. The exclusion clause combined with increases in real wages throughout the Mexican economy during the second half of the 1920s boosted CROM membership, which by 1929 had grown to 294,000, representing 5.5 percent of Mexico's economically active population.[56] Between 1925 and 1928, real wages in the textile industry increased by 43 percent.[57]

Preceding the CROM success in the textile industry was the formation of the Pan American Federation of Labor (PAFL). With the AFL and the CROM acting as its principal members, the PAFL sought to secure the model of business unionism in Mexico and for the rest of the Western Hemisphere where U.S. investment was growing. This effort coincided with Gompers's declaration of the "labor corollary" to the Monroe Doctrine. Approved by the delegates of the AFL's 1925 convention, the resolution connected all forms of labor radicalism to Bolshevism and condemned the Soviet Union's attempts to spread its influence into the Western Hemisphere.[58] Confident that it had secured labor peace, Mexico's leaders needed to rebuild its economy torn by more than a decade of revolutionary war. While the Mexican government sought infusions of American capital, the United States in turn needed the steady production of Mexican raw materials to boost its industrial capacity.[59]

The American acquisition of raw materials from both Mexico and Canada combined with Ford's assembly-line production to generate stupendous economic growth in the United States, where industrial output increased by 40 percent during the decade.[60] The corresponding increase in gross national product (GNP) resulted in American investment pouring into both Mexico and Canada.[61] In 1922, American investment in Canada surpassed British investment for the first time. By 1930, U.S. direct investment in Canada was more than five times that of Britain.[62] American corporations owned all automobile factories, 45 percent of machinery and chemical industries, and more than half of rubber and electrical companies. At the same time, 68 percent of Canada's imports came from the United States, while 46 percent of Canada's exports went to the United States.[63] In 1925, U.S. investments reached the $1 billion mark in Mexico and Henry Ford opened the country's first auto plant designed exclusively to manufacture and sell vehicles inside Mexico.[64]

In contrast to Mexico, the 1920s for unions in Canada were a decade of falling membership, division, and disarray. Membership declined by 16 percent over the decade as the Canadian population grew by 1.6 million. While the drop in membership numbers was in large part a result of the repression carried out by employers and the state during the Canadian version of the Red scare, the craft-based unions, much like the AFL in the United States, did not address the challenges of organizing the unskilled and semiskilled workers in many of the new American branch plants. This organizational inertia paralleled new employer strategies and tactics to stabilize industrial relations and create labor peace.

Major companies introduced so-called industrial councils to take advantage of the demoralized state of labor and to circumvent the development of independent unionism. These councils represented a form of company unionism, which often included profit-sharing schemes and restricted workers to playing an advisory role on a plant-by-plant basis. Under the council system, grievance procedures existed, but the employer generally held the right to make the final decision.[65]

While company unions in the United States had developed earlier in the twentieth century, their growth had mushroomed during World War I.[66] In the aftermath of the bitter 1914 Ludlow, Colorado, coal strike in which the Colorado National Guard killed 20 people, 11 of whom were children, John D. Rockefeller enlisted the help of Mackenzie King, who implemented elements of the Canadian company union model, to alleviate tensions and establish stable labor relations in the Rockefeller-owned mines. This included the development of the Colorado Industrial Representation Plan, a prototype company union structure.[67]

By 1919, increased employer militancy against unions had generated an epidemic of labor disputes, the most important of which took place in the steel industry. Elbert Gary, chairman of the board of the U.S. Steel Corporation, set the tone for employer militancy in the decade when he refused to meet and negotiate with a union committee, saying that he would only do so through a company union. When 367,000 steelworkers went on strike in mills all over the country, steel management quickly turned public opinion against the AFL-backed unions. The postwar Red scare had swept the country in the wake of the 1917 Bolshevik revolution in Russia. Capitalizing on the political climate dominated by the Red scare, the steel companies crushed the strike.[68]

Even more effective for eliminating the influence of unions in industry was the American Plan of Employment that promoted the open shop, the policy of no negotiations with unions. The American Plan adversely affected union membership. From 1920 to 1923, union membership in the United States shrank from 5 million to some 3.6 million, a 16 percent drop.[69] By 1932, employer hostility had reduced union membership to 2,689,000, or only about 4 percent of the workforce.[70]

Labor in the Great Depression and World War II: The United States and Canada

In effect, the reversal of labor's fortunes in the 1920s decade interconnected with the expansion of the U.S. industrial base into the rest of North America. Possessing a seemingly inexhaustible internal market, the United States had the decided technical and economic advantage over its European economic rivals. The American production model showed a direct link between increased profits, higher productivity, rationalization, and cost reduction, all of which rested upon the prevalence of management prerogative in the workplace.[71]

The American advantage, however, ran into the headwinds of chaotic forms of protectionism, which effectively erected barriers to its expansion on a global scale. France, Germany, Italy, and Britain all sought to bolster their own position against rivals by strengthening national controls and barriers to protect their own industries. At the same time, the United States was not prepared to open its market to European exports. In fact, in 1921 the United States raised tariffs in anticipation of an attempt by Germany and other European exporters to increase their penetration of the U.S. market through currency manipulations. In this environment of growing mistrust among the world's industrial powers, instead of modernizing their production methods, European industrialists responded to American protectionism by setting up cartels and other monopolistic restrictions in order to limit production and maintain prices.[72]

These conflicting ways of doing business and conducting trade led to autarkic economic policies based exclusively on national markets. As a result, nations sought protection not only through customs walls but also through hedges of bayonets. In the early years of the Great Depression, the world market had to all intents and purposes ceased to exist. After the United States enacted the Hawley-Smoot Tariff Act in 1930, the contraction of the world economy accelerated, further sharpening the already existing divisions between competing empires and spheres of influence. Accordingly, World War I had not resulted in a new leader of the capitalist world like Britain had been during the nineteenth century. These conditions gave rise to militarism and colonial-style wars such as those carried out by Japan in Asia and Italy in Africa, and they ultimately erupted into another world war when Nazi Germany overran Europe.[73]

In the United States, what the Great Depression meant for the masses of unskilled workers in such basic industries as steel, auto, electrical, and rubber were sweatshop conditions, rising unemployment, and declining wages. Many of these workers came from first- or second-generation immigrant families that had largely been ignored by the AFL leadership. By 1934, the intolerable conditions these workers suffered led to several major strikes in important industrial cities, many of which were carried out under Communist and Socialist leadership. In some cases, workers secured important gains and in so doing raised hopes and expectations among broad layers of the population who suffered under the same desperate economic conditions.[74]

But the American economic system handled these building social pressures because it still had at its disposal considerable resources. This enabled the administration of Franklin D. Roosevelt to embark on a program of social reform at a time when a large part of crisis-ridden Europe was going over to Fascism.

In 1935, organized labor received a shot in the arm when the U.S. Congress passed the Wagner Act. The legislation established a federal agency, the National Labor Relations Board (NLRB), with the power to investigate and decide on charges of unfair labor practices and to conduct elections in which workers would have the opportunity to decide whether they wanted to be represented by a union. This new legal and political environment encouraged UMWA President John L. Lewis, who headed one of the few mass industrial unions in the AFL, to lead a drive to unionize basic industry. In 1935, Lewis and other union leaders founded what eventually became called the Congress of Industrial Organizations (CIO). The CIO was a response to unmistakable signs that the working class was beginning to show signs of an uncompromising militancy that increasingly took on forms of a semi-insurrectionary character, reflected in 1934 when general strikes rocked three major cities: San Francisco, Toledo, and Minneapolis.[75]

Lewis also recognized that the labor movement could not survive without unionizing the industrial monopolies, like U.S. Steel, which controlled the coal mines and exercised overwhelming influence over the economy. Rather than engage in legal wrangling and rely on the court system, many CIO unions rejected the idea of using the NLRB in the first few years of its existence, choosing instead to strike for recognition. They employed the tactic of the sit-down strike that occurred in both the rubber and auto industries. The militant mood among workers swelled union membership. By September 1937, CIO ranks had grown to 3,700,000, from the 900,000 members it had counted in 1935.[76]

But the rapid increase in membership was only in part the result of militant struggles. U.S. Steel's agreement to recognize the CIO's Steel Workers Organizing Committee (SWOC) in March 1937 was a decision made by corporate executives, who calculated that the SWOC could help the firm avoid strikes and thus serve to stabilize labor relations. However, the drive to organize the second tier of major steel manufacturers, the so-called Little Steel firms such as Bethlehem, Republic, and Inland, met with violent resistance from employers and collapsed in the summer of 1937. The new union movement had reached an impasse.[77]

In a speech delivered on Labor Day on September 3, 1937, Lewis made it clear that the labor movement would avoid radicalization at all costs. His message clearly laid out the ideological trajectory of the labor movement. "Unionization, opposed to communism," Lewis said, "presupposes the relation of employment; it is based upon the wage system and it recognizes fully and unreservedly the institution of private property and the right to investment profit."[78] In 1941, the CIO's avowed moderate outlook helped break the deadlock with Little Steel. Receiving the tacit support of the Roosevelt administration, the CIO and its affiliates won union contracts at Ford, the Little Steel companies, and major electronics manufacturers.

World War II provided the laboratory for testing this new system of labor relations. The government entrusted the unions with the responsibility for preventing strikes (which reached record highs) and settling grievances peacefully while wages and other vital cost factors would be locked into the contracts for their duration.[79] At the same time, government patronage bolstered the status of labor's officialdom as they successfully integrated themselves into government. As early as 1940, Walter Reuther, president of the United Auto Workers (UAW), had presented a plan for union collaboration with corporate management and the government in the expansion and coordination of war production. Ultimately, trade unions affiliated with both the AFL and the CIO lined up with business and government in pursuit of these goals. Thus began the establishment of corporatist relations between the unions, employers, and the state, including the formation of industrial councils and other joint labor-management structures.[80]

Events in the United States during the Great Depression years also dramatically altered labor relations in Canada. Canadian unionists who had watched developments in the U.S. labor movement asked the CIO for support. At the start of 1937, the CIO began providing limited assistance to Canadian union organizing drives among loggers in British Columbia, women clothing workers in Montreal, and steelworkers in Sydney, Nova Scotia. The immediate result was the creation of a Canadian Committee for Industrial Organizing (CIO). Its first major victory came in a strike involving 4,000 workers at the General Motors (GM) plant in Oshawa, Ontario. The union won the eight-hour day, better wages and working conditions, a seniority system, and company recognition of the UAW.[81]

Although the Oshawa UAW and other unions were made in Canada, they still remained affiliated with the American-based CIO because they worked in the same industries for the same employers and under similar conditions. But unions bargained over local conditions, and this factor loomed large in 1940 when the CIO unions in Canada joined other independent labor organizations and formed the Canadian Congress of Labor (CCL). Yet, the CCL still recognized the necessity for cross-border cooperation by maintaining close fraternal and organizational ties with the American CIO. Within Canada itself, however, fragile links between unions in English Canada and Francophone Quebec continued when Catholic unions began to drift more toward clerical nationalism.[82]

Despite these obstacles, union membership in Canada exploded during World War II. Unlike in the United States, Canadian unions received no invitation from the government to join in wartime decision making. Union leaders did not offer no-strike pledges as a result, and workers went on strike for higher wages and better conditions in record number. Strikes doubled between 1941 and 1942 and did so once again in 1943 when one in every three union members in Canada was on strike.[83] By early 1944, labor's pressure forced the government passage of an emergency order in council, PC 1003, that protected the workers' right to organize and required employers to recognize unions chosen by a majority of workers. As in the United States with the Wagner Act, PC 1003 gave a big boost to union membership. By the end of the war, CCL membership had tripled to 314,000 and the craft-oriented TLC increased its membership from 132,000 to 356,000.[84]

When the government extended PC 1003 for two years after the war's end, in 1946 workers shut down the British Columbia logging industry, the Ontario rubber industry, the central Canadian ports, the Southam newspaper chain, the country's steel industry, and dozens of mass-production plants in the biggest industrial strike Canada had ever witnessed. These actions along with a strike in Windsor, Ontario, that involved 17,000 Ford workers influenced Canadian courts. In a landmark decision regarding labor, Justice Ivan Rand granted the Ford union the compulsory checkoff of union dues. Known as the Rand Formula, it combined with the decision of the federal government to codify PC 1003 into the 1907 Industrial Relations and Disputes Act. The legal framework for labor relations in postwar Canada had been established.[85]

Depression, Labor, and World War II in Mexico

When the Mexican economy recovered from years of stagnation caused by the revolution, it affirmed the Gompers formula for sound international political economy and jobs for American workers. When Mexico purchased U.S.-made capital and consumer goods, the country stabilized politically, trade union membership grew, and organized labor played an ever more crucial role in the nationalistic and "revolutionary" regime beginning to take shape. But the Great Depression years, as in the United States and Canada, generated waves of labor unrest and strikes, many against foreign-owned enterprises when management attempted to impose wage cuts and other measures that resulted in worsening job conditions.[86]

The now politically discredited and corrupt CROM, whose leadership had been blamed for the assassination of president-elect Alvaro Obregón, could not control the unrest. Under these conditions, the Mexican Congress enacted the 1931 Federal Labor Law (FLL), giving the federal government the legal mechanisms necessary for the enforcement of Article 123, which included the protection of Mexican workers from abuse by foreign employers. This shield of government protection helped many Mexican unions rebuild their membership. Because the FLL also codified the existing tripartite labor boards into federal law, most unions that had broken from the CROM and had since affiliated with the Confederación de Trabajadores de México/Confederation of Mexican Workers (CTM) moved closer to the government.[87]

This resulted from the government of President Lázaro Cárdenas encouraging and supporting strikes by workers against foreign-owned companies. By attaching himself to the nationalist struggles of the workers, Cárdenas distanced himself from his predecessors who had failed to establish a margin of economic independence from foreign capital, and especially the United States. In 1938, the government nationalized the petroleum industries during a strike by oil workers seeking higher wages and demanding that the mostly U.S.-owned companies share more of their profits as well as technical and managerial expertise with Mexican nationals. While Cárdenas and the Mexican unions viewed the nationalization as the long-awaited fulfillment of Article 27 and the idea of "Mexico for the Mexicans," it faced strong opposition from the foreign oil companies and temporarily disrupted commerce between Mexico and the United States. The nationalization, however, did win Cárdenas widespread praise both within Mexico and throughout much of the developing world, where nationalist sentiment was growing.[88]

The oil nationalization also drew tacit support from the CIO. Like Gompers and the AFL in the past, Lewis had pragmatic reasons for supporting Mexican workers and their government. The CIO hoped that its support would assist in its ongoing efforts of cooperation with the CTM on a myriad of issues affecting labor in North America, especially the organizing of Mexican workers in the United States.[89] Moreover, Mexican control of oil would provide workers with a larger share of national income. This would enable Mexican workers to purchase American goods made by unionized workers in the U.S. manufacturing sector, which constituted a substantial portion of CIO membership. The CIO position complemented efforts by the American government to expand trade and investment in all of Latin America. In a 1939 Labor Day speech, Lewis affirmed CIO support for U.S. commercial expansion in the hemisphere when he said, "Central and South America are capable of absorbing all of our excess and surplus commodities."[90]

Lewis added in his speech that increased volume in trade would also result in improved political and cultural relationships and thereby help the United States thwart challenges by foreign powers in the region, a political position that in effect resurrected and reinforced the American labor movement's support of Gompers's labor corollary to the Monroe Doctrine made a decade earlier.[91] In an effort to build better relationships with Mexican unions and others throughout the Western Hemisphere, Lewis and the CIO supported the creation of the Confederación de Trabajadores de América Latina/Confederation of Latin American Workers (CTAL) to replace the defunct PAFL.

The AFL, meanwhile, denounced the CTAL as Communist-inspired and opposed the Mexican oil nationalization. Refusing to be outflanked by the CIO through its relationship with the weakened CROM, the AFL and its representative Robert Haberman lobbied the Mexican government to rescind the nationalization decree on the grounds that governments should not intervene directly in the economy.[92] Although unsuccessful in achieving this goal, during the war years the AFL sent representatives to Mexico and the rest of Latin America in order to establish backdoor contacts with non-CTAL-affiliated unionists. Working closely with American officials and receiving U.S. government funding, AFL operatives identified cooperative union leaders who then would be involved in travel exchanges with American unions.[93] Despite this AFL maneuvering, Mexican unions grew more nationalistic as a result of their participation in the management of the oil industry and the railroads.[94] This development not only provided the opportunity for the government to cultivate a stronger relationship with the growing trade union bureaucracy, it also checked rank-and-file demands to place the nationalized oil industry and the railroads under workers' self-management.

The tighter CTM-government relationship and the federation's administration of state-run enterprises resulted in union membership growth. By 1940, union membership as a percentage of Mexico's economically active population had increased to 15.5 percent from 5.5 percent in 1930.[95] Higher rates of unionization translated into bargaining leverage for all unions, even those that faced strong employer resistance, such as the steelworkers local in

Monterrey that in the past had been the crown jewel of the company union model.[96] Between 1935 and 1940, real industrial wages increased by 26 percent.[97] The gains made by Mexico's industrial workers were a direct result of the wealth generated by the oil nationalization and other industries such as mining.

In 1942, the potential for industrial workers to earn more received a boost when the Mexican Congress amended Article 123 to place strategic industries like mining, petroleum, railroads, automobile manufacturing and assembly, and textile production exclusively under federal jurisdiction. The CTM moved even closer to the government as unions expanded their management role in many of these enterprises.[98]

The revenue from nationalized industries and increased government control over major sectors of the economy not only helped workers make gains and strengthen the position of unions, it also gave the Mexican state a margin of economic independence. This relative economic autonomy was instrumental in building Mexico's Import Substitution Industrialization (ISI) program. These ISI enterprises used government tariff and nontariff measures to protect them from imports. As the government expanded this program and gained outright ownership and control over the oil, railroad, electric power, telephone, and many other industries, Mexican unions, through their participation in the management of these enterprises, dug deeper material roots for integration into the state.

That integration, however, never resulted in the government-backed unions having complete control over the rank and file. During World War II, factions emerged within CTM unions that challenged organized labor's alliance with the government. They ignored the no-strike pledges labor officials had made to the government, and it precipitated a record number of strikes that protested the shrinking portion of national income going to the working class in the form of wages and benefits.[99] Ironically, these events in Mexico and in the rest of North America combined with the economic expansion of national industries in the war years helped stabilize labor relations. The efficacy of collective bargaining as a viable mechanism for stabilizing labor relations in the postwar period would depend greatly upon that continued economic expansion and success of national industries.

Labor and the Postwar Boom in North America

In his landmark study, *The Great Transformation*, sociologist Karl Polanyi attempted to explain the connection between capitalism and the outbreak of two global wars in less than a half century. He suggested that the emergence of the modern industrial economy and the economic changes that it generated had created markets beyond national control. He argued that these developments were impossible to sustain and therefore had led to armed conflicts between rival capitalist countries.[100] Published in 1944, Polanyi's work predated the end of World War II that effectively marked the beginning of the rapid demise of rival capitalist empires and the emergence of the United States as the world's preeminent power. This opened the way for the reconstruction of the world economy based upon the adoption of American production methods.

Complementing this process was the development of a postwar financial structure built on an American dollar backed by gold to provide a stable international system of payments to help rebuild the capitalist world. As historian Charles Maier writes, the extension of American production methods through the major capitalist countries in the postwar period, especially in Europe through the Marshall Plan, formed the basis of the postwar boom.[101] This "cult of productivity" promoted by the United States through economic and political channels around the globe helped profit rates reach record levels worldwide during the postwar decades.[102] For the first time since the nineteenth century, the capitalist world had an undisputed leader, one that could manage and control markets on an international scale, much like Britain had done a century earlier.[103]

Central to the management of the postwar boom were the Bretton Woods institutions: the International Monetary Fund (IMF), the General Agreement on Tariffs and Trade (GATT), and the World Bank. Created in 1944 under heavy U.S. influence, these institutions directed the progressive dismantling of the prewar trade blocs and the integration of the European market, formerly divided by cartels and tariffs. At the heart of postwar reconstruction, however, was the necessity to revive national economies as the focus for the accumulation of capital.[104] It is within this framework that Canada and Mexico, both under constant and relentless pressure from the United States to extend its economic influence into their respective countries, were able to build extensive networks of tariffs and other trade restrictions protecting many of their home industries that until recently allowed for a relative degree of autonomous development.[105]

Worldwide between the years 1950 and 1970, gross domestic product (GDP) and labor productivity grew twice as fast as they had in any other period.[106] In North America, this provided leverage for organized labor to bargain for higher wages and pressure the state for social reform. Programs such as workers' housing in Mexico, Medicare in the United States, and national health insurance in Canada constituted what became known as the social wage, and it helped boost living standards significantly. Because production was still a unified process primarily organized within the geographic framework of nation-states, organized labor could negotiate the distribution of profits resulting from worker productivity. The homespun accumulation of capital enabled the unions to exercise leverage through strikes and collective bargaining to win higher wages and effectively pressure their governments for social wage provisions.

The gains workers and their unions made depended greatly upon the continued success of their respective national economies and industries.[107] In the United States, this meant the American economy's continued expansion and domination of markets beyond its borders, particularly in Latin America. In 1945, U.S. Assistant Secretary of State Will Clayton unveiled the U.S. government's plan to secure this objective. Although never completely implemented, the Clayton Plan, as it became known, called for massive infusions of American capital to Latin America to ramp up production in agriculture and in extractive industries while, at the same time, lowering tariffs in those countries to increase the sale of U.S.-manufactured goods. Both the leadership of the AFL and the CIO supported the essentials of the Clayton Plan.[108]

Much like Gompers had done in an earlier period, the postwar union leadership linked the improvement of living standards for Mexican workers to their ability and readiness to supply the United States with agromineral materials. High levels of productivity would translate into purchasing power through collective bargaining, and workers would in turn consume goods made by unionized workers in the United States. The UAW claimed that, if implemented, the Clayton Plan would increase U.S. car sales south of the border and provide as many as 200,000 jobs for workers at home.[109]

Despite this display of organized labor's open support for American capitalism and its continued expansion abroad, many corporate leaders fiercely resisted the spread of unionism inside the United States. This was glaringly evident in 1946 when industry-wide strikes broke out in the auto, steel, meatpacking, and electrical industries. While winning only minimal gains, the strikes resulted in the passage of the 1947 Taft-Hartley Act, severely weakening the legal power labor had won a decade earlier. Organized labor felt the impact of Taft-Hartley almost immediately as the CIO suffered a crushing defeat in its much touted Operation Dixie organizing drive. Corporations then began to successfully use Taft-Hartley against labor everywhere.

Through the legislation's right-to-work laws, states prohibited agreements between unions and employers making membership or payment of union dues or fees a condition of employment, either before or after hiring.[110] The result was that Taft-Hartley allowed low-wage, low-tax regions to become the settings for the first wave of U.S. corporate globalization, undermining the strength of labor in the rest of the economy. As labor historian Jefferson Cowie shows in his study of RCA, *Capital Moves: RCA's 70-Year Quest for Cheap Labor,* the relocation of manufacturing plants, or just the threat of it, has long been a weapon in capital's arsenal to hold workers' demands in check. Through tracing RCA's moves from Camden, New Jersey, to Bloomington, Indiana, to Memphis, Tennessee, and finally to Ciudad Juárez, Mexico, to escape unions and keep wages down, Cowie explains the pre-NAFTA roots of the "runaway shop."[111]

For at least two decades, the full implications of the runaway shop in the American South and elsewhere were masked by the postwar economic boom and the hegemony exercised by the United States in the global marketplace. These conditions aided unions as they successfully bargained with employers in many major industries. In exchange for higher wages, benefits, and guaranteed pensions, unions conceded the basic prerogatives of management rights in the workplace. These negotiated agreements, the first and most of important of which were in the auto industry, set standards for unions in steel, mining, rubber, trucking, construction, and telecommunications. The pattern of steady wage increases together with increasingly stronger health and retirement benefit packages stretched well beyond heavily unionized industries, setting benchmarks for all the nation's employers, union and non-union alike.

But the agreements made by American leaders tied the future of organized labor and the broader working class to the assumption that U.S. capitalism and American companies would maintain a permanent hegemonic position within world markets.[112] Remarks made by Walter Reuther confirmed this outlook: "It is in our self-interest in terms of providing a market for finished goods from American industries, a market for goods manufactured by American workers, to see the living standards of others raised—to see their own indigenous economies developed and strengthened."[113] Although many independent-minded union locals, especially those outside the auto Big Three of GM, Ford, and Chrysler opposed Reuther and his support for American capitalism, his outlook prevailed not only within the UAW but also throughout the great majority of unions making up the American labor movement.

Facilitating the triumph of this outlook was the emergence of the Cold War, and both the AFL and the CIO aligned themselves firmly behind this anti-Communist crusade of American capitalism. In the process, they purged what was left of Socialist and Communist elements within their ranks and directly participated in U.S. government efforts to subvert radical and pro-Soviet labor organizations around the world. In many ways, the merger of the CIO and the AFL in 1955 occurred on the basis of this common political orientation. In 1956, it was a driving force that helped unite the CCL and the TLC into the newly formed Canadian Labor Congress (CLC) as both federations expelled Communists and Socialists from their unions.[114]

In Canada, the triumph of anti-Communist business unionism paralleled the ongoing American economic penetration of the country. Trade had expanded significantly between the two countries during the war when the United States provided about 70 percent of Canada's imports. In the postwar period, Canada's exports to the United States grew to unprecedented levels. By 1951, exports to the United States had more than doubled, representing 59 percent of total Canadian exports. The Cold War fueled the export boom as the American military purchased huge quantities of Canada's uranium, aluminum, lead, zinc, and other minerals.[115]

By 1960, U.S. investment represented three-quarters of all foreign investment in Canada, the majority of which went into manufacturing, oil, mining, and smelting. In 1967, American exports to Canada totaled nearly $8 billion, while Canada sent $7 billion worth of goods to the United States.[116] In no other country with Canada's level of industrialization was such a percentage of the economy controlled by foreign interests.[117] Closer economic ties also meant the strengthening of linkages between American and Canadian unions. By 1970, slightly more than 65 percent of Canadian union members belonged to U.S.-headquartered unions.[118]

In Mexico, government-backed trade union leaders worked with their American counterparts to oust militant and independent union leaders, whom they replaced with more reliable labor leaders called charros. In the process, the Mexican unions received crucial training and direct material assistance from the AFL, the CIO, and the U.S. government.[119] As in Canada, the involvement of American unions in Mexico paralleled increases in investment from the United States. In 1946, total investment from the United States had grown to $729 million, up from $525 million in 1942, and investment into manufacturing accounted for 25 percent of the total. By 1952, direct investment into Mexican manufacturing had climbed to 30 percent of all U.S. investment flowing into Mexico. Between 1952 and 1958, direct investment in the Mexican economy from the United States increased 60 percent, and half of it went into manufacturing.[120]

The flow of American dollars into Mexican manufacturing and the resulting economic "miracle" that took place between 1940 and 1960 depended greatly on the ability of labor officialdom to boost labor productivity. Acting not only as the legal bargaining representative for production workers, the union officialdom directly involved itself in the management of these enterprises.[121] Because union leaders in the United States had aligned themselves with government and business in seeing increased industrial exports as an important means in maintaining domestic economic growth and job creation, they stood ready to assist Mexican unions to ratchet up worker productivity.

Working closely with the American government's United States Information Service (USIS), labor leaders in the United States developed programs to train Mexican union leaders on ways to enhance labor productivity. Between 1953 and 1956, fifty-nine Mexican labor leaders visited the United States to study the adjustment of labor to problems regarding productivity in American business establishments.[122] Although it is difficult to establish a direct link between these trips to increased labor productivity, higher worker output in Mexican manufacturing enabled the labor officialdom to negotiate wage increases in a low-inflation economy that ticked real wages upward during the miracle years.[123]

The 1960s: The Beginning of the End of the Postwar Boom in North America

Although real wages did increase for Mexican industrial workers during the miracle years, an even larger share of national income went to the nation's growing layer of upper-middle-class technocrats and managers.[124] By 1958, this factor had taken its toll on the stability of the nation's labor relations system. Cracks opened up in the system when railroad workers and teachers went on strike to demand both higher wages and a loosening of government control over their unions. Unwilling to tolerate this direct challenge to the charro system, the Mexican government employed violent force to break the strikes and issue long-term jail sentences to prominent strike leaders on charges of attempting to "dissolve the state."[125]

Despite the repression, challenges to the charro system continued. In 1960, the electrical workers' union formed a new labor federation to rival the CTM. Instead of using force as it had done in the past, the government responded with a series of reforms to give workers and unions a greater voice in the nation's economy and political affairs. In 1962, the Mexican Congress passed laws that finally implemented profit sharing mandated by the 1917 constitution. In 1963, the Mexican government modified the system for setting minimum wages through the establishment of a tripartite Minimum Wage Commission, giving labor a greater voice in the country's economic affairs.[126] At the same time, the government expanded social wage programs. Workers began receiving supplemental benefits such as paid time off, social insurance, transportation allowances, and low-rent housing, all of which came to represent an average between 20 and 30 percent of the workers' total compensation package.[127]

In 1966, the Mexican government attempted to curry favor with smaller labor organizations and win their support for state policies by actively helping form the Congreso del Trabajo/Labor Congress (CT). An umbrella organization linked to the Partido Revolucionario Institucional/Institutional Revolutionary Party (PRI), the CT incorporated unions and federations independent of the CTM. The idea was to provide these organizations opportunities for greater participation in the state sector of the economy as well as to encourage their participation in the political system.[128] Despite these efforts to shore up the labor relations dimension of the Mexican miracle, its economic basis continued to unravel.

Reflecting this development was the initiation of the 1965 Border Industrialization Program (BIP) that established maquiladora manufacturing along the U.S.-Mexican border. Among other factors, American interest in supporting the creation of the BIP was a direct reaction to the beginning signs of a crisis in U.S. manufacturing, most notably the fall in the rate of profit.[129] While the postwar boom helped drive the Mexican miracle, more importantly it revived the economies of Europe and Japan. As labor historian David Brody writes, in the 1960s foreign firms based in these countries began to gain a larger share of the American domestic market. By the end of the decade, European and Japanese firms controlled 70 percent of the U.S. market for radios and television sets, 35 percent of apparel, and nearly 20 percent of steel.[130]

In the case of Japan, its increased share of the U.S. domestic market occurred within the context of developing what became known as lean production. In effect, lean production began acting as a counterweight to American production methods that had dominated industrial production around the world for decades. The continuing success of lean production and the new forms of work organization that characterized its operation allowed Japanese-owned auto firms like Toyota to take control of 15 percent of the U.S. market for automobiles.[131] The immediate consequence of these developments was the relative weakening of the U.S. economic position internationally, manifested by the depreciation of the dollar.

Management reacted to this crisis by demanding major changes in work rules from unions based in steel, the railroads, textiles, and many other industries. Soon, employers in a variety of other industries began contracting out work, implementing tougher production standards, and relocating plants away from the centers of union concentration, like the American South. As the so-called runaway shop took off and competitive pressures built as a result of foreign competition, American unions began what can be described today as a protracted decline in membership.

Offsetting this development in the 1960s, however, was organized labor's growth in the public sector. In Mexico, when federal employees gained the same constitutional rights as workers in the private sector, they joined unions en masse.[132] In the United States, public sector unionism resulted from the enactment of new laws and executive orders that encouraged unionization and collective bargaining. Most notable was President John F. Kennedy's 1962 promulgation of Executive Order 10988 giving federal employees the right to unionize. Although these laws and orders prohibited most public employees from striking, numerous work stoppages occurred nonetheless, highlighted by the massive 1970 postal workers' wildcat walkout in the United States.[133]

In all three countries, public employee unionism benefited from the almost uninterrupted period of postwar economic expansion, which gave governments the revenues with which to meet union demands for increased salaries and benefits. According to labor historians Michael Goldfield and Bryan D. Palmer, public employee militancy colored the climate of class struggle in Canada in these years.[134] Goldfield and Palmer suggest that Canada's booming economy driven by the stepped-up exploitation of natural resources in the 1960s enabled public sector unions to extract more from the Canadian state than was possible in the Vietnam War–entangled United States.[135]

Paralleling the emergence of militant public sector unionism was the development of a strident labor nationalism that affected many areas of the Canadian private sector. Essentially, this nationalism sought to challenge the legitimacy of American power in Canada. In the context of protesting the Vietnam conflict, many Canadians complained that their country had become a rich consumer market for American products, where U.S.-based transnationals had unfettered access to its natural resources and a flow of human resources trained at the public expense.

Although not clearly articulated, these left-nationalist political and ideological forces exercised considerable influence among west coast smelter and metal-working tradesmen, pulp and paper workers, energy and chemical labor, retail clerks, building tradesmen, and within the Ontario and Quebec garment trades. Fragmented into rival union centers by region and language, nationalism provided Canadian workers the opportunity for labor unity. As a result, unions seized the opportunity to exercise their clout politically by integrating into the New Democratic Party, founded in 1961.[136]

In 1965 and 1966, this new current of politicized nationalist and militant unionism resulted in the highest percentage of work time lost to strikes since 1950.[137] Providing an important backdrop for this renewed militancy was tacit recognition that the AFL and the CIO had controlled the fractured Canadian labor movement ideologically for most of the twentieth century. In many ways, the labor nationalism that filtered through unions in the 1960s was a response to this historical domination, and it helped build momentum for an eventual breakaway movement of Canadian unions from the U.S.-headquartered AFL-CIO.[138]

Statistics Canada, an agency of the Canadian government, has assessed the long-term affects of the nationalist current in Canadian unions begun in the 1960s. In 2002, forty-six international unions operated in Canada, and they represented three out of every ten union members. By comparison, in 1952 Canada had 108 international unions to which seven out of every ten Canadian union members belonged. In 1952, only two out of ten union members belonged to national or regional labor organizations. By 2002, slightly more than 70 percent belonged to Canadian national unions.[139]

As the 1970s began, the postwar economic boom in North America started to seriously fade. The slowdown was especially notable in the U.S. manufacturing sector, where the fall in the rate of profit had begun to accelerate.[140] This factor was crucial in the American government's decision to stop backing the value of the dollar with payment in gold, making it the first casualty of the Bretton Woods system and triggering a takeoff in the internationalization of finance.[141] When stagflation—the simultaneous development of high inflation and rising unemployment—began to infect the American economy, the trend toward global financial manipulation as well as the search for cheaper sources of labor to restore profitability advanced.

While this economic malaise and the proposed business solutions to remedy it seriously affected Canada and the United States, its impact on Mexico, the developing nation of North America, rocked both its economy and its political system. The major changes resulting from these factors were a transformation of Mexico's political system and its economic development strategy that had been based on the primacy of the national market. These transformations involved Mexico's ideological abandonment of the 1910 revolution, which had provided the nationalist political and ideological framework that had guided the state's economic development policies for more than sixty years. In the process of turning its back on the revolution, the Mexican state gradually began shifting its development strategy in a direction that was more in line with changes occurring in the global economy, especially as they related to the emerging new international division of labor.

2

The Politics of Mexican Labor and Economic Development in Crisis

On September 1, 2006, Mexican President Vicente Fox canceled his final state of the union speech before Congress after legislators seized the podium in protest of a massive police and military mobilization against antigovernment demonstrators. For only the third time in Mexico's volatile political history, political and social conflict prevented a sitting president from addressing the opening session of the legislature.[1]

The incident was an immediate result of Fox's unprecedented ordering of the deployment of thousands of troops to occupy the area surrounding the Mexican Congress. Fox ordered the troops to block a demonstration by supporters of Andrés Manuel López Obrador, the presidential candidate of the Partido de la Revolución Democrática/Party of the Democratic Revolution (PRD), the declared loser of the July 2 presidential election by a narrow margin of 240,000 votes. The PRD candidate had rejected preliminary rulings of the federal election tribunal in favor of Felipe Calderón, the candidate of Fox's Partido Acción Nacional/National Action Party (PAN). Supporters of the PRD candidate were taking to the streets in anticipation of the eventual September 6 tribunal ruling that officially declared Calderón the victor and cleared the way for his December 1, 2006, inauguration as Fox's successor.[2]

The scale of the military occupation reflected the serious nature of the political and social crisis gripping the nation. The military imposed a no-fly zone for over a twelve-mile radius covering the Congress at San Lázaro, Los Pinos (the president's mansion), and the Zócalo square. Authorities closed all streets leading into San Lázaro with police barricades, manned by 2,840 members of the Preventive Federal Police, 800 troops from the Presidential Corps, and 200 from the Group for Special Operations. Armed with forty antiriot tanks and equipped with water cannons, these forces subjected all those entering the security zone, including legislators, to operations that involved the use of canine units and inspecting the underside of cars with mirrors.[3]

These conditions caused uproar among the congressional delegates from the opposition parties. A few minutes before the scheduled speech time, scores of legislators from the PRD and its coalition partner, the Partido de Trabajadores/Workers Party (PT), took over the podium and demanded an end to the military occupation. Legislators cited Article 29 of the Mexican constitution, which guarantees the right to protest.[4] At that point, President Fox announced that he would not address the legislature. Instead, he handed in his report, left the scene, and two hours later delivered from a remote location a taped version of his speech in which he declared that Mexico was a stable democracy and on the road to solving many of its social problems. He emphasized his administration's success in keeping inflation low, stabilizing the financial sector and lowering interest rates, and balancing the budget.[5]

Without mentioning either López Obrador or his opponent Calderón, Fox defended the results of the election, declaring them "transparent," while calling on every segment of Mexican society to put aside partisan differences and work toward a greater Mexico. Prepared in advance and in anticipation of a protest, the broadcast was interlaced with prerecorded images of well-groomed, happy children in school, workers drilling for oil, and children waving Mexican flags.[6] Meanwhile, inside Congress, PRD legislators held up signs that denounced the president as a traitor and a dictator, while refusing to leave the podium. Following the event, PAN leaders threatened to push for the decertification of the PRD as a political party, making it clear that a similar disruption would not be tolerated during Calderón's swearing in on the first day of December.[7]

The conflict between the PAN and PRD in the early days of September 2006 had roots that went far beyond the results of the July 2 elections. The disputed election transpired in the context of rising popular opposition and growing social discontent over a number of factors, some of which came to light in Fox's videotaped speech. The cost of stability and low interest rates for a better-off segment of Mexicans that Fox mentioned in his speech had another side: the economic marginalization of millions. While a small minority in Mexico, those with access to international finance and capital have become fabulously wealthy as joblessness, unemployment, and underemployment have pushed millions either into the informal economy or have forced them to migrate to the United States.[8]

In his speech, Fox also ignored events in the state of Oaxaca where thousands of striking teachers and their supporters had occupied the center of town for months. Events already had turned violent in Oaxaca, when police killed three demonstrators and wounded many more during several attempts to remove the strikers from the center of town. Only a few hours before the September 1 events in Mexico City, vigilante elements in Oaxaca had pistol-whipped a prominent leader of the teachers' union.[9]

The deteriorating political and social climate worried not only Mexicans but also many observers in the United States, especially those in business circles. An August 31, 2006, front-page editorial in the *Wall Street Journal* raised the possibility that Mexico will "become a headache on the growing list of global problems" for the United States. Condemning what it called "mob rule" in Oaxaca and criticizing Fox's unwillingness to get tough in Oaxaca and with forces still supporting López Obrador, the conservative daily of the American business world urged the Mexican president to order police and military to use the kind of force that it employed in Michoacán in April 2006.

There, both police and military used lethal force against striking steelworkers at the Sicartsa mill, which resulted in the killing of two strikers and the wounding of seventy-three others. In addition, authorities arrested thirteen striking workers and charged them with a variety of crimes, all of which carried with them significant time in jail, if convicted. Although events in Oaxaca and at the Sicartsa mill developed independently of the PRD mobilization surrounding the election protest, the *Wall Street Journal* linked them to an overall social climate characterized by a growing political uncertainty.[10]

San Lázaro, Oaxaca, and Michoacán: The Social and Political Context

The crises that developed at San Lázaro, Oaxaca, and Michoacán reflected a profound and protracted social polarization in Mexico that has roots going back at least a quarter century. Characterized by a sharp decline in living standards for large layers of the working class and peasantry, this deep and ongoing social polarization has been accompanied by the destruction of social programs that have coincided with the liberalization of the nation's economy.

Reacting to the building up of competitive pressures of an increasingly globalized economy, successive governments of the last quarter century have gradually abandoned the economic nationalism that grew out of the 1910 Revolution and guided the country's development policies for more than sixty years. In the process, the Mexican state has reopened its economy to foreign domination and has scrapped the social compact between the government, workers, and peasants that provided political stability in Mexico during those years. Among developing countries, Mexico was a model to emulate in those years, especially those in Latin America.

Mired in mountains of huge external debt, Mexico bowed to the dictates of international capital. In exchange for restructuring its debt payment schedule, the International Monetary Fund (IMF) and the World Bank demanded the dismantling of state-owned industries and the parallel assault on the social compact. In reaction to a series of financial crises, funds were siphoned off from masses of workers and peasants to international financial institutions and Mexican banks. Cuts in social programs were combined with the sale of state enterprises to domestic and foreign capitalists, followed by capital flight, devaluations of the peso, interest rate hikes, and further rounds of cuts in social programs and privatizations.

The reforms that ended the social compact exacted a huge cost, from which workers and peasants have yet to recover. The social rights that had been guaranteed by the 1917 Mexican constitution increasingly came under attack as living standards plummeted for millions and a small group of elites accumulated great wealth. For the most part, the international financial community has welcomed these developments. By following these prescribed policies, Mexico has witnessed an explosion in foreign direct investment (FDI) since 1994, making the country the third largest recipient of U.S. investments, right behind China and Brazil.[11] While this has been beneficial to some, especially the export-oriented northern states, the majority of working people have not shared in the prosperity.

Once considered a bulwark of stability in a region of the world historically characterized by political crises, military coups, revolving-door governments, new constitutions, and general economic malaise, in the era of globalization and NAFTA Mexico increasingly exhibits the historical characteristics of its Latin American neighbors. Many of the country's national institutions established by the 1910 Revolution have weakened or disappeared altogether. Mexico's subordination to the demands of global capital and the new international division of labor has deepened, especially as compared to its Latin American neighbors. What follows is an in-depth look as to why and how this transformation has taken place.

The Politics of Mexican Development, 1920–82

When the major fighting of the 1910 Revolution ended with the writing of the 1917 constitution, Mexico initiated a tumultuous period of political turmoil in which the system that governed the country for more than seventy years began to take shape. The period of political turmoil started when Venustiano Carranza, who managed to rule until 1920, was assassinated in a plot involving one of his generals, Alvaro Obregón. As Mexico's president, Obregón initiated the tradition that the president should leave office after choosing his own successor. This put the finishing touches on the Mexican state structure, a self-perpetuating presidential autocracy in which power had passed from president to president within the ruling elite.[12]

In 1924, Obregón named Plutarco Elías Calles, another general in Carranza's army, to succeed him. While Calles's term technically expired in 1928, he was the power behind the next three presidents, and in 1929 he organized the founding of the Partido Revolucionario Institucional/Institutional Revolutionary Party (PRI), first called the Partido Nacional Revolucionario/National Revolutionary Party (PNR). The formation of the PNR—renamed the PRI after World War II—created a party that would subordinate all classes to the state and the military. Within this arrangement, the ruling party discouraged any independent political or industrial action by the working class and incorporated trade union officials into its ranks. The PNR received its baptism of fire at the start of the Great Depression, when, fearing growing labor and social unrest, it turned to Lázaro Cárdenas, who as governor of Michoacán state had initiated popular social reforms, such as land redistribution. When Calles designated Cárdenas as president in 1934, he was compelled to concede him real and not merely nominal power.[13]

Once in power, Cárdenas revived the radical democratic promises of the 1917 constitution by acting upon agrarian reform and nationalizing the foreign-owned oil companies. Meanwhile, the Great Depression and war for the United States meant no competition for native industrialists who raked in huge profits in steel, chemicals, banking, brewing, glass, textiles, and other industries.[14] At the same time, Mexico implemented the Import Substitution Industrialization (ISI) program as part of an economic policy that featured mixed enterprises composed of both public funds and private capital combined with a large state-owned sector, thus promoting the growth of both state and private capitalism.

This form of state capitalism depended greatly upon the PNR's promotion of class harmony under the aegis of a "progressive" military. In effect, the PNR employed repressive policies toward elements of the peasantry and the working class who resisted state policies while materially rewarding their leaders for subordinating their demands to the profit system and state economic development policy. During the Cárdenas years (1934–40), the PNR fully acquired its corporatist characteristics, analogous to Italian Fascism, formally incorporating workers, peasants, and the army as separate organizations within the party structure. In effect, the PNR acted as moderator, controlling the conflict and struggle between classes and subjecting all major sectors of Mexican society to the growing power and authority of state-building elites.

The Cárdenas presidency represented the high-water mark of the seventy-year history of rule by the PRI because it provided a laboratory for the resolution of the principal postrevolutionary question facing the Mexican ruling party: How are the popular demands of Mexico's laboring classes balanced with the interests of its own national elites and foreign capital? Cárdenas and the ruling party did so masterfully during the period of oil nationalization by casting off foreign domination in order to gain control of their own national market and undertake the extraction of surplus value from its "own" working class.

At the same time, Mexican state-building elites raised democratic demands while making use of the working class to help establish its independence from foreign capital. By taking a more or less defiant stance toward the United States, the ruling party balanced the interests of both foreign and domestic capital while subordinating the demands of the laboring classes. As long as productive capital remained organized largely within the nation-state framework, there existed a significant objective basis for the conflict between the national elites in countries like Mexico and the more developed capitalist world.

It is within this context that state-party bureaucrats and the Mexican capitalist class at first merely coexisted. Later, however, a process of both social and political integration occurred as both groups seized opportunities generated by the pursuit of capitalist development within the framework of the national market.[15] As the community of interests among Mexican state-party bureaucrats and the capitalist class in Mexico solidified, the economy registered spectacular growth. From the mid-1930s until the late 1970s, the Mexican economy grew at an average annual rate in excess of 6 percent, and manufacturing output rose at 8 percent per annum. Mexico's real gross domestic product (GDP) increased most rapidly from the mid-1950s until 1970, when it averaged about 9 percent per year.[16]

The Bretton Woods system effectively guaranteed the viability of the Mexican development model that generated this astonishing growth because it assured that the nation-state would provide the foundation for capital accumulation on a world scale. Bretton Woods held back the excesses of unfettered globalization of an earlier period and provided space for countries like Mexico to develop capitalism based on national markets. Both ISI and the trade of raw materials to the developed world, especially oil, generated a substantial amount of foreign exchange to sustain and expand this model called the economic miracle.[17] But beginning in the 1960s, the motor that had driven this miracle began to sputter when the national market started to diminish in comparison to the global market to which production in Mexico and all countries became increasingly directed.[18]

In recognition of these changes, state planners of economic development in Mexico had hoped that automobile manufacturing would complement ISI and generate a dynamic economy built around mass-production industries. By the end of 1964, Mexican law mandated that all automobiles sold in the country had to be manufactured within the nation's borders. The Mexican government granted major concessions to U.S. auto companies to make the necessary large-scale capital investments. But the move toward a more modern system of mass production in the 1960s and 1970s under the aegis of the transnationals did not stop the economic miracle from fading. The government borrowed heavily from international banks to prop up the economy, especially the ISI sector. By the mid-1970s, the Mexican economy was on the brink of collapse.

Only the discovery of new oil fields in Mexico prevented financial disaster, at least temporarily. Mexico's known oil reserves provided the necessary collateral to obtain large new loans in the late 1970s and early 1980s. Between 1976 and 1980, Mexican oil revenues jumped from $311 million to $14 billion, and international banks gladly lent billions of dollars to both the government and the Mexican private sector as a result.[19] The government borrowed billions for infrastructure, industrial development, and social programs. It used these monies to build long and winding highways and construct new hospitals, modern universities, and steel mills.[20] The price of oil in international markets was a boom for the state-supported sector of the economy, and it grew at an exponential rate. From 1950 to 1970, the number of state-owned enterprises in Mexico had remained below 300. By 1982, the number of state-owned firms had grown to 1,555, accounting for 18.5 percent of GDP and employing more than 10 percent of the economically active population.[21]

When the price of oil on the world market collapsed, Mexico was on the verge of bankruptcy, unable to service its massive foreign debt. Higher interest rates on the money borrowed combined with the collapse in commodity prices proved the overwhelming dominance of the world market over the economies of developing countries. Beginning in 1982, as the Mexican economy began to register negative growth, the country entered a transition phase in which successive governments cast off the nationalist economic model and embarked on a new growth strategy. And Mexico was not alone among developing nations to do so. One developing country after another abandoned national development projects in order to comply with IMF and World Bank structural adjustment programs. By the end of the 1980s, Mexico and its Latin American neighbors Chile, Argentina, and Brazil all had virtually abandoned ISI. Meanwhile, the autarkic economies of the Soviet bloc, also based on the primacy of the national market, collapsed with the fall of the Berlin Wall.[22]

The End of the Mexican Revolution

In the next twenty-year period, instead of nationalizing foreign-owned enterprises while developing national industries as it had done in the past, Mexico looked to attract more capital investment from abroad, especially into the maquiladora sector where cheap labor and conditions of unrestricted exploitation prevail. Mexico's elites also linked their fate more directly to world markets, exporting ever-increasing amounts of their own capital to global financial centers. In 1986, when Mexico joined the General Agreement on Tariffs and Trade (GATT) and in doing so opened its economy further to global trade, currency devaluations had driven the dollar cost of Mexican labor below that of South Korea and Taiwan.

These factors combined with its geographic proximity to the United States made Mexico a magnet for low-wage manufacturing.[23] During the five years prior to NAFTA, maquiladora employment grew 47 percent, and in the first five years after NAFTA, employment growth soared 86 percent. In 1990, Mexico counted 1,789 maquiladoras. Three years later, the number had reached 2,143. By 2000, the number of maquiladoras operating in Mexico had grown to 3,703.[24]

In the process, the maquiladoras came to dominate the export sector of the Mexican economy. In 1980, for example, maquiladoras accounted for just 14 percent of Mexican exported goods and services. By 1991, that number had reached 37 percent, and in 2000 production in maquiladoras accounted for 47 percent of all exports and 54 percent of all manufactured exports. As the economic importance of this sector grew, the rules that governed production and labor relations in the maquiladoras began to spread to the rest of the economy, especially in Mexico's traditional manufacturing sector. As the lines blurred between export and domestic production, labor relations in Mexico began to experience profound changes.[25]

For most of the postrevolutionary period, Mexican unions negotiated wage increases for industrial workers in line with growth in productivity and the rate of profit in the traditional manufacturing sector. This trend began reversing in the early 1980s when productivity and the rate of profit in manufacturing began to fall. Many firms reacted to these developments by downsizing their workforces and pressuring the unions to make changes in collective agreements that gave management more flexibility in determining conditions of employment. Although some unions protested these developments and went on strike, others acquiesced to management demands on the grounds that their organizational future depended on the survival of their membership base, which already had experienced sharp decline because of downsizing.[26]

Where this occurred, collective agreements began accommodating wage cuts and work speedup. By mid-decade, these measures had contributed substantially to restoring both productivity and profitability in the manufacturing sector. Between 1985 and 1988, worker productivity increased at an annual average of 4 percent while the rate of profit in the traditional manufacturing sector grew by 55 percent.[27] During the entire decade of the 1980s, the real wages of industrial workers declined, contributing greatly to the shrinking of labor's share of national income.[28] In 1980, payment in wages and benefits to workers accounted for 36 percent of Mexican GDP. By 1991, it represented just 21.1 percent.[29] At the same time, lower wages combined with rising unemployment began pushing large numbers of Mexicans northward to work in the United States.

These economic and social conditions generated a political crisis that coincided with the 1988 election and the eventual installation of Carlos Salinas de Gortari as president. Growing resistance by labor and the peasantry to the increasing liberalization of the economy had caused a split within the PRI. The result was the birth of the PRD, which acted as a left-wing political catalyst for uniting political opposition to Mexico's turn away from economic nationalism and the Revolution. Salinas and the PRI narrowly escaped electoral defeat at the hands of the left-wingers through what many claim was the use of voting fraud.[30]

As president, Salinas moved to discard the ideology of the Mexican Revolution and its corresponding economic model once and for all. As more foreign investment poured into the country, the sell-off of state-supported industries that had begun in 1982 occurred at a much more rapid rate. In the years between 1982 and 1992, the number of state-owned enterprises fell from 1,555 to 223.[31] These sales included mining operations, steel mills, the telephone company, and the railroads. In the process, Salinas and his close circle of supporters pocketed billions of dollars.

Salinas provided an ideological cover for his actions by replacing the "revolutionary" rhetoric of his predecessors with a new doctrine that he called social liberalism. In theory, while social liberalism was a mix of free-market economics with populist sloganeering, in practice it attacked what remained of the 1910 Revolution's social compact. Helping conceal the real nature of social liberalism, Salinas created programs to provide meager assistance for the nation's population living in extreme poverty.[32]

The social liberalism of Salinas was really neoliberalism, the ideological outlook that began sweeping the capitalist world in 1990 after the fall of the Berlin Wall and the collapse of the Soviet system. Neoliberalism promotes the rule of the market, deregulation, privatization of public services, and cuts in social spending. No matter how much Salinas tried to promote his image as a social liberal inside Mexico, outside the country he was well known as a neoliberal, an agent for the modernization of a "backward" nation.[33]

Salinas earned his reputation by deregulating the Mexican economy, facilitating the freer flow of imports and exports, investing in new technologies and research, and seeking to moderate wage demands while boosting worker productivity. For Salinas, increasing worker productivity was central to the success of the Mexican government's development policy goal of exporting the country into the First World fold of nations. If Mexican workers increased their productivity, Salinas and his technocrat advisers argued, a new labor relations environment would emerge, one that would establish labor peace, an essential condition for the country to attract more foreign investment, especially to the maquiladora industry.[34]

In his quest for labor peace, Salinas broke with his predecessors and challenged labor union power. This included the implementation of efficiency measures in the state-run railroad and oil companies. The result was massive layoffs of workers along with a significant reduction in the number of union-management personnel in these enterprises. When the head of the powerful petroleum workers' union leader resisted, Salinas had him charged, tried, and convicted to serve a thirty-year prison sentence for financial impropriety, illegal possession of firearms, and involvement in the death of a federal officer.[35] In addition, Salinas sought to put downward pressure on wages and impose work speedups in industries designated strategic by the federal government. Through the adoption of plant-by-plant collective bargaining negotiations, mixed state-private enterprises pit workers in the same industries against one another by threatening layoffs if wage cuts and productivity clauses were not agreed to by unions. This replaced the industry-wide bargaining method called *contrato ley* (labor contract) that since has ceased to exist almost entirely.[36]

These maneuvers by Salinas were touted by the government and business community as necessary to control runaway inflation, and they complemented the Economic Stability and Growth Pact (PECE) that capped wages and prices. Salinas also attacked the bargaining power of unions by linking an increase in the national minimum wage to levels of productivity for the first time. Labor union leaders traditionally had negotiated increases in the minimum wage, which during negotiations with employers always serve as the starting point for any increase in wages.[37]

These attacks on workers and unions emboldened many elements of the business community, reflected by their efforts to lobby Salinas directly to reform Mexican labor law and make it more business friendly. But Salinas rebuffed this request. He did so because his primary objective was to raise worker productivity and enlist the support of labor unions and their leaders in doing so. Francisco Hernández Juárez, for example, the president of the telephone workers' union, enthusiastically supported Salinas's initiative to link wage hikes to increases in worker productivity.[38] While Hernández Juárez headed a union in an industry undergoing a technological transformation that was sure to boost worker productivity, unions based in older industries had experienced rapid membership decline as a result of the privatization of many formerly state-owned enterprises. For these unions, the argument that higher worker productivity would attract foreign investment was compelling because it meant jobs and more members in their ranks.

More important, gaining the unions' support for increasing worker productivity was essential not only for attracting more foreign investment, but it was also ultimately a necessary step to win their support for Mexico's entrance into NAFTA. Productive workers needed markets to sell goods, Salinas argued. When the Mexican government entered negotiations on NAFTA in 1990, Salinas pitched NAFTA to the nation's unions with the idea of gaining more access to the American consumer market, the world's largest.

NAFTA, Salinas argued, was a hard-rock guarantee for Mexico to achieve sustained growth, which would enable the country's workers to enjoy increases in both the amount and quality of employment and earnings. Living standards for the Mexican people would eventually converge with those of the United States and Canada. All of this would happen when Mexican workers raised their levels of productivity, and many unions already had been buying into the idea.[39] By 1994, productivity bonuses showed up in slightly more than half of all collective bargaining agreements, which covered 78 percent of all workers employed in the federal labor jurisdiction.[40]

Perhaps equally as important as higher labor productivity for attracting foreign investment and getting Mexico into NAFTA was Salinas's 1992 declaration to end land reform and allow foreigners to own 100 percent title to Mexican lands. Land reform had been a central component of the 1917 constitution's Article 27, and for decades it served as a central pillar propping up popular allegiance to successive PRI regimes. PRI-controlled governments had always counseled patience from the masses of laboring people, claiming that the Mexican state was still at work trying to implement goals of the 1910 Revolution.[41] Ending land reform was a sign to foreign investors that the Mexican Revolution was over and that the country was now a safe place to put their money. The subsequent infusion of capital made Mexico a rising star among emerging markets, a category of nations that also included many former Socialist countries.

The foreign capital pumped into Mexico helped generate a 3.5 percent annual growth rate during the Salinas years. In reversing the negative GDP numbers of recent years, the upstart economy also created new employment by the hundreds of thousands.[42] More important, the influx of foreign capital helped bring inflation under control and boost the average manufacturing real wage, which increased by 19 percent between 1988 and 1993. Additionally, the government granted income tax credits to workers at the lower end of the earnings scale to increase their purchasing power. Cheaper and better goods flooding in from Asia via the United States to Mexico complemented these developments. Salinas pointed to the progress of the new model when he pitched for Mexico's entrance into NAFTA. Economic liberalization policies were already working, Salinas argued, and NAFTA would give Mexico the final push to transform itself from a Third World to First World nation.[43]

Although Salinas succeeded in obtaining much of organized labor's support for NAFTA, it did not change the fact that the government's policies of economic liberalization had unsettled labor markets, leading to a reconstituted Mexican working class. The new labor market included more female participation in the economically active population, more workers in the growing informal sector, and an industrial workforce that toiled increasingly for foreign employers who demanded labor flexibility.[44]

Most important, in regard to organized labor, much of the reconstituted Mexican working class remained outside the ranks of the "official" unions. One consequence of this development was that the wage premium that Mexican unions had once delivered to their members had all but disappeared. At the beginning of the 1980s, the wages of union workers were 40 percent higher than those earned by nonunion workers. By 1992, nonunion wages represented 97 percent of union wages.[45] The unions' ability to deliver good wages to their members received another blow when the peso crisis erupted in 1995, causing inflation to soar to record levels. This forced the unions to end provisions in collective agreements that linked increases in productivity to wage hikes.[46] These developments damaged both the credibility of the unions and the new economic model that they had supported. Even worse for the unions was that their traditional political ally, the PRI, was losing its grip on state power.

Under this weight, the once near monolithic Mexican trade union officialdom began to crack. By early 1996, twenty-one unions, including ten from the Congreso del Trabajo/Labor Congress (CT), formed the Foro group that initiated debate on the future of Mexican labor. In November 1997, the Telephone Workers Union, the National Union of Social Security Workers (SNTSS), and six other unions pulled out of the CT and joined independent unions such as the Union of Workers of the National Autonomous University of Mexico (STUNAM) and the Authentic Labor Front (FAT) to create a new labor federation, the National Union of Workers (UNT). The split within the trade union officialdom and the creation of new labor federations resulted from the economic restructuring that adversely affected membership and the change in labor relations practices by the unions themselves, most notably the abandonment of the strike.

The Decline of Union Density and the Strike

From 1984 to 1994, Mexican unions witnessed a 9 percent decline in membership, and it occurred across all economic sectors. The greatest decline came in the transportation, mail, shipping, and warehousing sectors, all of which experienced a 38 percent decline. Mining, electricity, water, and the gas transmission industry witnessed a 14 percent membership decline. In the same period, union density declined by 10 percent in manufacturing, 8 percent in the service sector, and 5 percent in the commercial sector.[47]

Between 1994 and 1997, restructuring in transportation, fishing, and the airlines that involved some 300 mergers or corporate partnerships between Mexican and foreign firms shrank union representation from 54 percent in 1984 to just 15.4 percent of workers in those industries.[48] In addition, large-scale restructuring of Mexican production through subcontracting and a rise in the number of "positions of trust" (*trabajadores de confianza,* or confidential employees) reduced the number of workers with a fixed-term contract who were represented by a union, which between 1992 and 1996 fell from 22.4 to 1.7 percent. Approximately 408,000 workers were involved in this transition.[49]

The exponential growth of the so-called informal sector also has adversely impacted union membership. Characterized by unstructured employment, self-employment, and microestablishments, the informal sector is difficult to unionize. Mexican law requires a minimum of twenty workers in order to establish a union, and because they are small businesses in which the employment relationship interfaces with family cooperation, they constitute more of a survival strategy rather than a traditional enterprise.[50] According to the International Labour Organization (ILO), in 2000 the informal labor sector in Mexico employed 25.5 million persons: 17 million (67 percent) men and 8.5 million (33 percent) women, constituting 63.4 percent of an economically active population of slightly more than 40 million [51]

Protection Contracts

Mexican union membership figures do not necessarily include those who are covered by protection contracts or "ghost unions," which are contractual agreements between employers and unions. In many instances, workers covered in protection contracts are unaware that they have union representation and never see the contracts that govern their terms and conditions of employment. The agreements give employers absolute authority in determining wages and other conditions of employment. In exchange, trade unions receive monetary compensation from companies for helping ensure peaceful labor relations.

Although the practice of protection contracts had existed in Mexico for decades, it accelerated when economic liberalization took off in the 1980s. Since NAFTA, protection contracts have become even more widespread.

Facilitating this development in the last several years has been an increase in the number of start-up services companies, designed to assist U.S. businesses in establishing operations in Mexico to better understand the nation's laws, regulations, practices and customs, and especially labor relations.

One such firm is Mexico Startup Services. On its Web site, the business offers to create a protection contract for U.S.-based companies that involve "help in choosing a union and union leader to deal with," "registering a contract with a labor court," and "the negotiating of a permanent agreement." The process allows for American companies to acquire a protection contract before ever setting up shop in Mexico.[52] In Mexico, since any strike without union authorization is illegal, protection contracts have afforded businesses a special type of legal shield to ensure a strike-free environment. Some analysts suggest that protection contracts constitute almost 90 percent of Mexico's 600,000 collective agreements and that government policies have encouraged the growth of these practices.[53]

Decline in strike activity has paralleled both the drop in union membership and the growth of protection contracts. The number of strikes, the number of workers involved, and the volume of strikes (i.e., the total number of working days lost due to strikes) have declined significantly in the last quarter century. In 1982, unions and workers in the federal jurisdiction carried out 675 strikes. By 1989, the number of strikes had declined to 118. The downward trend continued in the 1990s, when Mexico recorded an annual average of ninety-six strikes in the federal jurisdiction, involving an average of 36,000 workers each year and resulting in an annual average of 1.1 million working days lost. From 2000 to 2002, the annual average number of federal-jurisdiction strikes fell to thirty-eight, with an average of just 25,000 workers involved and an average of 529,000 working days lost each year.[54]

NAFTA and the Transformation of Mexican Politics

When Mexico signed on to NAFTA, it affected more than just workers and unions. It also signaled a major shift in power within the nation's ruling class. In effect, NAFTA represented the culmination of more than two decades in which governmental decisions began to reflect new socioeconomic institutional parameters resulting from the changing position of Mexico in the world economy. From 1940 to 1970, the dominant elements of Mexico's ruling classes were able to pursue state development policy within the framework of relative autonomy because favorable conditions in the world economy accommodated Mexican national interests. The viability of the ISI model initiated during World War II and sustained during the golden era of world capitalism bolstered the position of these dominant elite sectors within the Mexican governing class. It allowed them to unilaterally make the rules inside Mexico with regard to budgetary expenditures, taxes, labor, and social legislation and trade policy.

But when world capitalism headed into crisis during the early 1970s as a result of oil shocks, stagflation, and negative economic growth, the ruling elites of the advanced capitalist countries with the help of the IMF and the World Bank searched for ways to restore healthy profitability and restart economic growth. Working with governments, these institutions developed policies to free up the flow of capital, commodities, and labor. Within this context, both the IMF and the World Bank encouraged Mexico to privatize its state-supported enterprises and liberalize the financial sector to ostensibly offset its huge debt.

While these unfavorable external conditions for the continuation of the old economic model accelerated its collapse, the process also weakened the ruling political party and the once dominant elite sector that had organized itself around ISI industries. At the same time, Mexico's move away from the primacy of national markets toward the international market bolstered the position of Mexican elite sectors that had long advocated free-market capitalism, the dismantling of state-run enterprises, and the deregulation of labor. Accordingly, a transitional period began in which the established rules for governing Mexico were modified and adjusted to accommodate the specific composition of the ascending elite sectors and their foreign allies. These sectors were primarily members of Mexico's industrial and financial oligarchy hailing from the Mexican north where the benefits of increased economic openness were most apparent and where connections to U.S. capital traditionally had been strong.[55]

This sector of the Mexican elite had burrowed itself into the leadership core of the PAN, which emerged during the transition years as the PRI's most formidable opposition. Founded in the 1930s as a right-wing clerical party with historical roots in Spanish Fascism and sympathy for conservative Catholic doctrine, the PAN made a pragmatic turn during Mexico's process of economic liberalization. Posturing itself more as a probusiness, free-market-oriented political party, sections of the PAN hierarchy began to intermingle with elements of the declining elite sector who shared their neoliberal outlook. These developments gradually produced a PAN-PRI ideological fusion. These shifts in power within the governing elite mirrored the changing dynamics of the Mexican economy and paralleled even deeper changes taking place in the political system as the nation struggled to redefine its role and status in the emerging new world order.[56]

Major shifts in electoral politics characterized this transitional period, reflected in large part by the ending of seventy years of PRI rule and the PAN ascendance to power. This development unfolded gradually, and it first involved the PAN capturing a number of governorships in the north and west of the country. The process reached the federal level with the election of Vicente Fox in 2000, and the PAN consolidated its rule by winning the disputed 2006 presidential election. During the transitional period from the early 1980s to the election of Fox in 2000, the PRI gradually adapted itself to the emerging neoliberal political landscape.[57]

Through its repudiation of its old nationalist program, the PRI lost the basis for its appeals to workers and peasants and created a political vacuum that opened the door for the PAN. The abandonment of economic nationalism and the privatization of the nation's wealth enabled foreigners to capture ownership of significant portions of the Mexican economy. Meanwhile, a new group of capitalist billionaires emerged and international competition laid waste to many traditional sectors of the Mexican economy. The discarding of its time-honored doctrine of economic nationalism and widespread state intervention was not a matter of "betraying" a revolutionary program as some have claimed.[58] The PRI had been the ruling party of the Mexican elite, and its program always had centered on the defense of private property and the profit system. This had been confirmed in its repression of massive labor strikes in the 1940s and 1950s and in the 1968 massacre of students at Tlatelolco. The PRI had always blown with the winds of global capitalism. In the 1970s, when those winds began changing direction, the PRI followed.

A clear indication that significant changes were taking place within Mexico's governing elite, and that it was searching for political instruments that did not necessarily include the PRI, was evident at the party's seventieth anniversary celebration on March 4, 1999. At the event, President Ernesto Zedillo declared that, unlike previous presidents, he would not appoint a successor to serve as the candidate of the PRI for president in 2000. Every six years since 1934, the outgoing president of Mexico had selected his successor, after a process of private consultations among the power brokers of the PRI. This president-designate would then be rubber-stamped in elections whose outcome and even vote totals were determined not at the ballot box but in the central offices of the PRI. Instead, for the 2000 election, the candidate would be chosen by internal balloting at a party national assembly.

By taking this action, Zedillo had admitted that he could no longer control the factional struggle within the ruling party.

Both in 1987 and in 1993, the designation of a presidential successor led to divisions in the PRI. When President Miguel de la Madrid designated Salinas as his successor, Cuauhtémoc Cárdenas and Porfirio Muñoz Ledo led their faction out of the PRI and formed the PRD. In 1993, when Salinas designated Luis Colosio (who was assassinated soon thereafter) and then Zedillo as his candidates, Manuel Camacho Solís led his faction out of the PRI. By 2000, the PRI power structure had been badly shaken. It was now compelled, partly by international pressures, to make concessions to opposition parties. After many decades in which the PRI monopolized every office, the ruling party began to accept electoral defeats in state and local elections at the hands of the PAN and the PRD. In 1997, Cárdenas won election as mayor of Mexico City. By the time of the 2000 presidential election campaign, the PRI had already lost its majority in Congress and opposition parties controlled many state governments.

The new political realities forced Zedillo to preside over a considerable shift in the forms, if not the substance, of Mexican politics. The electoral institute received statutory independence from the Interior Ministry, media censorship of opposition candidates was loosened, and Zedillo followed through on his pledge not to select his successor in the traditional way. Instead, a PRI national primary held in December 1999 resulted in the selection of Interior Minister Francisco Labastida, who squared off in the general presidential election against the PRD's Cárdenas and Vicente Fox of the PAN.

The three major candidates all pledged to uphold Mexico's obligations to U.S. and international capital, represented by agreements with the IMF, the World Bank, and NAFTA. Fox personified a newer layer of Mexican businessmen who had risen to wealth and power through service to foreign capital. As the chief executive officer of Coca-Cola of Mexico, Fox was recruited by the PAN in order to run as its candidate for governor of Guanajuato in 1991. Denied victory by the PRI state machine, he ran again and won in 1995, after President Zedillo ordered the local PRI bosses to accept defeat. As governor of Guanajuato, Fox pursued a double strategy of attracting foreign investors, such as GM subsidiary American Axle, and aggressively slashing public investment and social benefits.[59]

Cárdenas, the PRD candidate, had lost considerable credibility by his performance in governing Mexico City since 1997, which included his role in the repression of the ten-month-long strike by university students at the National

University (UNAM). Throughout the campaign, Cárdenas made it clear to the business community that he would not challenge the policies of privatization and deregulation demanded by the IMF and Wall Street. On the eve of the 2000 presidential election, Mexico had still not fully recovered from the mid-1990s peso devaluation and debt crisis, let alone overcome the long-standing problems of underdevelopment and desperate poverty. Promising to attack Mexico's declining living standards and growing poverty through attracting more foreign investment that would create desperately needed jobs and to clamp down on out-of-control crime, Fox won a clear-cut victory in the presidential election.

The defeat of the PRI after seventy-one years in power marked a watershed in Mexican history. Long associated in the popular mind with the Mexican Revolution of 1910–17, the party still claimed, despite decades of corruption and bureaucratization, to represent the interests of Mexican workers and peasants. But millions of workers, peasants, small-business people, and students had arrived to associate PRI governments with political repression, bribery, corruption, and, in recent years, the drug trade. The PRI lost heavily in the more industrialized northern half of the country and finished a poor third in the capital, where more than 10 percent of Mexico's 100 million plus population lives. The ruling party's resounding defeat sent shock waves through Mexico's governing elite, and key members of that class began defecting from the declining PRI and jumping to the ascending PAN right from the outset. Fox placed two former prominent leftist intellectuals, Jorge Castañeda and Adolfo Aguilar Zinser, in charge of foreign policy, while Porfirio Muñoz Ledo, a former leader of the PRD, coordinated "political reform" for his administration.[60]

With regard to the masses of Mexican working people, Fox's populist campaign rhetoric raised their expectations and compounded his difficulties once in power. Although his talk of democracy, justice, prosperity, and equality helped win him votes, it proved difficult to reconcile it with his assurances to foreign and native capitalists that his administration would guarantee the unfettered exercise of property rights and the pursuit of profit. The charge of holding social tensions in check and managing discontent traditionally had fallen to the PRI-controlled trade unions, the CT, and the Confederación de Trabajadores de México/Confederation of Mexican Workers (CTM). The leaders of these federations, fearing that workers would stampede out of their discredited organizations now that they no longer had close connection to executive power, rushed to Fox's side.

Much like when the PRI was in power, for the most part, the official trade unions accommodated the continuing liberalization of the Mexican economy under PAN rule. During the Fox administration (2000–2006), the government was still selling off what remained of state-owned assets on very favorable terms to the buyers. Unions renewed the practice of placing productivity bonus provisions in collective agreements. In 2002 alone, their inclusion as clauses in union-management contracts in the federal labor jurisdiction nearly tripled from the previous year.[61] Paralleling this continuing trend was a renewed attempt to change the labor law in favor of employers and their need for workplace flexibility. These developments put further pressure on organized labor, and its ranks continued to fracture as a result.

In the last years of PRI rule, the Mexican Electrical Workers Union (SME) had declined to join the UNT and instead organized dozens of other unions, peasant organizations, and urban-based social movements in an independent labor coalition, the Mexican Union Front (FSM). The FSM disapproved of the UNT strategy of calling upon the major political parties to complete the nation's "democratization project," which had received a boost with Vicente Fox's election. The goal of the UNT was to reach agreement with the PAN neoliberal government on "a new social pact" with organized labor. The basis of the pact involved the UNT proposal to partner with employers and the government to increase productivity in order for Mexico to compete in the global economy and thereby attract corporate investors looking for labor flexibility.

Led by Francisco Hernández Juárez, the UNT advocated for union-management partnerships to boost labor productivity in the newly privatized telephone, airline, and other transport industries. But many workers in these industries were members of the newly recognized Federation of Unions of Goods and Services (FESEBES), affiliated with the FSM. In contrast to Hernández Juárez and the UNT, the FSM promoted what it called an anticapitalist unionism and rejected the notion of union-management partnership in the face of globalization.

But when the UNT and the FSM put aside their differences and worked together to oppose further privatization of the Mexican economy, particularly the Mexican Light and Power Company, for which most SME members worked, Fox's labor secretary, Carlos Abascal Carranza, quickly established a friendly relationship with Leonardo Rodríguez Alcaine, head of both the CTM and the CT. The CTM and CT generally supported the president's conservative political and economic agenda that included proposed cuts in social spending, continued privatization of industry, reform and privatization of the social security systems, regressive tax reform, and labor law reform.

In exchange, Fox and Abascal protected the labor leaders of the older federations and tried to help them maintain their tenuous grip on the reins of Mexican organized labor. By November 2003, in response to Abascal's moves toward reinforcing the corporatist system, the FSM and its forty union affiliates declared a new, independent labor federation, which split the Mexican trade union movement into three parts. Despite these fissures, in 2007 the CT and other labor unions close to the government still represented more than 90 percent of all workers covered in collective agreements negotiated during that year.[62]

It was in this context that the CT-Abascal alliance promoted a new labor culture, the idea that workers, employers, and governments should work together toward ensuring competitiveness in a global economy. Abascal is the grandson of the founder of a radical, anti-Communist Catholic group that in the 1930s opposed the Mexican government's prolabor orientation. His promotion of the new labor culture centered on workers and managers existing in a relationship framed entirely in terms of their common identities as individual human beings, rather than as something constructed by historical and economic processes. The rights of workers are understood as an extension of man's natural rights in the new labor culture, rather than as the product of historical struggles waged by the working class to protect itself against employer abuses and exploitation. Class struggle, the doctrine asserts, is antagonistic to human organization and especially the needs of private enterprise, which the new labor culture defined as the essence of "community."[63]

In the new labor culture, the basic rights of laborers are balanced with management's need for "flexibility." According to Abascal, the objective of any changes in Mexican labor law must seek to establish "equilibrium" between human rights on the one hand and corporate "flexibility" on the other. Through its focus on the individual worker rather than on labor's collective interests, the new labor culture complemented the changes taking place in labor relations as a result of globalization and NAFTA. And it filled a void in the context of Mexican labor union decline in terms of membership, organizational unity, and political influence.[64]

However, Mexico's poor economic performance during the Fox years stymied the conservative political and social agenda and in particular the initiatives to reform labor law and impose a new labor culture. Moreover, the Fox years had cast doubts on the viability of the neoliberal economic model in Mexico. For example, since NAFTA, Mexican manufacturing productivity had grown by more than 40 percent, while real wages had fallen. In 1975,

Mexican wages stood at 23 percent of U.S. wages; by 1994, the year NAFTA began, they had fallen to 15 percent; and by 2003, Mexican wages had dipped to 12 percent of what they were in the United States.[65] Mexico also had recorded weak per capita growth rates in the first ten years of NAFTA. From 1994 to 2003, Mexico registered per capita growth rates of just 1 percent compared to an annual average rate of 3.2 percent per capita between 1948 and 1973.[66] According to the World Bank, increases in income inequality also have characterized the NAFTA years. In 2000, the bottom 10 percent of the Mexican population earned only 1.5 percent of total income, whereas the top 10 percent earned 42.8 percent.[67] The number of working people living below the poverty line stood at 36 million persons, or 62 percent of the economically active population. The poverty line set by the Mexican government is two daily minimum wages for a family of five, which in 2000 was $8U.S. per day.[68] From 1993 to 2003, Mexico's working population receiving no benefits from social security (health insurance, pension contributions, etc.) reached 27.6 million, or 67 percent of the nation's labor force.[69]

By 2006, the dismal Mexican economy and the social misery it had inflicted on the nation's laboring classes had resulted in a full-blown crisis for the Fox government. The mounting social discontent parlayed politically into the reemergence of the PRD, which presented itself as a viable political alternative to NAFTA and the PAN. Recognizing the seriousness of the social volatility gripping the nation, especially in light of mounting labor protests by rank-and-file workers, the more farsighted layers of the Mexican governing class saw considerable value in a candidate like López Obrador. In the 2006 election, López Obrador struck a nationalistic posture, regularly winning ovations at campaign rallies with pledges to "renegotiate" sections of NAFTA so as to eliminate tariffs on imports of American corn and beans.[70]

His candidacy attempted to mobilize and control powerful social forces, driven by long pent up demands for jobs, a genuine land reform, an equitable distribution of income and wealth, and decent living standards, including health, education, and retirement. In the 2006 election, López Obrador and his elite backers had hoped to channel the explosive social discontent like the miners' strike and the Oaxaca rebellion through new institutions that would both ensure profits and allow for a minimum of social welfare.

But Mexican workers did not wait for the conclusion of the 2006 presidential election to act. Strikes by Mexican coal miners and steelworkers in the midst of the presidential election campaign and the violent and repressive actions taken by the government against the strikers shook the nation's already troubled labor relations and political systems. The labor department declared the strike at the Sicartsa mill of Villacero Steel, on the coast of west-central Michoacán, the largest wire rod and steel bar maker in Latin America, illegal only hours before President Vicente Fox's new labor secretary, Francisco Xavier Salazar Sáenz, sent in the police to take back the plant by force.

On April 20, 2006, state and federal police stormed the ocean-side complex with help from the Mexican navy. Armed only with slingshots and balls of iron ore, 600 striking workers stood their ground. Then police began firing live ammunition and the strikers set fire to dozens of cars to form a flaming barrier between themselves and their attackers. The workers eventually drove the cops out of their huge work shed using heavy machinery. Meanwhile, mothers, wives, and children marched from the Miners' Monument in downtown Lázaro Cárdenas to the port facility to protest the killing of two young workers.[71]

The strike at Villacero exploded on April 2, 2007, after Labor Secretary Salazar withdrew recognition of the miners' union president, Napoleón Gómez Urrutia, accusing him of having embezzled $55 million and looting a private pension fund. The action that occurred grew more heated when sixty-five miners died on February 19 in a huge explosion in the Pasta de Conchos coal mine, owned by Grupo México. Workers told the union they were required to weld while high concentrations of explosive methane gas filled the shafts in the days before the accident. The gas ignited in a huge fireball. Locals in Nacozari (Sonora), Sombrerete (Zacatecas), Taxco (Guerrero), and Lázaro Cárdenas struck when Salazar installed as union president the expelled retired union dissident Elías Morales, known for having negotiated an infamous productivity agreement with Grupo México.

In contrast, Gómez Urrutia had called more than thirty strikes in the last four years and, according to his supporters, helped defeat Mr. Fox's proposed labor reforms. He called the deaths of the miners at Pasta de Conchos "industrial homicide." In September 2005, the Mexican Miners and Metal Workers' Union won a forty-six-day strike against two steel companies in Lázaro Cárdenas. The local union and its 2,400 members secured an 8 percent wage gain, 34 percent in new benefits, and a lump sum payment of $7,250 Mexican pesos.[72]

In February 2006, Gómez Urrutia joined Isaías González, head of the Revolutionary Confederation of Workers and Peasants (CROC), to challenge the election of Victor Flores Morales, head of the Mexican Railroad Workers Union (STFRM), for control of the CT. Victor Flores had worked closely with the government to carry out the privatization of the Mexican railroads, which ended up in the hands of the Union Pacific and the Kansas City Southern railroads. When rank-and-file railroad workers protested, Victor Flores had them fired, and they joined 100,000 railroad workers already on the unemployment lines after having lost their jobs in the privatization. Both as a PRI congressman and a "friend of Fox," Victor Flores was a loyal adherent to the "new labor culture" and employer-driven labor flexibility.

Many union members viewed Morales as a tool of Villacero Steel and Grupo México enterprises. Grupo México is owned by the Carlyle Group, an international conglomerate with participating partners such as former U.S. President George H. W. Bush and former U.S. Treasury Secretary Robert Rubin. At the time, Salazar owned two companies that supplied chemicals to Grupo México. Carlyle Group has heavy investments in resource and defense and has dominated Mexican mining and steel production since their privatization in the late 1980s.[73]

Salinas had sent federal troops to the Cananea mining complex after it had been sold to Grupo México in 1989 at a bargain-basement price. Forty of the dead miners were contract or temporary workers who have no union or safety committee. They were paid $9 a day, working ten to twelve hours, well beyond the eight-hour limit defined in Mexican labor law. Contract employment is a growing development in Mexican labor relations. When the mines and mills belonged to the government, workers became permanent employees after finishing a probationary period. But when the mill was sold to the Carlyle Group, Sicartsa hired half of the workforce on temporary contracts.[74]

After the installation of Calderón as president, the Labor Ministry issued a report that found that management had routinely ignored between 90 and 120 safety regulations at the Pasta de Conchos coal mine. A federal court also ordered the reinstatement of Gómez Urrutia as miners' union president and cleared him of all charges. Yet Gómez Urrutia remains in self-imposed exile in British Columbia, fearing that returning to Mexico would jeopardize his personal safety.

But the political crisis that resulted from the 2006 election has given rise to more independent action by Mexico's laboring classes. The recent privatization of public employee pension plans and the reduction of benefits triggered massive sit-in protests and a series of intermittent general strikes. On July 30, 2007, the 1,293 unionized workers (plus 305 temporary workers) of Minera Cananea in Cananea Sonora, a division of Grupo México, went on strike. They demanded better safety in the mines, the opening of a local clinic to provide them with medical care, and recognition of their union representatives.

After the labor board declared the strike "nonexistent" on a technicality, the company took steps to fire all the striking miners. On the heels of this action, a new miners' union created with the support of Grupo México and in coordination with the federal government's department of labor claimed victory in a representation election held among more than 4,000 workers at la Caridad mine in Sonora. The new company miners' union is affiliated with the Federación Nacional de Sindicatos Independientes/National Federation of Independent Unions (FNSI), an organization of company unions headquartered in the northern industrial city of Monterrey. Founded in 1936 by a group of Monterrey industrialists, the FNSI opposed the leftist and nationalist politics of then President Cárdenas and the state-backed CTM.[75]

All of these incidents have taken place in the context of falling living standards for Mexican workers and full-scale assaults on their rights, a process that began with the liberalization of the nation's economy in the 1980s and that has accelerated since the beginning of NAFTA. The unfolding of these developments in the lives of Mexican workers and their impact on the nation's labor relations system have been documented extensively through the North American Agreement on Labor Cooperation (NAALC) and its complaint processes, the subject of the next chapter.

3

Mexican Labor and Workers' Rights under NAFTA and NAALC

While the NAFTA years for Mexico have reduced real wages, generated growth of the informal economy, and created conditions for massive migration of the working population to the United States, perhaps the most serious consequence of the period has been the assault on workers' rights. In their attempt to attract foreign investment, especially in the export manufacturing sector, Mexican government authorities have worked with corporate investors and compliant leaders of official unions in maintaining a low-wage economy, reinforced by more open and brutal systems of labor control. In the process, the legacies of more than a century of struggles—that is, the constitutional and legal protections that guaranteed workers' rights—are under relentless attack because they are viewed by the nation's elite and their foreign counterparts as obstacles to investment and creating a "good" business climate.

In the NAFTA years, the breaking of strikes and independent unions has been part of government and employer strategy to sweep away legal protections for workers and to crush any resistance to free-market-driven economic development. The evidence that this is occurring is overwhelming. It ranges from the attempts by the Mexican government to enact a new labor law more friendly to business interests to the documentation of workers' rights violations that are found in a plethora of complaints filed against Mexico since the inception of the North American Agreement on Labor Cooperation (NAALC).

The NAALC: Objectives and Limitations

In 1993, the Canadian, Mexican, and U.S. governments signed the NAALC, the first labor agreement negotiated as part of an international free-trade agreement, and it came into force along with its parent trade agreement, NAFTA, on January 1, 1994. In theory, the NAALC is supposed to provide "a mechanism for member countries to ensure the effective enforcement of existing and future domestic labor standards and laws without interfering in the sovereign functioning of the different national labor systems."[1] The goal is to "improve working conditions and living standards, and to protect, enhance and enforce basic workers' rights" via specific objectives, obligations, and labor principles that the three signatory governments are bound to uphold. The NAALC does not require the governments of the three signatory countries to raise standards or meet existing minimum international labor standards. The only issue addressed in the agreement is whether a country has persistently failed to enforce its own labor laws.[2]

Within this context, the NAALC has two broad goals: (1) to encourage the improvement of labor conditions in North America through cooperative activities, including the promotion of a set of eleven labor principles (discussed below); and (2) to provide a mechanism for mediating labor disputes. To fulfill these objectives, the NAALC created the Commission for Labor Cooperation (CLC), composed of a council of cabinet-level ministers from the three NAFTA countries and a secretariat. The NAALC also requires that each government establish a National Administrative Office (NAO) within its labor ministry. The NAO serves as a point of contact between the domestic government agencies, its NAO counterparts in the other NAFTA countries, and the secretariat. The NAOs are charged with responding to public requests regarding labor law matters in the other NAFTA countries and helping the CLC carry out its cooperative activities.

The NAALC provides a four-level dispute-resolution process to promote compliance with national labor laws: (1) NAO review and consultations, (2) ministerial consultations, (3) evaluation by a committee of experts, and (4) review by a dispute-resolution panel. The dispute-resolution process may be initiated in two ways. An NAO can independently request consultations with another NAO regarding any matter within the scope of the NAALC. Alternatively, individuals or organizations can make submissions to their domestic NAO if they believe a member country is not effectively enforcing its domestic labor laws. The NAO reviews these disputes and determines whether to proceed with the resolution process. To date, none of the complaints to the U.S., Canadian, or Mexican governments have resulted in serious action beyond what is called the ministerial consultation stage.[3]

One reason for this outcome is that coercive enforcement mechanisms in the NAALC are extremely limited. NAALC language obligates the agreement's signatories to protect workers' rights covering eleven labor principles: freedom of association, the right to bargain collectively, the right to strike, the right to minimum employment standards, prohibition of forced labor, labor protections for children and young persons, elimination of employment discrimination, equal pay for women and men, prevention of occupational injuries and illnesses, compensation in cases of occupational injuries and illnesses, and protection of migrant workers. They are pursued through cooperative activities and by means of mechanisms for intergovernmental consultations, independent evaluations, and dispute settlement.

However, the NAALC Ministerial Council can hear only complaints concerning forced labor, equal pay for men and women, worker compensation, and protection of migrant rights. Further, it is required only to respond to disputes in three areas: child labor, minimum wages, and occupational health and safety. Even then, the Ministerial Council may respond only if proof exists of a "persistent pattern of failure by the other Party to effectively enforce" its own labor laws. If the Ministerial Council declines to review a matter, then it may be referred to the Evaluation Committee of Experts, whose remedies are limited to "non-adversarial and non-binding recommendations" on the issue.[4]

The NAALC materialized as a mechanism to mitigate concerns that NAFTA would distort labor markets in both the United States and Mexico. The two main labor concerns were that, as a developing country, Mexico has substandard working conditions and lax enforcement of its own labor laws. These factors, along with significantly lower wages paid to Mexican workers, would pull more investment into the country and as a consequence would result in the loss of jobs and reduced wages for American workers. Accordingly, NAALC objectives linked compliance with the eleven labor principles to innovation, productivity, better working conditions, and quality of work life. The NAALC clearly spells out that only through adherence to the eleven labor principles could the three countries achieve higher living standards and thus reap the "benefits" of NAFTA and globalization.[5]

Since its inception in 1994, more than anything else, the NAALC process has exposed the Mexican government's failure to enforce the right of freedom to association. In Mexico, effectively this has meant denying workers their constitutional rights to organize unions of their own choosing and collectively bargain terms and conditions of employment. This is especially important in the NAFTA context because denial of this right deprives workers of the ability to negotiate productivity gains. Both the Mexican government and the official unions sold NAFTA to Mexico's workers on the grounds that higher labor productivity would mean increases in wages and thus a better standard of living. But real wages have not kept up with labor productivity growth in Mexico in the NAFTA years, and in fact they have fallen significantly behind.

What the NAALC process has revealed about the state of workers' rights, particularly with regard to freedom of association in Mexico, provides important insight into the consequences of the agreement's failure to impose a trinational set of labor standards. The domestic supremacy of labor law and especially how it is enforced preserves an incentive for businesses to invest in the territory with the least effective level of worker protection. This leaves the NAALC signatories with incentive to attract investment through the deregulation of their respective labor law regimes. The ongoing effort to reform Mexican labor law to allow more flexibility for business to determine wages and conditions is indicative of this development. The ironic result is that, instead of strengthening labor standards, the NAALC has contributed to their weakening. More specifically, the NAALC has been completely inadequate in correcting the verified record of nonenforcement of labor laws in Mexico, particularly with regard to freedom of association, the foundation upon which all other workers' rights rest.

Workers' Rights and Labor Relations in Mexico: An Overview

Article 123 of the Mexican constitution of 1917 was the first in the world to enact social and economic rights in a country's basic charter. Article 123, in effect, was a compilation of existing legislation that regulated labor relations in regions, sectors, and occupations in the United States, France, Belgium, and England. Because of its synergic character, it was unique in the world then, introducing a wide range of worker protections. Article 123 guarantees the right to organize, to bargain collectively, and to strike. It also secures a set of workers' social and economic rights, including the eight-hour workday and the six-day workweek, pregnancy and childbirth leave and pay, minimum wages, profit sharing, overtime pay, severance pay, worker housing and recreation, and occupational safety and health.[6]

A basic objective of Mexican labor law and Article 123 of the Mexican constitution is to ensure stability in the employment relationship and, in particular, to provide protection to workers against unjust dismissal for joining a union or waging a lawful strike.[7] The constitutional protections encompassed formal standards for collective bargaining, including interest representation and conflict mediation, substantive issues related to working conditions, health standards, remuneration, and many others as well as the tutelary role of the state, which at the time of their ratification recognized the weaker position of workers in a capitalist economy. Article 123 modernized labor relations centered on legal protection in a country where the vast majority of the labor force was made of rural workers and peasants, which by 1930 still constituted 71 percent of the economically active population.[8]

During the 1920s, a series of regulations emerged in the context of these constitutional standards, the most important of which were those pertaining to the right to strike and the developing system of labor-management relations. This process culminated in 1931 with the passage of the Federal Labor Law (FLL). In effect, the workers' rights ensconced in both the 1917 Mexican constitution and the FLL were a direct consequence of the political compromises arising from the revolution rather than through labor-management conflict over economic issues, and this is evident in the tutelary character of labor regulation. In exchange for legal protection, trade unions would deliver labor quiescence and political support for state policies, while state control over capital and labor organization and its internal affairs would help ensure labor peace.[9]

For example, Mexican labor law and regulatory mechanisms grant special powers to unions in terms of exclusion clauses (only union workers could be hired and keep their jobs). The creation of unions, collective bargaining, and the right to strike are all closely connected to the strong state control over unions' activities, processes of organization, and institutionalization. The state also exercises discretionary prerogatives in terms of the control of strikes and of conflict resolution based on a tripartite, albeit state-dependent, judiciary system, where political and/or economic reasoning intervenes in the interpretation of the legal codes. Over time, trade union presence in these tripartite structures as well as inside the state apparatus and the judicial system became institutionalized, and they eventually included workers' representative participation in the administration of state-owned enterprises, exemplified by the petroleum and railroad industries. In Mexico, strong state control over unions via administrative and repressive measures, including the possibility of control of elections, deposition of leaders, ratification of contracts strikes, and union decertification, has been the hallmark of the labor relations system.[10]

NAFTA and globalization have resulted in the increased scrutiny of the nation's labor relations system and the enforcement of workers' rights. Besides NAFTA and the NAALC, Mexico has entered into numerous free-trade agreements with other regions and countries around the world. Under the Mexican constitution, international agreements signed by the president of the republic and ratified by the Senate, including those dealing with labor matters, are considered "self-executing" and become an integral part of domestic law.[11] Even before NAFTA and the NAALC, Mexico had become party to several international instruments that require the government to protect workers' right to freedom of association. Mexico is signatory to the International Covenant on Civil and Political Rights (ICCPR), the International Covenant on Economic, Social, and Cultural Rights (ICESCR), and the Additional Protocol to the American Convention on Human Rights in the Area of Economic, Social, and Cultural Rights (Protocol of San Salvador).[12]

Similarly, the International Labour Organization (ILO) Declaration on Fundamental Principles and Rights at Work (ILO Declaration) has recognized freedom of association as one of the "fundamental rights" that all ILO member nations have an obligation to protect. Although Mexico has ratified ILO Convention no. 87, the right to freedom of association, it has not ratified ILO Convention no. 98, the right to organize and bargain collectively, despite the fact that Mexico's constitution protects these same rights. In all, Mexico has ratified seventy-eight ILO Conventions, sixty-seven of which are in force.[13] Mexico's entrance into the NAALC reinforced many of the nation's long-standing commitments to protect workers' rights as found in the ILO conventions. NAALC obligations and labor principles in fact supersede other international commitments because they are grounded in the realities of NAFTA and the country's specific economic trajectory, which is characterized by an ever greater deepening regional integration with its more developed neighbors to the north.

The NAALC and Workers' Rights under Assault in the Maquiladoras

Thirty-five complaints have been filed under the NAALC. Of those submissions, nineteen involved allegations against Mexico. Fifteen of those have involved issues of freedom of association, and seven have dealt with the right to bargain collectively. One complaint concerned the use of child labor, one raised issues of pregnancy-based gender discrimination, two concerned the right to strike, four concerned minimum employment standards, and six raised issues of occupational safety and health. The ones filed against the United States typically have involved Mexican workers on issues such as freedom of association, protection of migrant workers, various worker standards, and safety and health.[14] The majority of NAALC complaints filed against Mexico have centered on the maquiladora industry, which expanded rapidly in the years following NAFTA implementation. In the first six years of NAFTA, maquiladora employment grew 110 percent, compared with 78 percent over the previous six years.[15] In the process, the maquiladoras became a major engine of Mexico's economy.

The history of the maquiladoras has developed in three stages. In what is called the first generation of maquiladoras, intensive manual labor characterized the operations. The maquiladoras were based exclusively in light industries that involved routine assembly using unsophisticated and obsolete equipment with a preference for hiring young women. These maquiladoras were largely free of genuine worker organization; wages were low ($5.00 a day), and management ignored workplace regulations as defined by Mexican law.[16]

In 1972, when Congress made changes to the Mexican constitution that allowed overtime and night work for women, the maquiladora industry began to grow. In 1971, only 205 maquiladoras were in operation, and they employed just 20,000 workers. By 1974, there were 455 maquiladoras that employed 75,000 workers.[17] The Mexican government then granted exemptions to maquiladoras from the rules limiting foreign ownership and from Mexican labor laws, such as lengthening the probation period during which employers did not have to pay the minimum wage and allowing dismissals without having to pay severance, among many others.[18]

During this stage of growth, the technological and organizational progress of the automobile and auto parts sector resulted in a second generation of maquiladoras characterized by new production technologies that made operations less labor intensive. In the 1980s, continuing advancement of technologies for automobiles, electronics, new materials, and shipping combined to generate new industrial conceptions and methods for final assembly, such as the modularization and expanded use of mechanical subsystems and platforms (motors and transmissions), and gave birth to a third generation of maquiladoras.[19]

In 1989, the Mexican government passed the Decree for the Promotion and Operation of the Maquiladora Export Industry (1989 Maquiladora Decree), which extended many of the exemptions granted to the maquiladoras to the rest of the economy. For example, it had removed foreign ownership limits in most sectors, save mining, petrochemicals, auto parts, and communications. Firms that did not have maquiladora status could shift to export production if they had idle capacity, thereby creating part-time maquiladoras. More important, it made maquiladora licenses valid for an indefinite period, versus the previously imposed two-year limit.[20] By 2000, more than 3,500 maquiladoras were in operation, and they employed more than 1.2 million workers representing one-third of the country's manufacturing employment.[21]

As the NAALC complaints reveal, these advantages for employers combined with the low wages paid to a majority female workforce lure mostly U.S.-based transnationals into the maquiladora business. In 2000, the real wages of Mexican workers in the maquiladoras were less than they had been in 1990, and this occurred as labor productivity outpaced labor costs by an average of nearly 40 percent in the same period.[22] In addition to earning lower wages than their male counterparts in the maquiladoras, women were still most likely to have unskilled jobs and very few had been able to gain entry into the new supervisory or technician jobs that had grown with the industry's expansion.[23]

Several complaints claiming workers' rights violations in the maquiladoras help shed light on why wages had not kept up with productivity. Most of those complaints alleged violations of the right to free association and to organize unions of the workers' own choosing, the only means available to improve their terms and conditions of employment. Presented in the following paragraphs are just a sampling of NAALC complaints in its early years, and they represent only the tip of the iceberg in terms of describing ongoing and persistent violations of workers' rights.

The NAALC recorded its first complaints in 1996, and they involved allegations of workers' rights violations against U.S. and Japanese corporate giants General Electric, Honeywell, and Sony. The complaints involving subsidiaries of Honeywell and General Electric operating maquiladoras in Mexico claimed that workers had been deprived of their freedom of association insofar as they had not been permitted to organize into the unions of their choice. Filed by the International Brotherhood of Teamsters and the United Electrical, Radio, and Machine Workers of America (UE), the complaints alleged, among other things, that workers had been fired in order to impede the formation of a union. After accepting the submissions and conducting a hearing of the complaints, the U.S. NAO did not find the Mexican government guilty of failure to enforce the relevant labor laws. The U.S. NAO did, however, recommended that the NAFTA countries develop cooperative initiatives to address the issues raised in the submissions.[24]

The 1996 submission filed by the International Labor Rights Fund Corporation and others alleged that the Sony Corporation in Mexico had deprived workers of their freedom of association and their right to organize. Specifically, the submission asserted that Mexico was not promoting compliance with its labor laws regarding dismissals, union elections, work stoppage, and union registration. Evidence uncovered in the U.S. NAO investigation of the complaint found that the company had collaborated with the leadership of the Confederación de Trabajadores de México/Confederation of Mexican Workers (CTM; the officially registered union) to thwart the organizing drive by an independent union. Working with the "official" union, the company threatened, suspended, and fired workers involved in the organizing drive.[25]

Additionally, there was gross misconduct of union elections, such as giving workers less than a day's notice of a union election, voting not being held by secret ballot, and intimidation. The petitioners also alleged that the company had collaborated with the police in violently suppressing industrial actions following the elections and that the Mexican government thwarted attempts by the workers to register an independent union to represent workers at the plant.

After investigation, the U.S. NAO issued a report concluding that the submission raised serious questions about the workers' ability to form an independent union under Mexico's current union registration procedures. The U.S. NAO recommended ministerial consultations to address union registration and the certification process, including union elections. The ministerial consultations resulted in a two-year program of activities that included seminars, workshops, meetings, and studies. The U.S. NAO also recommended various cooperative activities to address the other issues raised in the submission.[26]

On October 11, 1996, the Communication Workers of America (CWA), the Union of Telephone Workers of the Republic of Mexico (STRM), and the Federation of Unions of Goods and Services Companies (FEBESES) filed a submission with the U.S. NAO concerning freedom of association issues at Maxi Switch Company in Cananea, Sonora, Mexico. The substance of the complaint by the CWA was that Maxi Switch, with the collusion of government officials and representatives of the conciliation and arbitration board of the state of Sonora, consistently violated the law to prevent Maxi Switch workers from joining a union of their own choosing. The independent union that fought for recognition and bargaining rights represented four hundred mostly teenage women. These women worked ten-hour shifts for only $3.50 in a plant where fumes had incapacitated workers on a regular basis.[27]

The complaint alleged that as soon as the union indicated to management that they were in the process of organizing, company officials began a series of illegal threats and intimidation. Management told the workers that they ran the risk of being fired if they joined the independent union and suggested that those who already had joined would benefit if they renounce their membership. Additionally, the workers had no idea that they already were in fact members of a CTM-affiliated union that had signed a protection contract with the company. They became aware of the sweetheart agreement when they attempted to register their own union with the labor board. The U.S. NAO accepted the complaint for review and scheduled a hearing. This development pressured Maxi Switch to negotiate a resolution of the conflict that at least partially satisfied some of the workers' demands. The petitioners withdrew the complaint as a result.[28]

On May 15, 1997, Human Rights Watch and others alleged that the Mexican government failed to enforce its labor law prohibitions on discrimination against pregnant women and that the Mexican government had been denying victims of sex discrimination access to impartial tribunals. Specifically, the submitters alleged that companies in Mexico's maquiladora sector regularly required prospective female employees to verify their pregnancy status as a condition for employment and denied employment to pregnant women. The submitters further alleged that some maquiladora companies mistreated, and sometimes dismissed, pregnant employees in order to avoid payment of maternity benefits. Further, pregnant workers reported that maquiladora employers frequently used probationary contracts of thirty to ninety days as a mechanism to refuse permanent positions to pregnant workers. A number of the women interviewed by Human Rights Watch reported that company management had coerced and intimidated them into submitting resignations after it was discovered that they had become pregnant.[29]

The complaint also addressed the institutional failure of the appropriate administrative labor tribunals or courts to protect workers' rights, particularly with regard to gender discrimination issues. The submitters also maintained that the labor boards had no clear position on whether preemployment pregnancy-based discrimination is illegal. Further, they asserted that the labor board process is time consuming and that they lack transparency as well as credibility among the workers. Consequently, few workers use the labor boards for redress of grievances. In January 1998, the U.S. NAO recommended ministerial consultations to determine the effectiveness of Mexican laws and law enforcement in protecting against pregnancy-based gender discrimination. As a result of the consultations, several conferences were held in Mexico and the United States to address issues related to women's rights at work.[30]

In 1998, the Support Committee for Maquiladora Workers et al. alleged that the Han Young maquiladora factory in Tijuana, Baja California, Mexico, denied workers freedom of association and the right to organize. The submission also alleged that the Mexican government had failed to enforce its laws on safety and health, dismissal from employment, and profit sharing. Specifically, their major concerns were illnesses, burns, injuries such as broken bones, and loss of vision due to lack of basic protection such as ventilation systems, safety shoes, glasses, gloves, masks, and facial shields. Management determined workers' pay individually on the basis of personal favoritism irrespective of experience, skill, and seniority. Another part of the complaint and subsequent investigation revealed low wages for such positions as welders and assembly workers ranging between $19 and $30 for a forty-eight–hour week, which required many workers to have a second job in addition to their forty-eight hours or more with Han Young in order to support their families.[31]

The submitters asserted that the company used threats and firings to keep workers from forming an independent union to break away from the one in which Han Young had a protection contract. The complaint also alleged that the union organizations holding the protection contract colluded with the local government to defeat the union-organizing effort. The submitters further alleged that the responsible Mexican labor tribunal overturned the results of an election held on October 15, 1997, won by the independent union. The U.S. NAO found that the conciliation and arbitration board acted in a manner inconsistent with Mexico's obligations under the NAALC. It recommended a ministerial level of consultations to address these issues to ensure the rights of freedom of association and collective bargaining.[32]

On June 23, 1998, a joint U.S.-Mexican government "Seminar on Union Freedom" took place in a Tijuana hotel as apart of the ministerial consultations process growing out of the Han Young complaint. When twenty-four Han Young workers tried to attend the meeting, a gang of toughs hired and led by officers of the "official" government-controlled Confederation of Workers and Peasants (CROC) physically assaulted them and drove them out of the room, through the hotel lobby, and into the parking lot. The meeting continued as if nothing had occurred, and the four official representatives of the U.S. Labor Department who witnessed the attack remained in the meeting until its conclusion and raised no objection to what was occurring. Afterward, Mexican Assistant Secretary of Labor Javier Moctezuma Barragán left the meeting to visit with the battered workers outside the hotel. Acting U.S. NAO Secretary Lewis Karesh later commented, "I was disappointed to see what happened." At the same time, however, Karesh attempted to minimize the damage done to the credibility of the Mexican government in enforcing its own labor laws when he remarked, "I was glad to see Moctezuma came out to talk to the workers."[33]

On December 15, 1997, the Echlin Workers Alliance that included the Teamsters, the Canadian Auto Workers (CAW), the Union of Needle Trades and Industrial Textile Employees, the UE, the Paper Workers, and the United Steelworkers of America (USWA) filed a submission with the U.S. NAO. The submission received backing from twenty-four other human rights groups and labor unions from the three NAFTA countries. The submission was noteworthy for the reason that for the first time in the NAALC process, labor centrals from each of the three countries were signatory to the complaint as co-petitioners. The Canadian Labor Congress (CCL) and the AFL-CIO filed parallel complaints with the Canadian NAO. Although based in the United States, the Echlin Corporation operated in all three NAFTA countries in the production and distribution of automobile parts. In 1997, at the time of the filing, Echlin's sales totaled $3.6 billion, and it employed 32,000 people worldwide.[34]

The charges against Echlin claimed that the company collaborated with the government and the CTM unions in worker intimidation and voter fraud to keep an independent Mexican union out of the plant and that the employer conducted operations under a protection contract, of which none of the employees had a copy. The complaints included allegations that not only were the Mexican workers denied their right to exercise freedom of association, but the companies also failed to comply with health and safety regulations as workers faced regular exposure to asbestos and other health hazards. In addition to earning low wages ranging between $33 and $45 per week, workers complained of abusive supervisors and sexual harassment along with an extraordinary level of surveillance. The petitioners also complained of production speedup, which forced increased exposure to asbestos dust and more dangerous working conditions.

In addition, Echlin had fired about fifty employees it had suspected of supporting the independent union. During the election, the company brought in approximately one hundred seventy armed men, whose activities were coordinated by the industrial relations manager and by an officer of the CTM. Some of the armed were members of the judicial police force. They physically prevented large groups of employees, who were known as supporters of the independent union, from participating in a vote. During the voting itself, several of the independent union supporters received severe beatings. Despite this hostile and unfair environment, the conciliation and arbitration board refused to suspend the election and, in fact, later certified the representation election in favor of the government-sanctioned union.

After conducting a hearing on July 31, 1998, the U.S. NAO issued a report that recommended ministerial-level consultations on the freedom of association and safety and health issues raised by the petitioners. On May 18, 2000, the U.S. secretary of labor and the Mexican secretary of labor and social welfare signed a ministerial agreement to make every effort to ensure that workers are provided information pertaining to collective bargaining agreements existing in their place of employment and to promote the use of eligible voter lists and secret ballot elections in disputes over the right to hold the collective bargaining contract. Under the ministerial agreement, Mexico agreed to conduct a trilateral seminar to discuss law and practice governing Mexican labor boards, including the rules and procedures to assure their impartiality.[35]

On July 3, 2000, current and former workers at Auto Trim and Custom Trim/Breed Mexicana, the Coalition for Justice in the Maquiladoras (CJM), and more than twenty additional unions and nongovernmental organizations in Canada, Mexico, and the United States filed a submission that raised more concerns about occupational safety and health and compensation in cases of occupational injuries and illnesses at the Auto Trim of Mexico in Matamoros, Tamaulipas, and at Custom Trim/Breed Mexicana in Valle Hermoso, Tamaulipas. The submitters claimed that workers at Auto Trim and Custom Trim/Breed Mexicana suffered skin, respiratory, eye, central nervous system, and reproductive health problems due to their exposure to chemicals in their work. They also alleged that workers had suffered ergonomic ailments such as carpal tunnel syndrome and back and shoulder pain due to the repetitive nature of their work. Furthermore, they made the claim that workers who suffered these conditions had not been properly treated and compensated.

Significantly, for the first time in the NAALC complaint process, the submitters argued that Mexico had shown disregard for the principles set out in the preamble to the NAALC to protect, enhance, and enforce basic workers' rights and to promote high-skill, high-productivity economic development in North America by encouraging employers and employees in each country to comply with labor laws and to work together in maintaining a progressive, safe, and healthy working environment. Moreover, the petitioners complained of pressure on workers to meet excessively high production quotas, poorly designed work stations, inadequate personal protective equipment, lack of properly functioning safety and health committees, failure to stock medical supplies on-site, and government failure to institute workplace monitoring, all required by Mexican labor law and the 1917 constitution. After conducting a hearing on the complaint, the U.S. NAO once again recommended ministerial consultations.[36]

Frustrated with the NAALC process, some maquiladora workers took matters into their own hands. On January 9, 2001, the workers of Kukdong International, an apparel contractor in the town of Atlixco, in the central state of Puebla, seized control of their factory. Protesting the factory's rancid cafeteria food, low wages ($30 for a forty-five-hour week), the failure of the company to pay the Christmas bonus in accordance with Mexican labor law, the lack of representation by the official union that enforced its protection contract with the employer, and the firing of five workers for demanding better treatment, approximately eight hundred workers, mostly young women in their teens and early twenties, left their stations at midday and went on strike. Shortly thereafter, a battalion of riot police, led by the existing union's secretary-general, marched into the area wielding clubs and guns, injuring more than seventeen strikers. A week later, almost the entire Kukdong workforce went on strike. After first agreeing to reinstate all of the fired strikers, Kukdong and official union representatives reversed their decision.

Kukdong, now called Mexmode, is a Korean-owned factory that makes sweatshirts for Nike, Reebok, and the universities of North Carolina, Maryland, Michigan, Arizona, Penn State, Georgetown, Michigan State, and Oregon, to name just a few. As a result, labor and nongovernmental organizations (NGOs) in the United States and Mexico, the most prominent of which was United Students against Sweatshops (USAS), conducted an international campaign to pressure multinational corporate buyers to exert influence on Kukdong management to remedy its violations of workers' rights. By mid-February, the company had allowed most workers to return to the factory, and by September 2001, workers had established an independent union (SITE-MEX) and signed a collective agreement with the company that increased wages by 40 percent. Although the NAALC process had nothing to do directly with the outcome, it is arguable that previous complaints filed under the NAALC produced a "sunshine effect" on worker abuses in the Mexican maquiladoras, which over time facilitated the development of cross-border labor solidarity and was a key to the victory of the Kukdong workers.[37]

Mexican and international law gives rights to workers to select their own union representation and negotiate improvements in their terms and conditions of employment, including health and safety. Under Mexican law and the NAALC, workers have a right to request Mexican agencies to fulfill their legal mandates by enforcing existing labor. It is clear that in complaints filed under the NAALC during its first six years, the Mexican government had failed to uphold its responsibilities as outlined in the trinational agreement. Moreover, while the Mexican government at the local, state, and federal levels had failed to do so, U.S.-based employers also had refused to comply with court orders, national laws, and international agreements. By documenting the conditions workers endured in the maquiladoras, the sunshine effect of the NAALC process has provided opportunities for more cross-border cooperation and actions of solidarity between labor advocacy groups and trade unions.

At least to some degree, the revelations that have grown out of the NAALC process have pressured the countries to push for an upward harmonization of workplace regulations and enforcement. At the same time, as transnational corporations are shifting production across borders in search of cheaper labor and other advantages, as shown by the NAALC complaints, Mexican workers are refusing to work under almost any conditions, and their efforts in resisting and defying government authorities, corrupt trade unions, and the transnational corporations' management practices are playing an important role in building opposition to the international business strategy of pitting workers of one nationality against another in a "race to the bottom."

The Euzkadi Struggle

Perhaps nowhere was growing worker resistance to the forces of globalization and organized labor solidarity more on display than in the three-year struggle waged by the workers employed at the Hulera-Euzkadi tire plant in El Salto, Jalisco. Founded in 1935 by a businessman from Spain's Basque Country, it was the leader in the tire industry in Mexico for decades. In 1981, the American-owned B. F. Goodrich Tire Company purchased the firm, and in 1992 Mexican billionaire Carlos Slim bought controlling interests in the company. In 1998, Slim sold Euzkadi to the German-based Continental Tire Company.[38]

Immediately, Continental Tire management attempted to unilaterally impose a "flexible" collective agreement, which in the case of the Mexican rubber industry meant altering a national, industry-wide contract called *contrato ley*, which had been in place for decades. Acting with impunity, Continental Tire management implemented continuous twenty-four–hour, 365–day-a-year work schedules, pay for production schemes, mandatory overtime, stricter attendance policies, wage givebacks, increased management rights, and higher production quotas.[39]

On June 11, 1999, the company terminated eighteen longtime Euzkadi employees and union activists who opposed management's plans. The union representing the fired workers, the Revolutionary National Union of Euzkadi Workers (SNRTE), insisted that the firings were illegal and stated that it would reject the unilaterally imposed changes to the collective bargaining agreement. The resolve of the SNRTE members reflected the history of its union, which has been one of the few genuinely democratic and independent labor organizations in Mexico.

Born in 1935 at the height of the Great Depression and in the midst of Mexican state support for organized labor in their battles with employers, both foreign and domestic, the SNRTE remained independent from the tutelage of the Mexican CTM until the years immediately following World War II when, with government backing, the large federation gained control of the union. On January 3, 1959, in a period of renewed union and rank-and-file militancy in Mexico, the SNRTE expelled CTM president Fidel Velásquez and his entourage from a general assembly meeting. In the process, the union reestablished its fighting and democratic traditions and once again exercised organizational autonomy. In the decades following its breakaway from the CTM, the SNRTE won many hard-earned gains for its members in battles with Euzkadi management and repelled countless attempts by the CTM to reestablish control. Those gains included the five-day workweek and wages well above the national average.[40]

Ignoring the militant character of the SNRTE and its militant traditions, Continental Tire management persisted in its efforts to unilaterally change work rules and impose its own collective bargaining agreement on the 1,164–member union. Management sent letters to the homes of every Euzkadi worker, outlining its proposals and stating that if the union refused to accept the new conditions, the company would lay off hundreds of workers and impose a shorter workweek on those who remained. Inside the facility, Continental Tire management threatened workers by saying that closing the plant was a real possibility if the SNRTE refused to acquiesce to its demands.

The union held its ground, and on December 16, 2001, Continental Tire management shuttered the plant and stopped paying workers their wages.

In response, in January 2002 the SNRTE declared a strike claiming that it considered the plant's closing an illegal interruption of labor and the company's actions violated Articles 434–439 of the Mexican FLL, which stipulates that permission for closing production facilities must be submitted to the relevant Mexican authorities for approval. Meanwhile, Continental Tire pleaded to the Mexican government that it had to close the plant because it was not possible to implement international production standards. In so doing, it asked the Conciliation and Arbitration Board (CAB) to declare the Euzkadi workers' strike illegal on a technicality, asserting that the plant already had been closed. In order to prevent Continental Tire from dismantling parts of the factory and installing these in other factories bought by the company in Mexico, the Euzkadi union workers picketed the factory around the clock, seven days a week. The SNRTE also conducted mass protest marches in Jalisco and Mexico City, bringing more attention to their plight.

Even after the CAB declared the strike illegal, workers continued their picketing while enlisting the support of prounion activists in Mexico and workers at another Continental Tire factory, General Tire in San Luis Potosí. There, a union allied with the Euzkadi SNRTE won a certification election by a wide margin over a CTM-backed union. In May 2002, the SNRTE conducted a lobbying tour through Germany, visiting the Mexican embassy, the German Foreign Ministry, German parliament, the Economic Ministry, the German Union Confederation, and Continental's main shareholder meeting. While in Germany, SNRTE representatives and the German environmental and development agency Germanwatch presented an official complaint against Continental Tire with the Organisation for Economic Cooperation and Development (OECD), arguing that the company had violated OECD directives for multinational companies. One month later, the SNRTE officially presented the complaint in Mexico.

In February 2003, the Mexican CAB affirmed its initial decision that declared the strike illegal. The SNRTE then submitted a constitutional complaint on the basis of the right to strike. At the same time, labor advocacy groups around the world begin pressuring Mexico to comply with international agreements on workers' rights it has signed. In May 2003, representatives of the Euzkadi union again traveled to Germany and, with Germanwatch, the case was once again presented at the main shareholders meeting of Continental Tire in Hanover. In June 2003, the Mexican Supreme Court declared the union's constitutional complaint as lawful. On February 18, 2004, the Mexican CAB declared the SNRTE strike against Euzkadi as legal. In October 2005, delegates from unions representing Continental Tire employees in four countries met in San Luis Potosi, Mexico. Union members from Brazil, Argentina, Mexico, and the United States announced their intention to contact the unions of Continental Tire employees across the world to agree on a joint strategy to combat the antilabor policies of this transnational company, which had shut down ten plants in Europe and the United States since 1995. Finally, with support from labor organizations around the world, the SNRTE succeeded in forcing Continental Tire to permit the creation of a workers' cooperative, the Cooperative Society of the Democratic Workers of the West (TRADOC), which now owns and runs the former Euzkadi plant.[41]

Labor Law Reform: Making Mexico Competitive

The successful rank-and-file Euzkadi struggle and other efforts by Mexican workers documented in the NAALC process rocked Mexico's economic elites and political governing class and put a dent in their efforts to shore up the nation's labor relations system and make it more compatible with its development strategy of export manufacturing. Soon, however, they redoubled their efforts, which built on actions taken in the early years of the new millennium when an economic recession and a sudden reversal of fortune for the maquiladora industry created a renewed a sense of urgency. Companies shuttered Mexican facilities and in some cases moved production elsewhere, such as China, where wages were lower and conditions worse than in Mexico.

Compounding the situation for the Mexican government were the murders of almost four hundred women in Ciudad Juárez, which remain unsolved. After years of investigation and international pressure from the United Nations, human rights groups, unions, and other organizations, the government failed to provide a plausible explanation for the crimes, to indict and convict those responsible for the murders, or to protect women. Many of the women abducted and murdered were maquiladora workers waiting for company buses to transport them to their workplaces. The violence against women has spread from Ciudad Juárez to other border cities, northern towns, and into the interior of Mexico and seems to follow the dispersion of the maquiladora industry. Instead of making a serious effort to solve these crimes and protect workers' rights such as protection against pregnancy discrimination, the Mexican government placed reforming the nation's labor law at the top of the political agenda.[42]

To continue attracting direct investment from foreigners, Mexican labor law, which on paper appears as "labor friendly," needed to change. And any changes would require measures that minimized the possibility of future labor unrest such as that which occurred at Kukdong and the solidarity exhibited by the workers at Euzkadi. Essentially, Mexico's whole economic development strategy was at stake, and it was inextricably linked to reforming labor law and making it "employer friendly." Moreover, the Kukdong incident was also important because the facility was just one among an increasing number of maquiladoras in the center and south of Mexico, which as a result of NAFTA rules and regulatory changes had become a developing trend, and it would accelerate in future years.

The regulatory changes reflected the evolution of a program that began as a simple "twin-plant" concept. Maquiladoras allowed U.S. manufacturers to establish capital-intensive operations on their side of the border, ship goods to Mexico for labor-intensive assembly, and return them to the United States. Inputs moved into Mexico duty-free if returned to the United States in assembled form within a fixed period. U.S. tariffs applied only to the value added by assembly. Over the years, the maquiladora industry evolved to include imports of machinery and equipment along with inputs, and it expanded from manufacturing to services, such as engineering, call centers, and coupon processing.

The original maquiladora program forbade domestic sales, but NAFTA completely removed the restriction by 2001. After these changes, maquiladoras became similar to companies operating under the Program for Temporary Imports to Promote Exports (PITEX), created in 1990 to allow qualifying domestic producers to compete with maquiladoras. Under PITEX, the export-services parts of domestic plants received maquiladora-like benefits, allowing them to import materials and export-oriented machinery. In recent years, no significant differences existed in the customs status of maquiladoras and PITEX plants' export operations, and income tax differences persisted only to the extent that maquiladoras qualify for treatment as foreign entities.[43]

By March 2007, the states along the border had a combined total of 3,552 maquiladora and PITEX operations, compared to 2,391 in other states. From 1990 through the end of 2006, the interior states' share of maquiladoras alone had increased by nearly 23 percent.[44] The changes in the regulatory environment complemented the lower pay earned by those working in maquiladoras in the interior states compared to along the border, where wages were on the average 40 percent higher.[45] Within this context and with efforts to reform Mexican labor law, workers and their supporters filed more submissions under the NAALC. In the process, more allegations of workers' rights violations by export manufacturers in the Mexican interior states surfaced.

On September 30, 2003, the USAS and the Centro de Apoyo al Trabajador filed a NAALC complaint concerning conditions at a the Tarrant garment factory in the state of Puebla, which produced denim apparel for its parent company, Los Angeles–based Tarrant Apparel Group. The specific allegations included nonpayment of legally entitled benefits, dangerous working conditions, an end to forced overtime, and verbal and sexual harassment by management and plant security guards. That filing, along with two amendments submitted subsequently in support of the original complaint, alleged violations under the NAALC concerning what had become the standard for workers' rights violations in Mexico: freedom of association and the right to organize, collective bargaining, occupational safety and health, minimum employment standards (minimum wage and overtime pay), and access to fair and transparent labor tribunal proceedings.

After both the U.S. and Canadian NAOs conducted investigations and extensive hearings on the case, they reached the same general conclusions. Testimony given by former Tarrant workers like Salvador García Sánchez, a twenty-eight-year-old female employee, heavily influenced the conclusions drawn by government investigators. Describing the day-to-day working conditions in the plant, she said the company was not very well ventilated and the chairs were uncomfortable, "which made us very tired. We [were] forced to sit all day long in those chairs and when they permitted us to go to the bathroom they clocked the time in which we were away from the job. They also timed us when we wanted to get a drink of water, which was always very hot." She added: "When we didn't produce enough, we had to stay overtime and we were not paid for that." García Sánchez also testified that on very few occasions were the Tarrant workers paid overtime, and the company forced them to work on holidays. When production quotas were not satisfactory to management, the company forced the employees to work on Saturdays and Sundays without pay. The company also forced workers to continue sewing garments even when they had been cut by the machines and suffered other types of injuries. According to testimony, the company also hired fifteen- and sixteen-year-olds by falsifying their birth certificates. García Sánchez also testified of female workers receiving sexual harassment.

The government hearings on the case of the Tarrant México workers revealed a pattern of systemic, fundamental nonenforcement of labor law by the Mexican government. Specifically, the Mexican government had failed to protect its citizens through the enforcement of labor law relating to the right to freedom of association and collective bargaining, minimum employment standards, and occupational health and safety. Further, the continued denial of union registration on minor technical grounds, which occurred to maintain protection contracts, neither served the interest of NAFTA nor the NAALC.[46]

Also, as the U.S. NAO report pointed out, the failure of the Mexican government to ensure that workers are paid a minimum wage, that they are paid their wages as scheduled, that they enjoy job security without regard to their union support, and that they work in a safe and healthy environment reveals that "there is a fundamental problem with the enforcement of national and international laws in Mexico."[47] The U.S. NAO report concluded by stating that NAFTA and the NAALC exist to provide not only free trade but also the furtherance of labor rights and assurance that trade will not deteriorate labor rights. As in the past, however, the remedy suggested was more government-to-government consultation to resolve these issues.[48]

A year before the Tarrant case hearings and U.S. NAO report, some unions in the United States that had participated directly in the NAALC complaint process had expressed their frustration with the lack of remedy for workers' rights violations and particularly the inevitable recommendations of ministerial consultations, seminars, and cooperative activities. Representative of this sentiment was a July 24, 2002, letter written by UE President John Hovis to U.S. Secretary of Labor Elaine Chao. Hovis pointed out that despite the Mexican government's commitment in ministerial agreements to protect the associational rights and safety of its workers, Mexican workers continue to have their rights violated and have suffered abuse by company management and official unions. As a result, Hovis concluded, the UE would cease its participation and thereby not lend credibility to a process that has totally failed to protect workers' rights.[49]

Facing increasing international scrutiny for violations of its own labor laws and independent unions looking to scrap laws that favored established trade unions, the Mexican government felt pressure from international financial institutions like the World Bank, which were making calls for less regulation and greater labor flexibility. In this context, the Mexican government hurried to push labor law reform through Congress. On December 12, 2002, ruling Partido Acción Nacional/National Action Party (PAN) deputies submitted the proposed changes for consideration by the Mexican Congress. Popularly known as the Abascal Project after Labor Secretary Carlos Abascal, its roots went back to the late 1980s when the Partido Revolucionario Institucional/ Institutional Revolutionary Party (PRI) and the Mexican Employers Association (COPARMEX) put forward their vision of a New Labor Culture that emphasized linking labor productivity to compensation and management flexibility in terms of work organization, shop-floor rules, and the hiring and firing of workers. Facing resistance from many unions and elected officials, the proposal failed to gain any real traction in the 1990s.[50]

In 2000, however, after the election of PAN candidate Vicente Fox, Carlos Abascal, a former head of COPARMEX, began developing a proposal for labor law reform. In July 2001, Abascal initiated the talks between the Secretary of Labor and Social Welfare (STPS), the Business Coordinating Council (CCE), and the labor unions, both the Congreso del Trabajo/Labor Congress (CT) and the National Union of Workers (UNT), with a commitment that no legislation would be introduced in the absence of a consensus. However, the dialogue never moved forward, and the proposal that reached the Mexican Congress at the end of 2002 was the exclusive product of STPS. Its final version contained provisions that would maintain even tighter government control over the labor unions and their right to strike, while at the same time granting employers a greater role in labor relations and giving them more flexibility in the use of labor.[51]

Labor market flexibility, a central feature of the proposal, would have made it easier for employers to hire temporary and contingent workers, who may be fired at any time with no penalty. Employers could issue individual contracts that would unilaterally determinate the length of employment, whether temporary, for initial training (probationary), or for an indeterminate length. The existence of these new contracts, temporary and probationary, would radically change the legal structure of labor relations and eliminate job security through the use of short, fixed-term contracts of employment. The reforms would have also allowed firms wide latitude to change hours of work by permitting employers to count maximum hours on a weekly or monthly basis, thus eliminating maximum daily hours of work, a violation of Article 123 of the constitution. Also, the proposed changes would have given employers additional rights to substitute productivity bonuses for wages but without specific obligations to share the benefits of increased productivity with the workers.[52]

The reform proposal also contained language that would have made it harder for workers to organize unions of their own choosing. Outside of the limited exception of the Federal District, there is no public registry of unions and no public access to collective agreements in Mexico. Accordingly, even in cases when workers have union representation, they have no legal right to obtain information as to the name of their union, the name and addresses of the leadership, or copies of their collective agreements, which allows for the proliferation of protection unions. If workers filing a petition with a labor board are unaware of the existence of a protection contract and file the wrong type of petition, it is subject to summary dismissal, exposing the petitioners to discharge either directly by the employer or at the behest of the incumbent union pursuant to the exclusion clause.[53]

The proposed reforms created a procedural obstacle course that would have made it virtually insurmountable for workers seeking to establish an independent union or to bargain collectively. It would have functioned by requiring workers to reveal their individual identities in order to initiate the processes leading to collective bargaining or union recognition, thus exposing them to discharge, and by prohibiting consideration of more than one representation petition at a time, enabling employers and protection unions to preclude consideration of legitimate petitions and to create interminable delays.

The Abascal Project would have also added burdensome provisions requiring workers to obtain various certified documents before they could strike, compel their employers to bargain collectively, or call a vote to oust a preexisting union. These documents are only available from authorities who have been historically hostile to independent unions: the Labor Ministry in federal matters and local boards of conciliation and arbitration in local ones. The proposed reforms would also have kept the practice of nonsecret votes in union certification elections. Under the Abascal Project, an election to gain workplace representational rights could occur only after workers supporting the vote presented to the relevant board the requisite legal documents and papers containing their names and signatures, thus negating the notion of a secret ballot and exposing workers who signed the petition to discharge either from their employer or existing union.

The Abascal Project immediately faced opposition. It came not only from independent unions but also from international human rights groups, social movements of peasants, and indigenous groups. It even drew criticism from Mexico's official labor unions, but in the end it received the full support of the Mexican CT. Perhaps most important, more than twenty Canadian, Quebecois, Mexican, and U.S. unions came together in filing an objection under the NAALC. In a follow-up letter written by Representative Marcy Kaptur and signed by thirty-seven members of the U.S. Congress to U.S. Secretary of Labor Elaine Chao, the elected representatives urged the U.S. government to accept the submission and conduct an investigation into the Abascal Project. The twenty-page NAALC complaint, filed on February 17,

2005, with the United States (NAO) alleged that the Abascal Project violated NAALC language that obligates all parties to "ensure that its labor laws and regulations provide for high labor standards, consistent with high quality and productivity workplaces, and [that it] shall continue to strive to improve those standards in that light."[54]

The Abascal Project, the complaint asserted, would significantly worsen those standards, not improve them. The weakening of existing laws combined with no remedy to address problems that already exist was clear evidence that Mexico was not striving to improve its standards, the petitioners asserted. Furthermore, the submission suggested that the obligations of the countries under the NAALC would be rendered utterly meaningless if laws that protected workers were repealed and new laws were put in place that would violate the principles set forth in the NAALC. Additionally, the petitioners claimed, the reform proposals failed to address the pattern and practice of violations of the NAALC principles documented time and again in recommendations by the U.S. and Canadian NAOs, the ILO, and other international bodies.

The Abascal Project also failed to provide sufficient protections for workers facing pregnancy-based discrimination in hiring. The complaint summarized its concerns by stating that failure to address these violations is not only unconscionable, but it also violates commitments made by the federal government of Mexico in resolving previous cases under the NAALC. While international pressure and mounting internal political difficulties for the PAN killed labor law reform during the Fox years, it resurfaced once again in the Mexican Congress at the behest of Mexico's Secretary of Labor Javier Lozano Alarcón.[55]

Helping resurrect discussion of labor law reform in Mexico was the U.S. NAO's rejection of the complaint against the Abascal Project on the grounds that a review would not further the objectives of the NAALC.[56] The U.S. NAO decision not to review the complaint took place within the context of heated debate over immigration reform in the U.S. Congress as well as another NAALC complaint against the United States. Filing the submission on April 13, 2005, with the Mexican government was the Northwest Workers' Justice Project, the Brennan Center for Justice at New York University School of Law, and the Andrade Law Office.

The submission raised issues concerning rights of migrant workers under the H-2B Visa program in Idaho, including prohibition of forced labor, minimum employment standards, elimination of employment discrimination, equal pay for women and men, prevention of occupational injuries and adequate compensation in such cases, and protection of migrant workers. The complaint was the second filed against the United States within a two-year period that alleged the lack of protection of migrant workers in government-sponsored temporary worker programs.[57]

By 2006, NAALC complaints as well as increasing focus on migrant rights by human rights groups, labor unions, and other organizations had brought the issue of labor mobility to the forefront. In North America, labor mobility has aggravated the issue of workers' rights in the context of a global economy, meaning that all workers, regardless of wherever they are employed or their national origin, have internationally recognized labor rights. What follows is a detailed examination of the inherent connection between labor mobility and workers' rights in North America, both in its historical context and contemporary setting.

4

Labor Mobility and Workers' Rights in North America

On May 1, 2006, International Workers' Day, millions of immigrant workers, comprising an overwhelming majority of Mexicans, took to the streets in several major cities and towns across the United States. The demonstrations, both in their size and national scope, were unprecedented in U.S. history. Many who participated in these actions also went on strike and called for boycotts, despite being warned by politicians of both major political parties and President George W. Bush. Those who participated did so in the face of nationwide workplace raids by U.S. immigration authorities, threats of arrest, deportation, and even violence by extreme right-wing elements.[1]

On the Mexican side of the border, miners and steelworkers carried out waves of wildcat strikes in protest of sixty-five miners losing their lives as a result of unsafe job conditions and the shooting of four striking steelworkers by the nation's police and military. Also protesting the killings of miners and steelworkers on May Day were 500,000 union members marching through the streets of downtown Mexico City. Demanding justice not only for the slain strikers, the marchers also called for union democracy and labor autonomy in response to the Mexican government's imposition of leadership on the mine workers' union and rank-and-file union members.[2]

Meanwhile, many unions and civic groups joined their counterparts in the United States by organizing International Workers' Day as "a day without gringos," a boycott of American-owned businesses like Wal-Mart, McDonalds, and others operating in Mexico.[3] On May 1, 2007, despite a sharp increase in workplace raids and deportations since the events of the previous year by American authorities, immigrant workers once again took to the streets in the hundreds of thousands demanding their right to work and earn a living in a global economy.[4] While these recent collective actions are linked directly to developments associated with NAFTA, they are deeply rooted in a broader historical setting, one in which Mexican workers have demanded and exercised their rights in a region of the world that has been undergoing a process of economic and demographic integration for more than a century.

Inside Mexico: Social and Economic Factors that Propel Migration

U.S.-Mexican economic and demographic integration has accelerated and intensified since NAFTA. The impact of NAFTA on the economies, labor markets, and conditions of employment in both countries is reflected in large part by the presence of at least 8 million undocumented Mexican workers in the United States. Nearly half of these workers are from rural Mexico, where NAFTA rules that have allowed cheaper agricultural imports from the United States to flood the country have had a devastating impact on farmers. While a substantial number of those affected by NAFTA policies have trekked northward to the United States in search of employment, others remain, trying to scratch out a living in the nation's growing informal sector.[5]

Many also migrate to the United States because NAFTA has either destroyed or resulted in the privatization of many Mexican industries, wiping out thousands of jobs. At the same time, the Mexican economy falls short in the area of employment in the formal sector, leaving many new workers just entering the labor market either unemployed or underemployed. For those who find work, real wages have declined and stagnated. By many accounts, especially those that have surfaced as a result of the North American Agreement on Labor Cooperation (NAALC) and its complaint process, working conditions have eroded while the enforcement of workers' rights has been rolled back.

Meanwhile, union density has declined and the relative power that trade unions had once exercised within the Mexican political system has significantly weakened. Declining union membership along with diminishing economic power and political influence are reflected in organized labor's almost complete retreat from the strike and struggles to resist the employer assault on the Mexican working class. The ousting from power of the Partido Revolucionario Institucional/Institutional Revolutionary Party (PRI), organized labor's long-standing ally, also has contributed to the decline of union power. Since the crisis of Mexican political economy that began in the 1980s, organized labor has been increasingly hemmed in by the PRI shifting to a probusiness stand and by the Partido Acción Nacional/National Action Party (PAN), long associated with free-market capitalism and rolling back workers' gains and winner of the last two presidential elections. The result is that rank-and-file workers are left virtually defenseless, forced to rely on their own initiative to mount any resistance to eroding working conditions and declining living standards. These are the economic and political realities that propel Mexican immigration to the United States.

Labor Conditions in the United States: The Social and Political Context

On the other side of the border, the growth of the immigrant workforce is only one dimension of a broader transformation taking place in the world of work and labor markets. The ranks of American workers have been vastly expanded since NAFTA, and not just through immigration. Substantial layers of what had been previously considered part of the American middle class are being forced into employment that is characterized by stagnating or declining real pay, disappearing pensions, and increasingly expensive health care plans and other amenities.[6]

As in Mexico, union membership has experienced sharp decline in the United States, strikes have dropped, and the political clout that trade unions once wielded no longer exists. Many workers caught up in this transformation, especially those who possess low levels of educational attainment and have lost high-paying jobs in the shrinking manufacturing sector, are pushed into the low ends of the labor market where they potentially compete with immigrants for jobs.[7] In the midst of this labor market volatility, the millions of Mexican immigrants in the United States who have escaped desperate conditions in their native land are confronted with open hostility by some media pundits and politicians. These forces claim that they are motivated by concern for American workers whose jobs are allegedly being taken away and whose wages are depressed through the presence of the immigrant population.[8]

Those who claim immigration puts downward pressure on the wages of low-skill workers also suggest that it has been a major cause of growing income inequality in the United States.[9] A similar discussion took place in the period between 1870 and 1914 when arguments were made that mass immigration played an important role in keeping the domestic real wages of unskilled labor low. But a recent Organisation for Economic Cooperation and Development (OECD) study found that wage inequality has been rising in both developed and developing countries. In sixteen of the nineteen countries covered in the study, the earnings of the 10 percent best-paid workers have risen relative to those of the 10 percent lowest-paid workers since the mid-1990s.[10] The study included every country in North America, and its findings have been confirmed in three studies of labor market conditions conducted by the NAFTA-created Commission for Labor Cooperation since the late 1990s.[11]

Immigration, while having increased in the United States substantially in recent decades, has had far less impact on Canadian and Mexican labor markets.[12] Accordingly, other explanations are needed to explain that downward pressure on the wages for unskilled workers is a factor in all the NAFTA countries, not just the United States. The OECD study suggests that the globalization of production has contributed to shifting labor demand away from less skilled workers and in the process has kept wages down for the unskilled and hence has produced rising earnings inequality. Advances in information and communications technology have made it possible for firms to fragment the production of goods and services and to outsource certain tasks to other countries. This "great unbundling," according to the OECD, has extended the reach of globalization to domestic activities where workers had been previously sheltered from direct international competition.[13]

This at least partially explains why a World Bank report finds that migration today is less than it was between 1870 and 1914 when 10 percent of the global population migrated to find work. Since 1980, global migration has constituted just 3 percent of the world's population.[14] Competitive pressures resulting from the globalization of finance and of production expose the workforce to greater insecurity and weaken the bargaining position of workers. Employment is less stable, and the wages of workers who continue in the same job are more affected by changing economic conditions.

This is particularly true for workers with relatively low levels of education and job tenure. In addition to being exposed to import competition, these workers are the least prepared to navigate in labor markets characterized by intensive restructuring, rising skill requirements, and employers who are increasingly sensitive to differences in labor costs. These factors, most economists argue, put much more downward pressure on the wages of workers in low-skill jobs than does immigration.[15]

Despite strong evidence that vintage early twenty-first-century global capitalism better favors the movement of goods and money across national borders than the movement of people and that immigrants have little or no effect on the wages of unskilled native-born workers in the United States, media pundits and politicians continue to scapegoat these workers. The hostility toward the immigrant population in the United States picked up steam in the economic downturn beginning in 2007. In addition to the continuing public relations blitz against immigrants in the news media by pundits like Lou Dobbs, the Immigration and Customs Enforcement (ICE) of the Department of Homeland Security has stepped up workplace raids. Further militarization of the U.S.-Mexican border by National Guard troops also occurred, and Congress passed legislation mandating the building of a wall to keep migrants out.

The attempt to wall off the U.S. national economy against immigrants to protect "American jobs" in many ways resembles the long-term efforts of American unions to convince workers that they share a common goal with business in defending "American jobs" against foreign companies and workers alike. The union strategy, however, has failed to keep jobs in the United States. Between July 2000 and January 2004, the United States lost more than 3 million manufacturing jobs.[16]

But organized labor's position on the immigrant workforce has taken a recent about-face. For more than a hundred years, the policy of the labor officialdom in the United States had been welded to the notion that the presence of immigrant labor pressures wages downward for native-born workers.[17] In 1897, the American Federation of Labor (AFL) endorsed a literacy test as a prerequisite for immigration, and in 1917 the U.S. Congress included it into a new immigration law. In the late 1940s and early 1950s, the AFL-affiliated National Agricultural Workers' Union fought undocumented immigration and threw up picket lines on the border and made citizen's arrests of alleged illegal aliens. In 1954, many unions supported Operation Wetback, a series of raids that resulted in the deportation of more than 1 million migrants. In the 1960s, even the United Farm Workers' Union, an organization historically associated with defending immigrant workers' rights, agitated to remove undocumented migrants from the fields. In doing so, the union reported undocumented workers to the Immigration and Naturalization Service (INS) and demanded their deportation.[18]

In recent years, however, Mexicans and other immigrant workers have poured into the ranks of the unskilled, especially in the low-wage service sector. In the heavily unionized manufacturing sector, the workforce is being downsized and jobs are being destroyed; however, unions in other sectors are viewing immigrant workers as targets ripe for organizing and see their inclusion into the ranks of organized labor as key to reversing membership decline.[19] Organized labor's change in thinking about immigration is also a response to increases in union membership among new arrivals to the United States and the difference affiliation makes for those workers in both wages and benefits.

Unionized immigrant workers obtain a premium comparable to other workers, whether they have immigrated relatively recently (within ten years) or earlier.[20] Obviously, this is one reason why between 1996 and 2003 the number of foreign-born union members rose from 1.4 million to 1.8 million, or by 24 percent. In 2003, the number of working immigrants with union representation increased from 1.6 million in 1996 to 2.0 million, or by 23 percent. During the same period, the number of native-born union members decreased from 14.8 million to 14.0 million, or by 6 percent. And the number of native-born workers with union representation decreased from 16.5 million in 1996 to 15.4 million in 2003, or by 7 percent.[21]

Despite its new outlook on organizing immigrants into its ranks, much of organized labor still clings to a nationalist position with regard to the immigration question.[22] In doing so, these elements of organized labor join politicians in calling for border security, while saying nothing to oppose capital and business expanding upon their rights to cross national borders freely. The AFL-CIO leadership opposes open borders on the basis of defending "American jobs" against foreign competition and calls for toughening up immigration controls and border enforcement. In its position paper on immigration found on its Web site, the AFL-CIO recognizes the constitutional right of the U.S. government to set and enforce limits on immigration.[23] At the same time, however, the AFL-CIO says nothing about the constitutional right of the U.S. Congress to regulate commerce and thus restrict the movement of capital and commodities across national borders. In so doing, the AFL-CIO surrenders crucial political terrain on the question of workers' rights and in effect waives its right to have any voice in how the government establishes guest-worker programs.

While commodities and capital keep crossing borders, workers seeking to provide for themselves and their families are confronted with the ever greater militarization of these same borders, and the AFL-CIO gives a pass to businesses and politicians who call for a greater crackdown on those crossing the border without authorization. The resulting tougher border security has forced migrants to take more dangerous, remote routes to cross into the United States, leading to a sharp increase in the number of deaths of people trying to enter the United States through places like the Arizona desert. At least 275 bodies of Mexican nationals had been found in the first six months of 2007, according to a Mexican congressional report that both U.S. and Mexican academics confirmed. The same report claimed that at least 4,500 Mexicans have died trying to cross since 1994, when the United States drastically increased border controls.[24]

The demands for border security in the United States are complemented by proposals for the creation of various types of temporary guest-worker programs, which if implemented would satisfy employer needs for cheap labor in industries like agriculture, construction, food processing, health care, and home care. According to a recent study by the Southern Poverty Law Center entitled "Close to Slavery," existing temporary- and guest-worker programs sanctioned by the U.S. government deprive workers of their rights and allow employers to impose substandard working conditions.[25] Based on these findings, one can assume that any new or similar program would essentially institutionalize a large pool of low-wage immigrant workers with limited or very few rights and who would be forced to repatriate to their own countries once their labor is not needed. Although the AFL-CIO is on record opposing guest-worker programs, organized labor is fractured politically on the issue, and some powerful and influential unions actually support the creation of more guest-worker programs.

One such union is the Service Employees International Union (SEIU). The SEIU backing of more guest-worker programs is rooted in the union's organizational character and reflected in its approach to organizing and political lobbying. While the SEIU advocates "partnerships" with business to foster competitiveness, it accepts the establishment of more guest-worker programs as an inevitable result of political compromise. The SEIU hopes that, by throwing its support behind guest-worker programs, the workers in any such program would have the right to union representation. Joining the SEIU in its position on resolving the status of undocumented workers is UNITE/HERE, a union that represents workers in the immigrant-worker-dominated hospitality industry. Like SEIU, UNITE/HERE believes that organizing rights in guest-worker programs could give the union a substantial increase in dues-paying members. Both unions belong to the Essential Worker Immigration Coalition (EWIC), an association of the forty largest manufacturing and trade groups in the United States, which includes Wal-Mart, Tyson Foods, and Marriott.[26]

The extent of SEIU support for guest-worker programs is illustrated by the union's president, Andy Stern, joining with U.S. Chamber of Commerce President and CEO Thomas Donohue to coauthor a statement in support of guest-worker programs. In doing so, the two leaders openly declared that the antiunion Chamber of Commerce and the SEIU had "discarded our many differences on other subjects to pursue what we believe are policies in the nation's best interests."[27] "We need legislation that will create a carefully monitored and essential guest-worker program," Stern and Donohue wrote.[28] While calling for stronger border enforcement that would carefully screen workers, they also claimed that immigrant labor was essential for America's economic growth and its ability to remain competitive in today's global economy.[29]

The notion that U.S. national security concerns trump labor mobility and workers' rights also has been the theme of a major campaign conducted by the Teamsters union to keep Mexican truck drivers off U.S. highways. When NAFTA came into effect in 1994, Mexican trucks were to be allowed to travel anywhere in four states—Arizona, California, New Mexico, and Texas—and they were to freely deliver goods throughout the United States by the year 2000. After heavy lobbying by the Teamsters, the Bill Clinton administration, citing supposed concerns over truck safety, blocked implementation of the cross-border provisions in 1995 and restricted Mexican trucks to a narrow strip along the border where freight is picked up by U.S. trucks.[30] In 2000, President Clinton extended the ban, which was later ruled a violation of U.S. obligations under NAFTA. After President Bush announced his intention to reverse Clinton's measures and open the borders to Mexican truckers, the Teamsters mounted an all-out appeal to Congress to stop it.

The Teamsters claim that their opposition to the entry of Mexican trucks has been based on a concern for the safety of American motorists rather than the union having a Canadian franchise in which it collects dues from drivers there, unlike in Mexico. But even without the presence of Mexican trucks on U.S. highways, it appears that the Teamsters have done very little in the area of trucker safety, at least according to statistics compiled by the U.S. Department of Transportation. In 2005, accidents involving trucks recorded 10 percent of all occupational fatalities in the United States, an all-time high.[31] Teamsters President James P. Hoffa also suggests that truckers from Mexico could pose homeland security risks. On the Teamsters union Web site, Hoffa asks: Will the drivers be checked against the terror watch list? Will our borders be open to anyone with a Mexican driver's license?[32]

Despite the chauvinistic attacks carried out by politicians and some union leaders, some of which accuse migrants of being criminals, these workers reject status that relegates them to a malleable and disposable workforce. Many migrants have expressed indignation about their status and especially charges that they are criminals. "We are not criminals or bad people," one immigrant worker said in a recent interview, "We just want a way to work here and provide for our children."[33] Another added: "People do not believe it but we really do come to work, we are not delinquents here."[34] Migrant labor's mass protests, strikes, and boycotts pose a demand of a profoundly social character, that of defining workers' rights in an environment where laws of nation-states regulating labor mobility no longer correspond to the socio-economic realities created by an increasingly integrated global economy.

By viewing labor mobility within the broader context of workers' rights, a fundamental contradiction of global capitalism comes to light. Commodities and capital are allowed to flow freely across national boundaries, but labor mobility remains regulated. While NAFTA continues to transform the North American labor market, a strategic role to Mexican labor is being assigned as American capital and industry undergo restructuring both within and beyond the country's borders.[35] This ongoing process is producing a set of complex challenges for nation-states.

While the governments of North America grapple with the tasks of both managing and coordinating labor mobility in the era of globalized production, Mexican workers are pressuring those same governments to enhance and protect workers' rights. This pressure is highly visible through massive rallies and street protests organized around the demand that labor has the right to move freely across national borders to earn a living. A better grasp of these recent developments first requires recognition that they are linked directly to the long history of North American economic integration, a process that has been highly uneven and characterized by Mexico's subordination to U.S. economic interests.

North American Integration, Labor Mobility, and Workers' Rights: The Historical Legacy

Mexico's modernization effectively subordinated the nation and its people to the geopolitical and economic interests of the United States. Ever since the United States came to control substantial quantities of Mexico's wealth and the economies of the two countries began experiencing integration, migratory labor has played a strategic role in the development of capitalism in North America. For more than a century, Mexico's border with the United States has effectively functioned as an artificial boundary for millions of migrants who have crossed it to work in a myriad of occupations and industries, and in many cases for the same enterprises.

In the age of globalized capital and production, migrants labor for firms that are increasingly transnational in their operations as they set up shop not only in North America but also around the world. Because substantial numbers of the Mexican working class began toiling in workplaces owned by firms involved in international business, they developed a consciousness that reached beyond national borders. Accordingly, the notion of worker-employer partnership in order to assist a national-based enterprise to compete against international capitalist rivals is historically inconsistent with the real-world experiences of many Mexican workers. This factor trumps the narrow nationalism and chauvinism promoted by the unions in all the NAFTA countries. The result is that the Mexican worker has developed an international labor consciousness that is usually not found among American and Canadian workers.

The demands raised by Mexican workers for a living wage and decent working conditions, among others, are connected with the workers' right to mobility and to earn a living where they and their families can survive as human beings. In many ways, the special conditions that Mexican workers endure have broadened the meaning of workers' rights in the era of globalization and NAFTA. The significance of this development has helped launch the idea that workers' rights are human rights that move far beyond the narrow confines of the place of employment.

Wages and the Causes of Labor Mobility

Much like today, low wages in the early period of Mexican modernization provided a powerful incentive for migration to the United States. But during the reign of Porfirio Díaz, many of the nation's elites ignored this fact as illustrated in a report written during the late years of the nineteenth century by Matías Romero, Díaz's foreign minister. In a study of Mexico that included a chapter on wages, Romero wrote, "the rate of wages keeps moving upwards" and "there is no sign that it has reached its limit." He concluded that "our peons are not starving, and are, for the most part, a quiet and philosophic people . . . complaining very little, while a Patriotic government has their interests at heart."[36]

Yet as early as 1900, nearly 200,000 Mexican migrants were in the United States working in mines and smelters, construction, and on the railroads.[37] And they were not "quiet people" who rarely complained. As early as 1901, Mexican migrants working construction went on strike against the El Paso Electric Street Car Company for higher wages and better conditions. In 1903,

Mexican migrants joined Japanese agricultural laborers in Oxnard, California, and struck the Western Agricultural Contracting Company (WACC), protesting poor working conditions and low wages.[38] In 1906, on the Mexican side of the border, striking miners at Cananea, many of whom had worked in the United States, revolted against American management practices, the most important of which was wage discrimination. The struggles at Cananea and elsewhere played an important role in bringing the Díaz regime down.

After the fall of Díaz in 1911, an article in *El Economista Mexicano* suggested that the most pressing problem facing the nation was the problem of the distribution of wealth and what it called the "social question." It noted that internal peace depended greatly upon how successful government could be in obtaining an agreement between capital and labor.[39] Soon, management signed agreements with unions in the textile industry that granted the demands of 30,000 workers who had staged a strike for higher pay. From 1914 to 1916, regional military commanders of the revolutionary armies issued decrees establishing minimum and overtime wages in areas under their control. The 1917 constitution contained provisions for a national minimum wage, overtime pay, and profit sharing, and the state labor codes that implemented Article 123 of the document generally included language on wages.[40]

Although the situation for workers regarding wages generally improved, the economic integration of North America continued to advance and the need for Mexican labor in the United States increased. Record numbers of Mexicans crossed the border to work, especially in the 1920s when the U.S. economy boomed. Mexicans were pulled to the United States in this period also because major changes occurred in immigration law in 1921 and once again in 1924 that restricted Europeans but did not bar Mexicans. Between 1920 and 1930, approximately 400,000 Mexican migrants entered the United States legally, and it is estimated that nearly the same number entered and worked illegally during those years.[41] Although the vast majority found jobs in agriculture, many ended up working in steel mills and meatpacking plants in places like Chicago and Pennsylvania, while Henry Ford actively recruited and employed Mexicans to labor in his sprawling auto factories inside and around Detroit.[42]

The effects of the Great Depression discouraged Mexican migration, as economic conditions in the United States initiated a reverse movement of migrants back to Mexico. From 1931 to 1942, an average of only 2,013 Mexicans migrated to the United States per year, representing a considerable drop of the previous twenty-year flow.[43] Besides the effect of the Great Depression on employment availability in the United States, an increase in real wages for

Mexican workers during the period also acted as a deterrent to migration. According to one study, real industrial wages increased 26 percent between 1935 and 1940.[44] A report issued in 1942 by the General Motors Company of Mexico suggested that real wages grew considerably between 1935 and 1940, with a 44 percent improvement in base salary and benefits measured in dollars.[45] Finally, and perhaps the most important factor curbing Mexican migration to the United States in these years, was the acceleration of land reform.[46]

Despite the slowdown in migration and open hostility toward Mexicans that included their deportation and forced others to voluntarily expatriate from the United States, Mexican nationals joined millions of other American workers to form unions and fight for workers' rights.[47] In many organizing efforts, however, Mexican workers had to overcome opposition from their own government. Mexican consuls in the United States worked with growers in agriculture to break strikes, undermine the efforts of organizers, and even help set up company unions.[48]

Many successful organizing efforts involved the employment of the tactics of cross-border cooperation and interracial unionism that mobilized workers to protest discriminatory hiring practices. These actions demonstrated that Mexicans were no longer willing to accept inferior status assigned to them by employers or by those in the political establishment who sought to deny them full political rights and exclude them from citizenship.[49] Moreover, the struggles waged by Mexican workers in the 1930s in agriculture, tobacco, garment, and other industries gave the American labor movement a broader context in which to build organizing momentum.

As the U.S. economy recovered from the Great Depression as a result of World War II, full employment was in force as more than 13 million men and women entered the armed forces. Acute labor shortages resulted, and in 1942 the United States and Mexico agreed to a contract labor arrangement known as the Bracero Program. Lasting until 1964, more than 4 million laborers participated. Rising unemployment in Mexican rural areas caused by increased mechanization of agriculture after the war and a slowing down of government-sponsored land redistribution programs also helped generate illegal migration to the United States, which totaled some 20 million during the life of the program.[50] Although most Braceros worked in agriculture and on the railroads, some also labored in other industries.[51]

When the Bracero Program ended in 1964 and Mexicans returned home, the U.S. and Mexican governments sought to integrate their respective economies further by establishing the maquiladora industry along the border.

Through generating employment that paid higher wages than in the rest of Mexico, but at the same time were much lower than across the border in the United States, it was hoped that the Border Industrialization Program (BIP) would attract workers to the border region. There Mexicans could provide a potential source of labor for insertion into the U.S. economy, which at the time was beginning to experience deindustrialization and the parallel growth of the service sector.[52] These developments, coupled with the 1965 ending of quotas for legal immigration into the United States, generated a new wave of Mexican migrants crossing the border without documentation.

The significance of the increase in the flow of undocumented migrants is reflected in the rise of border apprehensions, which in 1965 the INS reported at 55,000. In just one year, that figure had jumped to 90,000, and by 1969 it had reached 200,000. During the 1970s, INS apprehensions continued to climb, as 710,000 were reported in 1974. By 1979, the number of apprehensions had jumped to 978,000.[53] For Mexican migrants able to escape INS authorities and find work during this period, their occupational characteristics also began to change. Although many continued to labor in agriculture, increasing numbers took jobs in the expanding service sector while others secured employment in light manufacturing and the meatpacking industry, both of which were undergoing restructuring.[54]

As migration increased sharply during the 1970s, Mexican labor inside the United States made significant advances in the area of workers' rights. The struggles for dignity, better conditions, and a living wage were heard first from those working in the fields, trapped at the bottom of the occupational ladder. Not protected by minimum wage statutes and other labor laws, the United Farm Workers of America (UFW), led by César Chávez, dropped its demands to remove undocumented workers from the fields and deport them. The UFW then began to include them in strikes and in the organization of national boycotts against grapes and lettuce, actions that eventually forced a significant section of agribusiness to recognize their union, pay higher wages, and improve conditions.[55]

By the mid-1980s when the liberalization of the Mexican economy was in full swing, migratory flows to the United States had increased substantially. Migrants came to the United States from all parts of Mexico, including some urban areas. They arrived to work not only in the traditional destinations of years past, such as the Southwest, but also in major U.S cities, like Las Vegas, Chicago, and the New York metropolitan area. Mexican migrants continued the trend of filling an increasingly broad range of jobs, moving from the agricultural sector into food processing, low-value-added manufacturing, and personal services. With the capping of certain permanent immigrant admissions from the Western Hemisphere in 1978, demand for family immigrant visas began to exceed supply. Legal permanent immigration from Mexico continued to grow through the 1980s, averaging 65,500 admissions per year from 1980 through 1986. With opportunities for legal admissions remaining grossly inadequate to meet demand, illegal immigration from Mexico increased substantially, and it alarmed many in the U.S. political establishment.[56]

In 1986, the U.S. Congress passed the Immigration Reform and Control Act (IRCA). Among other things, IRCA provided for the legalization of unauthorized immigrants who could show they had been resident in the United States since January 1, 1982, or had worked in agriculture for a specified time. IRCA also created a system of graduated sanctions for employers who hired undocumented immigrants "knowingly." From 1989 to 1994, almost 2.5 million Mexicans received permanent residency, and 2 million of these were a result of IRCA legalization provisions.[57]

NAFTA: Promises Made and Not Kept

Mexico's 1994 entrance into NAFTA was supposed to stop the migratory trend once and for all. The proponents of NAFTA claimed that both the creation of jobs at higher wages and the resulting growth of a Mexican middle class would serve to discourage migration to the United States. Instead, migration to the United States continued, as reflected in the increase of apprehensions along the U.S. southwestern border, which grew from about 700,000 in 1994 to more than 1.3 million by 2001.[58]

Also, the number of Mexicans in the United States without authorization rose from 2 million in 1990 to 4.8 million in 2000, meaning that 79 percent of the total unauthorized population between 1990 and 2000 was due to migration from Mexico.[59] Further proof that NAFTA caused a spike in Mexican migration to the United States is that the number of people immigrating to the United States from Mexico decreased by 18 percent in the three years preceding NAFTA. However, the number of annual immigrants from Mexico surged from 332,000 in 1993 (the year before NAFTA went into effect) to 530,000 in 2000, a 60 percent increase over the period.[60]

The Pew Hispanic Center reported that in 2005 almost 11 million of the nearly 13 million undocumented workers in the United States were Mexican nationals.[61] Other factors illustrate the acceleration of U.S.-Mexican demographic integration since NAFTA. While Mexicans still have a comparatively lower tendency to become U.S. citizens, the number of naturalized citizens from Mexico rose by 144 percent from 1995 to 2005, which was the sharpest increase among immigrants from any major sending country.[62]

The trend toward geographic and economic dispersion of Mexican-born individuals in the United States also has continued in the NAFTA years. The 2000 Mexican census revealed that several states that did not have a tradition of northward migration had begun sending large numbers of migrants to the United States. Among those states were Oaxaca, Guerrero, Puebla, Hildalgo, Veracruz, Morelos, the state of Mexico, and the Distrito Federal.

In the United States, Mexican migrants could now be found in states such as North Carolina, Kentucky, Minnesota, and Arkansas, all places that witnessed increases of their Mexican-born population of more than 1,000 percent between 1990 and 2000.[63] The broader geographic dispersion of Mexican migrants within the United States paralleled the continuing trend of diversity with regard to occupational characteristics. In 2005, the undocumented migrant in the United States represented 36 percent of all insulation workers, 29 percent of all roofers and drywall installers, and 27 percent of all butchers, other food-processing workers, and construction helpers. In the leisure, hospitality, and construction industries, the share of unauthorized workers in 2005 was one in six and one in every five workers, respectively.[64]

Evidence strongly suggests that demographics and the failure of the Mexican economy since NAFTA to create sufficient levels of employment are the primary reasons why migration to the United States has increased. High population growth rates through the 1970s resulted in women joining the workforce at an increasing rate during the 1980s and 1990s. They did so because of both declining reproductive rates and the increasing need to support household incomes resulting from several severe economic crises that occurred in those decades.

The result was an increase in the growth of the Mexican labor force, from 33.7 million in 1993 to 43.4 million in 2003. Mexico needed to create almost a million jobs a year simply to absorb the growth in labor supply.[65] A study by the Worker's University of Mexico using official Mexican government statistics shows an annual jobs deficit during the period of nearly 600,000. During the first five years of the Vicente Fox government (2000–2005), Mexico's jobs deficit climbed to 5,289,853 overall.[66]

Although Mexico did manage to create employment in export manufacturing, growth in that sector failed to keep pace with jobs lost in agriculture due to increased imports, especially cheaper corn from the United States. Between the years 1993 and 2002, employment in the agricultural sector declined from 25.7 to 17.3 percent of the economically active population.[67] And while the manufacturing sector did create employment, in 1995 real manufacturing wages declined by 12.9 percent due to the collapse of the Mexican peso.[68]

Other long-term developments regarding wages have provided powerful incentive for Mexican workers to migrate to United States. First, the minimum wage in Mexico lost 80 percent of its purchasing power between 1976 and 2004.[69] Second, in a ten-year period (1975–1985), the wage disparity between Mexico and the United States increased 60 percent.[70] Connecting migration to job losses and declining real wages, Joseph Stiglitz wrote in 2004: "The disparity in income across the Mexican border is among the largest anywhere, and the resulting migration pressure is enormous."[71]

Studies and surveys conducted by the Mexican government's Consejo Nacional de Población (CONAPO) have documented this pressure.[72] From 2001 to 2003, 390,000 persons, or an average of 1,068 per day, left Mexico for the United States. These figures are in stark contrast to an earlier period when Mexico geared its development toward the national rather than the international market. From 1961 to 1970, Mexico lost fewer than 30,000 persons annually to the United States, or an average of 82 persons per day.[73]

According to a 2006 report published by the International Federation for Human Rights (FIDH) produced at the request of the United Nations Committee on Economic, Social, and Cultural Rights (CESCR), NAFTA has created conditions inside Mexico that have contributed to the increase in migration to the United States. The FIDH investigation focused on employment and working conditions in the northern part of the country, in particular the maquiladoras and in the informal economy. It found that national manufacturing production capacity has been dismantled, the agricultural industry destroyed, and a growing dependence of the Mexican population on American firms. NAFTA particularly had benefited the maquiladoras and the transnational corporations that own them, the report found, but its effects on employment and wages have been deeply detrimental to Mexican workers. In the context of NAFTA, the report suggested that the main competitive advantage of Mexico lies in the maintenance of low wages and precarious working conditions, along with state control of trade unions.[74]

At the same time, migrants working in the United States send remittances back to their family members in Mexico, helping to sustain a substantial portion of the population. A recent study of trade agreements by Oxfam International concurs with the FIDH report that Mexico has lost more control of its economy to U.S.-based transnationals since NAFTA. Mexico is experiencing greater income inequality as a result, making the government and the population increasingly dependent on the infusion of remittances from nationals working in the United States. According to the Bank of Mexico, remittances are now estimated at slightly more than $20 billion annually. These transfers have become an important contributor to Mexico's external accounts, providing capital inflows estimated to be as much as 2.5 percent of Mexico's gross domestic product.[75]

Accordingly, data that measure outcomes on employment, wages, and trade policies since the inception of NAFTA strongly suggest linkages between these variables and increased migration. Evidence also shows that the integration of Mexican workers into expanding segments of the U.S. labor market has been steadily increasing for decades. The restructuring of both the U.S. and the Mexican economies that predated NAFTA has resulted in the assignment of a more strategic role for Mexican labor on both sides of the border.[76]

Labor Mobility and Workers' Rights under the NAALC

In 1993, when the Canadian, Mexican, and U.S. governments signed the NAALC, the countries pledged to uphold the protection of migrant workers. Article 1 of the NAALC sets forth the agreement's objectives, and Article 2 details its obligations. Together, these objectives and obligations define the scope of the agreement. One of the objectives is to ensure the effective enforcement and transparent administration of labor laws, defined in the NAALC to include laws and regulations that are directly related to the protection of migrant workers. In accordance with these objectives, the NAALC countries agreed to promote to the maximum extent possible the same legal protection afforded to migrant workers as the party's nationals with respect to working conditions.[77]

The NAALC complaints that have been filed involving the rights of migrants inside the United States have argued that migrant workers do not receive the same treatment as domestic workers. Because of this discrimination, petitioners have asserted that their rights to minimum employment conditions and their right to organize a union have been violated. Allegations that the right to organize a union surfaced almost immediately after the NAALC went into effect. On February 9, 1995, the Mexican Telephone Workers' Union filed a complaint alleging that a subsidiary of the Sprint Corporation in San Francisco, California, closed its facility to avoid the possibility of 240 workers winning a certification election after having organized a union. The company shuttered the plant shortly before the date of the scheduled union representation election.

The Communications Workers of America (CWA), which had organized the workers, filed an unfair labor practice case with the National Labor Relations Board (NLRB). The Mexican National Administrative Office reviewed the submission and issued a public report on May 31, 1995, requesting ministerial consultations on the effects of such a plant closure on union organizing efforts. As part of the Ministerial Consultations Agreement between the U.S. secretary of labor and the Mexican secretary of labor and social welfare, the U.S. Department of Labor held a public forum in San Francisco, California, to allow interested persons an opportunity to convey their concerns about the effects of sudden plant closings.

The labor secretaries further instructed the Secretariat of the Commission of Labor Cooperation to conduct a study on the effects of sudden plant closings on the principle of freedom of association and the right of workers to organize in the three countries. In June 1997, six months prior to the Secretariat completing and releasing the study, the NLRB ordered Sprint to reinstate the dismissed workers and awarded them back pay. The Sprint Corporation appealed the decision to the federal courts. On November 25, 1997, the U.S. Court of Appeals for the District of Columbia reversed the NLRB and ruled that Sprint closed the facility for legitimate financial reasons.[78]

With respect to safety and health issues, petitioners in a number of complaints alleged the existence of a persistent violation of U.S. law in matters of ergonomic protection, claiming a complete lack of safety measures to prevent injuries caused by repetitive movements affecting workers. Also alleged by petitioners in a number of complaints was that the U.S. federal and state authorities had not set a standard regulating the information provided to workers on the handling of pesticides or the provision of protective equipment for these types of toxic substance. Many accidents involving these substances have been recorded in which the worker was not given the necessary medical assistance; many other accidents are not even reported. Additionally, petitioners claimed in a number of cases that the U.S. government had failed to ensure for compensation in cases of occupational injuries and illnesses.[79]

Most of these issues came to light in early 2003 when the Farmworker Justice Fund and the Mexican-based Central Indepediente de Obreros Agrícolas y Campesinos (CIOAC), jointly filed a NAALC petition concerning use of the U.S. H-2A temporary agricultural visa program in North Carolina and the alleged failure of the U.S. government to enforce labor laws with respect to freedom of association, the right to organize, minimum employment standards, and protection of migrant workers. It was the first petition filed jointly by U.S. and Mexican organizations specifically to defend the rights of Mexican migrant workers in the United States. Unlike other public submissions concerning abuses of migrant workers' rights in the United States, the petitioners in the North Carolina case tied labor violations to interstate trade between the United States and Mexico as well as to mutually recognized labor laws.[80]

For example, both the United States and Mexico have laws concerning the recruitment, hiring, transport, and housing of migrant workers. According to Article 28 of the Mexican Federal Labor Law, employers are responsible for paying migrants' round-trip transportation costs between Mexico and the United States. Likewise, the U.S. Department of Labor is obligated by its own regulations to require H-2A employers to pay transportation costs for migrant workers. In practice, however, the North Carolina employers had been retaining recruitment firms to hire and transport workers. Employers claimed that the recruitment firms were solely responsible for compliance with laws regarding recruitment, but in reality workers end up bearing the transportation costs.[81]

This effectively meant that H-2A workers had been earning less than the minimum wage of $5.15 per hour, when in fact they would have been entitled to receive $7.06 per hour.[82] By linking the effects of migration to the U.S. and Mexican economies, the petitioners made an exceptionally strong case, eventually forcing the hand of the U.S. government. That pressure, combined with a five-year boycott against the Mount Olive Pickle Company and the North Carolina Grower's Association (NCGA) by the Farm Labor Organizing Committee (FLOC), resulted in a September 2004 agreement that covered more than 8,000 migrants working in 1,000 farms. It guaranteed employer payment not only of the transportation costs but also of the $100 fee a migrant worker had been paying for an interview with the U.S. consulate and the $100 visa to enter and work in the United States.[83]

A sidebar provision extended the influence of this agreement as far as Ohio, and an understanding with the Mount Olive Pickle Company increased wages to workers and prices to growers by more than 10 percent through 2007, which settled the boycott. The agreement between the NCGA and the FLOC includes the development of a system of seniority based on the number of years worked, growers' requests, and union membership. The contract's nondiscrimination clause, a three-step grievance procedure, and representatives in labor camps monitor implementation and protection of workers' rights.[84]

The agreement also included an initiative to bring the entire agricultural industry of North Carolina together to work on different issues that require investigation and long-term development. Standing committees with the NCGA and other public entities were established to improve housing and health care and to examine issues of fair trade regarding competitive growers and industries that compete with workers and growers under this agreement. The FLOC and the NCGA also pledged to approach the Mexican government together concerning graft, bribery, and blackmail committed by recruiters and Mexican police.[85]

A recent study by historian Leon Fink of North Carolina poultry workers in the early 1990s provides valuable insight in explaining how the FLOC succeeded in making gains for migrant workers. As Fink suggests, migrants rely much on a sense of community in a culturally alien world.[86] They carry with them the customs and traditions of their rural past, and in the process they reshape them to fit their new environment. New cultural forms of resistance emerge as a consequence, and the sense of community is strengthened rather than fragmented. These forms of resistance that are built through struggle are never retired. Especially in places like North Carolina, where larger numbers of migrants have settled in recent years, it is evident that when confronting abusive management practices and forms of hostility in the communities in which they live, the resistance strategies developed by migrants who arrived in an earlier period are resurrected, embraced, and then reconfigured to fit new circumstances and challenges.

Not all alleged violations of the NAALC obligation to uphold the protection of migrant workers have resulted in the official filing of a complaint, as was done in North Carolina. In fact, most that have been filed with the U.S., Canadian, or Mexican governments have not resulted in serious action or have had successful outcomes. Despite these shortcomings of the NAALC process, it has managed to create a so-called sunshine effect for exposing numerous violations of the right of migrant workers to freedom of association and collective bargaining. One of the more publicized cases occurred in 1999 at the Minneapolis Holiday Inn Express, where workers had voted in favor of union representation in an NLRB election. Days later, the manager called eight of the workers, all Mexicans, into the office, where the workers were met by immigration authorities, who asked them whether they had papers. When the workers admitted that they did not, they were handcuffed and taken to an INS detention facility.[87]

In 2002, the U.S. Supreme Court created a powerful new incentive for employers to carry out such actions by its decision in *Hoffman Plastic Compounds v. National Labor Relations Board*. In that case, the Court determined that an undocumented worker is not entitled to back pay, the only monetary remedy available to workers under the National Labor Relations Act when fired illegally for trying to organize a union.[88] In practice, the ruling has made it much more difficult for migrant workers to exercise the right to join a union and bargain collectively. This has been reflected in the 2003 case of mine workers in Utah when they attempted to organize the Kingston Co-Op Mine. Workers at the mine earned $5.25 to $8.00 per hour, with virtually no health care or other benefits, substantially less than the approximately $20 per hour that unionized mine workers earned.[89] Many miners had worked for the company for many years, and some had returned to Mexico annually. Company representatives even had assisted some of the workers to leave Mexico and come to the United States, and they often turned a blind eye to the lack of work authorization, until the miners began to organize a union.[90]

Just prior to the union election, the employer sent a letter to most of the workers who would be voting, requiring that they provide proof of work authorization. The employer then fired those who failed to present the documentation. The union filed charges with the NLRB, alleging that the employer had fired the workers in retaliation for their attempt to join a union. Even though the NLRB found merit to the charges, it refused to seek reinstatement or back pay for the great majority of the workers because the it determined that the workers lacked work authorization.[91] Despite these legal obstacles, as recent studies have shown, Mexican workers in the United States have registered increasing success in demanding their rights reflected by successful union organizing drives in Los Angeles, Houston, and elsewhere.[92]

Some U.S. employers, however, like the Smithfield Meat Company, continue to try to intimidate migrant workers by calling on the government to deport them. Undeterred by deportation threats, beatings, harassment, firings, and defeats in union elections in 1994 and 1997, hundreds of workers walked out of the plant on November 16, 2006, in defense of seventy-five immigrant coworkers fired over "no match" letters from the Social Security Administration. The "no matches" are often the product of name changes and wrong data entry.[93]

Open defiance of employers and federal authorities at Smithfield and elsewhere shows that Mexican migrants continue to struggle for their rights as workers. And the international border that divides Mexico and the United States is no deterrent to these struggles. South of the Rio Grande, workers defy employers, corrupt unions, and government officials, often at enormous risk to the well-being of themselves and their families, as illustrated in the Monterrey, Mexico, murder of FLOC organizer Santiago Rafael Cruz, a Mexican national who had played an instrumental role in bringing about collective bargaining rights for H-2A workers in North Carolina. Cruz was murdered while working in Monterrey in the FLOC hiring hall, established in the 2004 agreement reached between the growers' association of North Carolina and the union to circumvent the traditional costs charged by labor recruiters (coyotes) to migrants for processing visas to work in the United States.[94]

North American Integration and Labor Solidarity

As NAFTA creates a more integrated continental economy, the fate of the working class in all three North America countries is increasingly tied.[95] Yet despite deepening economic integration, with products manufactured and sold regionally that require a mobile labor pool, nation-states continue to insist on national borders to control the flow of workers in search of a cheap source of labor.

But Mexican workers, as they have done throughout the history of North American economic integration, continue the struggle for workers' rights. In spite of political obstacles in doing so, Mexican workers are leading the fight to defend freedom of association, the right to bargain collectively, and the right to strike. In North America, the struggles of migrant workers must form an integral component of any strategy to revitalize a labor movement needing a boost after experiencing years of decline. For working people and unions in North America, building strategies in support of migrant workers' rights are linked to strengthening labor's position versus capital overall, especially within the dimension of union-management relations in Canada and the United States, the subject of the next chapter.

5

The Crisis of Union-Management Relations in the United States and Canada

> If workingmen and capitalists are equal co-partners, composing one vast firm by which the industry of the world is carried on and controlled, why do they not share equally in the profits? Why does capital take to itself the whole loaf, while labor is left to gather up the crumbs? Why does capital roll in luxury and wealth, while labor is left to eke out a miserable existence in poverty and want? Are these the evidences of an identity of interests, of mutual relations, of equal partnership? No sir. On the contrary they are evidences of an antagonism.[1]
>
> —Karl Marx

A little more than a quarter century ago, experts, commentators, and scholars began writing about the changing environment in the world of union-management relations. Typical of this commentary was a 1981 *Business Week* article that noted: "Quietly, almost without notice, a new industrial relations system with a fundamentally different way of managing people is taking shape in the U.S."[2] The new system, the article pointed out, was seeking "to end the adversarial relationship that has grown between management and labor and that now threatens the competitiveness of many industries."[3]

In 1986, a group of employment relations scholars wrote in their now classic book *The Transformation of American Industrial Relations*: "We see the current moment as one of those historic periods of transformation in which existing institutional structures have been challenged and opened up to experimentation."[4] Observations that a new era of union-management relations was emerging reflected deep changes taking place in the structure of global capitalism, and they affected unions, collective bargaining, and workers' rights not just in North America but around the world in both developed and developing nations.[5]

Today, even more so than in 1981, the building up of competitive pressures in the global economy is a constant challenge to maintaining the profitability of many industries, and they have placed great stress upon nationally anchored union-management relations systems. This process is linked directly to a fundamental contradiction inherent in the capitalist system. More specifically, the nation-state system, in which the rules of commerce and ownership are written, designed, and regulated, increasingly comes into conflict with a capital accumulation process that stretches across national borders in search of markets, cheaper labor, lower costs, more efficiency, and higher profits. The result is a closer integration of the global economy characterized by social productive processes that are more international in scope and yet in most ways still subject to national laws. Many contemporary academics and analysts increasingly connect the changes taking place in union-management relations with these larger developments.[6]

In today's global economy, trade and finance liberalization, new technologies and production methods, and an expanded labor market have strengthened the bargaining leverage of employers and weakened unions. Declines in union membership and fewer workers covered by collective agreements are marginalizing the influence of the postwar, union-centered industrial relations model in the world of work. In this new environment, low-wage, human resource management, Japanese-oriented, and joint team-based employment relations strategies are challenging the viability of the older industrial relations model.[7] Moreover, the waning relevance of that older model is reducing the capacity of unions to organize workers and influence government policy.

As early as 1976, John T. Dunlop, former U.S. secretary of labor and Harvard professor, identified the beginnings of this historical development and its implications for the future of labor relations in the United States. He wrote that greater interdependence between America and its trading partners would bring pressures on the employment relations and collective bargaining systems in the United States as a result of the effect of foreign wage rates and labor market policies. Dunlop predicted that these developments would destroy many American jobs, and he described the challenges produced by these developments as "transitional pressures," insisting that they were inevitable and would require adaptation by both unions and management.[8]

The "transitional pressures" on union-management relations that Dunlop describes beginning in the 1970s are now well-established trends. Prior to the 1970s, the outcomes of union-management relations in the context of bargaining were characterized by workers obtaining lifelong job security, payment of wages that reflected the general cost of living, and generous employer-provided health and retirement benefits. Union and nonunion workers alike enjoyed rising living standards, giving them entrance into what became known as America's "middle-class."

This stable union-management relations environment depended greatly on American dominance of the world's industrial economy. In the 1970s, that dominance began to crack under the weight of global competitive pressures. Although most of these pressures resulted from Japanese- and European-based corporations capturing greater market share around the globe, other factors, such as the 1973 oil embargo and disruptions to the oil supply in 1979, also contributed to the decline of American economic dominance, especially in manufacturing. Also characterizing the 1970s were long periods of inflation, recession, and high unemployment. From 1970 to 1974, the average annual unemployment rate was 5.4 percent, while the average annual change in the consumer price index (CPI) was 6.6 percent. In the years between 1974 and 1979, unemployment rose to 7.9 percent and the CPI shot up to 8.1 percent.[9]

This economic malaise combined with increasing competitiveness triggered a crisis for American manufacturing, reflected by an accelerated fall in the rate of profit, a trend that began developing in the 1960s. In the 1970s, industrialists reacted to these developments in two ways. First, they actively lobbied the government for protection against imports. Second, industrialists launched an all-out assault on labor through speeding up the pace of work and attempting to roll back the gains made by workers in earlier periods. In the process of carrying out this strategy, employers also benefited from the government imposition of wage and price controls.

Serious attention began being paid to these developments in the 1980s when Barry Bluestone and Bennett Harrison published two books on the subject of deindustrialization. While those studies found that job losses in manufacturing were due to plant closings and their relocation to cheap labor havens outside the United States, they also revealed that deindustrialization was having a significant impact on jobs that remained in the United States.[10] Those jobs had been downgraded significantly through the increasing prevalence of part-time employment, wage cuts, and work speedup.[11]

The trends that began to take shape in the American economy and in the world of work identified by Bluestone and Harrison provoked resistance among broad sectors of the American working class. With the exception of 1973 and 1976, the number of workers involved in major strikes never fell below 1 million between the years 1967 and 1979. In 1970 and 1971, the number of workers involved in strikes was 2.4 million and 2.5 million, respectively. In 1979, strikes numbered 255 and involved a total of approximately 1 million workers.[12]

Perhaps most important, many of these work stoppages were wildcat strikes, conducted in many instances in defiance of union leaders and without their authorization. In early 1978, officials from many large unions reacted to these rank-and-file challenges by seeking to build stronger relations with management. In doing so, Douglas Fraser, then president of the United Auto Workers (UAW), along with AFL-CIO head George Meany, served on a nongovernmental organization called the Labor-Management Group. Consisting of an equal number of union officials and representatives of corporate management, the Labor-Management Group met regularly to discuss ways to tackle inflation, unemployment, rising health costs, and other matters, including labor legislation designed to remove obstacles that prevented workers from organizing unions.

In July 1978, when the group refused to back a labor law reform bill in Congress designed to make it easier for workers to join unions, Fraser and other union heads resigned.[13] The legislation defeated in Congress was an urgent attempt by the unions to reverse declining membership, which during the 1970s began to accelerate at an alarming rate. In 1978, for example, 26.6 percent of nonagricultural workers belonged to unions as compared to 34.7 percent in 1954. Between 1974 and 1978, unions in manufacturing lost more than 1 million members (from 9,144,000 to 8,119,000), more than 11 percent.[14]

Besides attempting to reverse declining membership through legislative measures, unions also followed the lead of many industrialists in lobbying Congress to enact laws that would protect American manufacturing from foreign imports. Owing their very existence to the success of national industries and economies, the unions combined their lobbying efforts by conducting a massive public relations campaign to urge consumers in the United States to "Buy American." Underlying the "Buy American" campaign were union efforts to enhance U.S. industry's global competitiveness through the building of "partnerships" with U.S.-based transnational corporations.

The hope was that through these partnerships labor productivity would rise and businesses would once again earn healthy profits that they would in turn share with unionized workers. As a report issued in 1983 by the AFL-CIO noted: "Profits can only be created in a well-managed enterprise, where both capital and labor contribute to the result."[15] In 1985, the AFL-CIO issued another report that reaffirmed the belief that the only way to reverse organized labor's declining fortunes was to help strengthen the competitive position of U.S. industry in the world economy through union-management cooperation and developing partnerships with employers.[16]

Reflecting the new union outlook of cooperation and partnership was a notable reduction in the number of work stoppages. In the 1980s, the annual average of work stoppages involving 1,000 or more workers (large strikes) fell to 83 from an annual average of 207 in the 1970s.[17] According to the Federal Mediation and Conciliation Service, the most strikes in a year during the decade occurred in 1985, when 1,016 strikes were started that included large and small work stoppages. This compared to 3,005 small and large work stoppages in 1975. The downward trend continued in the 1990s as the number of strikes involving 1,000 workers or more declined to a yearly average of just thirty-five. In 1995, unions and workers conducted 385 strikes, large and small. The number represented a drop of 20 percent from the previous year, and it was the lowest number of strikes recorded in the United States in fifty years.[18]

The decline in strike activity paralleled the increasing practice of employers using replacement workers during work stoppages. The use of replacements took off after 1981 when President Ronald Reagan fired air-traffic controllers for violating federal law that prohibited federal employees from striking. The firing of the strikers made replacement workers permanent. Before 1980, employers hired permanent replacements in less than 2 percent of strikes. In the 1980s, employers used permanent replacements in 14 percent of strikes. Moreover, permanent replacement was often a feature of many large, highly publicized strikes, such as those that occurred at Hormel, Phelps-Dodge, International Paper, and Greyhound, all of which ended in defeat for the unions.[19]

This wave of defeats severely weakened the unions both in the workplace and politically. In 1994, despite employing a highly charged public relations campaign, the unions failed to stop NAFTA. Moreover, their efforts to get Congress to pass legislation banning the use of striker replacements collapsed. These two defeats, combined with continuing membership decline, accelerated the trend of fewer strikes.[20] In 2002, the number of workers idled, the number of days of idleness, and the percentage of estimated working time lost because of strikes and lockouts reached historic lows. Only nineteen strikes began during that year, idling 46,000 workers and resulting in 660,000 workdays of idleness, representing less than one out of every 10,000 available workdays.[21] February 2003 marked the first month since the Bureau of Labor Statistics started keeping track in 1947 that not a single strike of more than 1,000 workers was begun anywhere in the United States.[22]

The unions' abandonment of the strike and their pursuit of cooperation and partnership with employers along with conducting the highly visible "Buy American" campaign failed to stop the protracted decline in membership. From 1971 to 1989, union membership in the public sector dropped by 10 percent, while the private sector witnessed a decline of 42 percent.[23] In 2000, less than one out of every ten workers in the private sector belonged to unions, or less than 9 percent of the total workforce. This compared to a high of 35.7 percent of the workforce organized in 1953. In 2006, private-sector unionization dropped to 7.4 percent, down from 10.3 percent in 1995.[24]

The 2006 figure was the lowest private-sector unionization rate since 1900, when U.S. unions represented just 6.5 percent of the workforce. In 1905, unionization in the private sector had risen to 11.1 percent, well above the 2006 figure.[25] The protracted decline in the last quarter century is even more evident when considering that, in 1983, about one in six private-sector workers was in a union. By 2006, the share had fallen to about one in fourteen.[26] More significantly, in 2006, for the first time in U.S. history, union membership rates were lower in manufacturing (11.7 percent) than in the rest of the economy (12.0 percent). In 2006, the number of unionized workers in manufacturing was 9 percent lower than in 2005 and down from 38.9 percent in 1973.[27]

Union defeats in decertification elections also have contributed to the decline. From 1997 to 2006, unions in the United States lost a total of 2,704 decertification elections of the 4,045 conducted by the National Labor Relations Board (NLRB). In those elections, unions never received as much as 36 percent of the vote in any one year. During that period, trade unions in the United States lost 123,661 members through decertification elections.[28] Adding to the woes of organized labor and contributing to its membership decline in recent years has been the rapid growth of employer antiunion strategies that has featured the proliferation of consulting agencies and firms solely dedicated to union avoidance for employers.[29]

Astonishingly, union membership decline occurred even while the U.S. government enacted protectionist legislation. In the 1970s and 1980s, while the U.S. auto industry faced major challenges from foreign competition, the Big Three U.S. automakers—Ford, Chrysler, and General Motors—convinced the federal government to impose a cap on the number of cars Japan could ship to the United States. In the 1980s, the government imposed quotas limiting imports to 20 percent of the U.S. market. The steel industry also received protection through voluntary restraint agreements on imports. In 2000, American steel companies and the United Steelworkers (USW) and its president, George Becker, worked together to convince the Bill Clinton administration to curb imports by imposing a twelve-point plan to protect the domestic industry from the "dumping" of Japanese steel.[30]

Despite these few examples of protecting noncompetitive industries, in an ever more integrated global economy, the U.S. government pursues a free-trade agenda, characterized by its efforts to enter into bilateral agreements with low-wage countries. For the most part, while the unions have lobbied hard to stop these trade deals, they have failed to stop their proliferation. Since NAFTA, the United States has entered into numerous trade agreements with low-wage countries. The United States has entered into free-trade agreements with Jordan, Chile, Peru, and the Dominican Republic-Central American Free Trade Agreement (DR-CAFTA). At the same time, the U.S. government has several other similar trade pacts pending.

Concessionary Bargaining

Organized labor's failure to stop NAFTA and halt the momentum of free-trade expansion to low-wage countries has exposed the ineffectiveness of its nationalist orientation, reflected in large part by the collapse of its "Buy American" campaign. These developments are manifested in the process of collective bargaining in which the increasing globalization of production and finance has weakened union leverage. Evidence of this fact is the unions' growing practice of concessionary bargaining and the abandonment of the strike, the twin tactics that underscore their strategy of cooperation and partnership with management in the hope of saving jobs and reversing membership decline.

Concessionary bargaining is defined to include "some kind of 'give-back' from workers to management in the terms of some earlier specified agreement."[31] In her study of concessionary bargaining from 1975 to 1985, Linda Bell divided concessionary bargaining into two categories: "hard concessions" and "soft concessions." In the period between 1975 and 1985, Bell found an increase in the incidence of both "hard concessions," in the form of wage freezes or rollbacks and the erosion of cost-of-living allowance (COLA) clauses, and "soft concessions," including a shift away from guaranteed annual wage increases toward lump-sum payments, two-tiered pay scales, and bonuses.[32]

Instead of basic wage increases, many unions could secure only lump-sum bonuses or deferred compensation packages such as gain sharing and stock option plans that provided a payout only in the event that the company survived and reached a certain level of future profitability. In many instances, work rules were relaxed and job classifications reduced in an effort to improve labor productivity by increasing internal flexibility. From 1982 to 1988, the percentage of workers affected by at least one of these concession instruments grew from 48 to 76 percent.[33]

Indeed, throughout the 1980s, the paramount issue in union-management relations in the United States was on meeting foreign competition head on, especially in manufacturing. Soon, the mantra of making American businesses more "competitive" versus their international rivals spread from manufacturing to other economic sectors, such as retail, construction, telecommunications, and transportation. With their fate tied directly to the success of nationally based industries, unions joined management in "partnership," concentrating on ways to restrain labor costs, increase productivity, and preserve jobs.

Long-standing bargaining patterns disappeared as the parties sought to adjust to the shifting conditions in all forms of economic activity, ranging from individual plants to entire industries. Reflective of the efforts to restrain labor costs during this period is data on 1986 major collective bargaining settlements involving 1,000 workers or more in private industry. In that year, wage adjustments began to average less than 2 percent annually over the life of a typical three-year agreement, compared to an average of almost 3 percent at the beginning of the decade. In most major collective agreements, provisions began to appear that attempted to address other costs as well, such as health care insurance and pensions.[34]

In exchange for significant wage concessions and the "chipping away" at benefits, for the most part workers received only marginal (if any) quid pro quos from management. Generally, these consisted of promises to share in the sacrifices or that trade union leaders were put on company boards of directors without giving them voting rights and the power to effectively influence corporate strategic decision making. In those instances where job security improvements were negotiated, management for the most part agreed only to suspend employment cutbacks instead of giving explicit employment guarantees for the future.[35]

The trend of concessionary bargaining accelerated during the recession years of the early 1990s. By 1994, when NAFTA went into effect, two-tier wage systems were appearing in nearly 40 percent of collective agreements.[36] A 1996 study shed light on ways in which NAFTA affected bargaining. Produced by Cornell Industrial Relations Professor Kate Bronfenbrenner and commissioned by the North American Commission for Labor Cooperation, the study examined more than five hundred union organizing campaigns and more than a hundred negotiations for a first contract. It found that a majority of employers threatened to close all or part of the plant during the organizing drive, either in captive audience meetings, in letters to employees, or in conversations between supervisors and one or more employees. Among those campaigns in which threats were made, in 10 percent of the cases the threat was specifically to move to Mexico, while in other cases the threats were vaguer but sometimes made reference to NAFTA.[37]

The employer strategy was effective. When threats were made in organizing drives, unions won 33 percent of the time. No threats during a campaign meant a union win rate of 47 percent. Moreover, in 15 percent of the plants where the union won, the employer shut down all or part of the plant within two years of the election, and in most cases this occurred before a first contract was ever reached. The 15 percent shutdown rate within two years of a union winning an election was three times the rate found by researchers looking at the late 1980s.[38] The plant closings study showed how NAFTA, at least indirectly, provided workers' incentives to vote no in representation elections while at the same time encouraging unions to practice concessionary bargaining in the event of an election win.

In recent years, concessionary bargaining and the trends it had established in reducing wage increases and benefits and in increasing worker productivity accelerated to the point where they are now almost considered the norm in union-management relations. In 2002, for example, nearly 73 percent of collective agreements in the manufacturing sector of primary goods (metals, paper, etc.) had provisions for incentive pay rather than regular wage increases. In the same year, only 16 percent of agreements contained cost-of-living provisions, down from 34 percent in 1995.[39]

These trends continue even while U.S.-based corporations have racked up record profits. In March 2006, the U.S. Commerce Department reported that corporate profits increased 21.3 percent n 2005, which accounted for the largest share of national income in forty years. Strong productivity gains and subdued wage growth boosted before-tax profits to 11.6 percent of national income in the fourth quarter of 2005, the biggest share since the summer of 1966. For all of 2005, before-tax profits totaled $1.35 trillion, up from $1.16 trillion in 2004 and just $767 billion in 2001. Meanwhile, the share of national income going to wage and salary workers has fallen to 56.9 percent. Except for a brief period in 1997, it was the lowest share for labor income since 1966.[40]

Typical of record profits resulting from concessionary bargaining is an agreement signed in 2005 by the UAW and the Caterpillar Corporation. The six-year contract followed a series of failed strikes going back to the 1980s. It established a two-tier wage system in which new hires would be paid around 50 percent of veteran workers and included provisions that called for lump-sum payments instead of actual wage increases. Fixed monthly pensions go now only to veteran workers, and job security is effectively canceled for new hires, who must work twelve years without interruption to become immune to layoffs. Management boasted after signing the agreement that the arrangement gave Caterpillar leeway to shed the new workers when demand turns down for the company's products. Employee co-payments for health insurance also rose in the current contract, for retirees as well as for active workers.[41]

The Caterpillar-UAW agreement represented a significant turning point in the labor cost-cutting trend in the United States, particularly at old-line manufacturing companies. Until recently, cutbacks in the wages and benefits of hourly workers occurred primarily at money-losing companies, such as failing steel mills and the struggling airlines. But now healthy and highly profitable companies like Caterpillar are engaging in the practice. In 2005, for example, Caterpillar reported revenue of $36.34 billion, up 20 percent from 2004. That was on top of a 33 percent increase in 2004 from 2003. Net income was up 40 percent in 2005, to $2.85 billion, and it had almost tripled since 2003. At the same time, Caterpillar invested tens of millions of dollars into research to develop a great variety of products that sell against those of Komatsu and Volvo, the company's' two biggest foreign competitors.[42]

Christopher E. Glynn, the director of corporate labor relations for Caterpillar, summed up the agreement's objectives. "Our target is competitiveness," he said, adding that the new contract reflected the company's success in imposing a "market competitive" pay scale much in line with the manufacturing hourly wage, which traditionally had been higher than in other economic sectors. Through most of the 1990s, the manufacturing hourly wage premium was 10 percent or more, but by 2005 it had fallen to just 7.45 percent above the average in other industries, according to the Bureau of Labor Statistics.[43] Jim Owens, Caterpillar's chief executive officer (CEO), explained the significance of the bargaining process and outcome by saying, "We finally have a labor cost that is viable."[44]

The labor cost described by Caterpillar management in Illinois was now also more compatible with wages and benefits the company paid to its workers in the network of small, low-wage plants it had opened in the South in recent years. This southern network, as it is called, also includes plants in

Mexico, and it provides parts and other inputs to the big Illinois factories, where most of Caterpillar's tractors and earth movers, backhoes and excavators, giant off-highway trucks, and other heavy equipment are assembled for sale in the United States and around the world. CEO Owens called the domestic plants the hub of a "globally cost-competitive" industry that could not succeed without the concessionary UAW contract, combined with the network of lower-wage "focus plants" in the Sun Belt and in Mexico. "It's a beautiful North American equation," said Owens.[45]

Two-tier systems are appearing in sectors well beyond manufacturing, and like the Caterpillar-UAW agreement, they include not only lower wages for new hires but also significantly lower benefit provisions. In early 2004, the United Food and Commercial Workers (UFCW) and major supermarkets in Southern California agreed to a two-tier plan that cut pay and benefits for new hires. For 139 days, 60,000 UFCW members fought Albertsons, Ralph's, and Vons to block the two-tier system and deep cuts in benefits.[46]

Despite the militancy of the grocery workers and the broad-based support for their struggle, the 2003–2004 strike/lockout ended with the UFCW accepting all major employer demands, despite the fact that millions of customers honored and even joined picket lines, costing the stores more than $2 billion in lost business. The supermarkets claimed they had to cut labor costs to compete with Wal-Mart and other nonunion stores in the region. Under the agreement, new hires would top out at $2.80 an hour below their veteran co-workers and pay a higher share of their health benefit costs. Safeway, the parent company for Vons, even offered buyouts to push out its higher-paid veteran workers and hasten the shift to a low-wage workforce.[47]

The UFCW agreements with the supermarkets were not cataclysmic events in the retail food industry. Rather, they were significant steps in a larger trend of declining wages for the unionized retail grocery workforce, one that predated the emergence of Wal-Mart as the industry behemoth. From 1980 until the present, the wage differential (average hourly earnings) between the mainly nonunion retail stores compared to the highly organized retail grocery component of the industry sector has all but disappeared. Average hourly earnings in the grocery store sector in 1980 were $1.57 an hour above the rest of retail. In 1983, union retail workers made 35.5 percent more than their nonunion counterparts. By August 2000, the average hourly earnings in the retail grocery store sector were 18 cents an hour below the highly nonunion retail industry as a whole. Since the merger between the Amalgamated Meat Cutters and Retail Clerks in 1979, which created UFCW, the $1.57 an hour advantage in retail grocery has not only been eliminated but the mostly nonunion average hourly earnings in the retail industry now exceed that in retail grocery.[48]

According to the Research-Education-Advocacy-People (REAP), a UFCW rank-and-file advocacy organization that monitors the history of wages, conditions, and benefits bargained by their union, the 1983 wage differential of 35.3 percent between union retail workers and that of their nonunion counterparts had by 2003 narrowed to a mere 1.3 percent. REAP places the blame for the decline in union wages squarely on the UFCW leadership and describes the 2004 events in Southern California as a "mop up" to a successful national employer strategy to force workers into concessions around the country for some two decades. For example, in the mid-1980s, Kroger succeeded in getting major concession from workers in Ohio, Indiana, Kentucky, and in Atlanta, Georgia. During the decade, Safeway and Giant in the Washington, DC, and Baltimore area initiated two-tier wage structures. Rollbacks in wages and benefits continued in the 1990s in other parts of the country, while the industry raked in huge profits.[49]

The rank-and-file grocery workers' organization points out that the high salaries made by UFCW officials are in sharp contrast to the "sacrifices" that workers are asked by both union leadership and company management to make. Greg Conger, for example, the president of UFCW Local 324, earned $221,615 in 2006, according to a union filing with the U.S. Department of Labor. Seven other employees of Local 324 earned more than $100,000, while another seventeen took home more than $90,000 in 2006. In that same year, Rick Icaza, president of UFCW Local 770, the largest in Southern California, received a salary of $281,896. By comparison, a union member at the top of the supermarket's "first-tier" wage scale earned $37,232 a year for full-time work. On the second tier, top pay for full-time work was $31,408.[50]

The higher salaries among UFCW officials and the lower wages of union members are part of a larger trend involving the entire organized labor officialdom. Recent data filed under the Labor Management and Recording Act show that the number of union officials making more than $100,000 more than doubled between 2000 and 2004, while those getting paid more than $150,000 annually increased by 84 percent. Over the course of those years, 5,646 union officials and staff received a total of $733.6 million in salaries higher than $100,000, including multiple salaries, while 870 were paid $181.7 million in salaries higher than $150,000.[51]

In pursuit of lower wages for their employees through negotiating settlements with highly paid union officials, supermarket chains cite the need to reduce costs in the face of a greater competitive environment, often referred to as the "Wal-Mart factor." Unlike manufacturing enterprises that take advantage of globalized production to lower costs, supermarkets are forced to target specific consumer markets in which they are geographically and strategically anchored in order maximize their share of that market. Yet, like any capitalist enterprise in the era of globalized capital and production, they must seek to reduce costs relative to their rivals.

Thus, supermarkets that successfully establish two-tier wage systems, reduce workers' wages and benefits, and introduce flexible work rules are better positioned to maximize their rate of profit and attract capital, even while they may lose market share, as illustrated by the gains major chains have made in recent years. Kroger Company, for example, which operates the Ralph's chain, saw earnings jump 16 percent to $1.11 billion in 2006.[52] Safeway, Inc., posted its biggest numbers in 2006 since 2001, earning $870.6 million and increasing its fourth quarter gains by 77 percent.[53] Even Supervalu, Inc., which acquired much of the Albertsons chain, collected $332 million in profits in the last nine months of 2006, which enabled it to post a profit of $2.3 billion for the year.[54] At the same time, the salaries of company executives have soared. Between 2003 and 2005, total CEO compensation for Ralph's (Kroger), Safeway (Vons), and Supervalu (Albertson's) increased by 37.6 percent, 817.3 percent, and 142.9 percent, respectively.[55]

Recent concessionary bargaining carried out by the International Association of Machinists (IAM), representing workers at Harley-Davidson, perhaps best illustrates the abject failure of the trade union policy of economic nationalism and partnership with employers in the face of higher executive pay. In early 2007, after a brief strike and lockout, the IAM agreed to a two-tier wage structure and increases in the level of out-of-pocket costs that employees could incur for health insurance deductibles and co-payments. Under the agreement, new hires were to receive a lower company match of optional contributions that employees can make to the contributory portion of the plan. IAM International President Tom Buffenbarger commented: "There is a time for sharing sacrifices and a time for sharing success," adding that "after eighteen straight quarters of record profits and sales at Harley, these workers know what time it is."[56]

The concessions made by the Harley-Davidson workers occurred in the context of the company earning nearly $1 billion in profits in 2006 amid surging worldwide demand for the company's iconic line of motorcycles and related products.[57] In 2007, the company paid $7 million in salaries and bonuses to its top executives. Harley-Davidson CEO James Ziemer raked in $5,560,650, giving him the lion's "share of success" to which Buffenbarger had referred.[58]

Moreover, the 2007 concessionary bargaining at Harley-Davidson by the IAM occurred within the context of the company being touted by the trade union officialdom as a business model for other firms to emulate. In 2005, the AFL-CIO–funded American Rights at Work praised Harley-Davidson for keeping jobs in the United States instead of going to Mexico or elsewhere. The group credited the "partnership" Harley-Davidson had made with the IAM and other unions for "saving jobs." Unions and management established partnerships through participation in a model of cooperation called the High Performance Work Organization (HPWO). In the HPWO model, employees and management reach consensus on implementing measures to keep the company globally competitive, such as higher labor productivity and greater product quality control.[59]

The Harley-Davidson HPWO is a variation of union-management collaboration strategies that collectively fall under the rubric of employee involvement. These programs involve the implementation of new types of work design and practices that include the use of teams, quality circles, and the concept of total quality management (TQM). For employers, especially firms in manufacturing, gains in productivity and financial performance in the late 1980s and 1990s occurred for those that implemented the HPWO. At the same time, however, wage gains for workers involved in these schemes were almost nonexistent. Also, employers that had introduced the HPWO by 1992 had bigger layoffs by 1997 than firms that refrained from introducing the HPWO. Yet employee involvement programs and joint union-management committees are still favored strategies pursued by trade unions as they struggle to find answers for the globalization of production.[60]

Concessionary bargaining and the notion of union-management partnership were on full display during a dispute between workers represented by the United Steelworkers of America (USWA) and the Goodyear Tire and Rubber Company, despite some initial rank-and-file resistance. On October 5, 2006, 15,000 workers walked out at sixteen Goodyear plants in the United States and Canada, three months after the expiration of the labor agreement between the world's third-largest tire maker and the USWA. The Goodyear workers resisted company demands for a two-tier wage system and a further erosion of pensions, medical coverage, and working conditions. The October strike followed an August 2006 USWA concessions agreement with Michelin's B. F. Goodrich Company, which was designed to set the pattern for the industry as a whole. The contract called for wage cuts of 20 percent over five years and other givebacks that included a lower pay scale for new hires and the diversion of one dollar from a cost-of-living pay increase scheduled for current employees into a retiree trust fund. This transferred, at least in part, the responsibility of funding retiree benefits from company management to the unionized workforce.[61]

Despite the union's recommendation to approve the new contract, nearly 40 percent of rank-and-file tire workers voted against it. The agreement set the minimum wage for new hires at $13 per hour. Goodyear, however, rejected the industry-wide pattern and demanded even bigger concessions, which included a 50 percent wage cut for new hires, which would have reduced wages to $10 per hour. According to Goodyear management, the demands for wage reductions were consistent with recent developments in the U.S. manufacturing sector. In fact, the Goodyear demands were similar to those granted by the UAW at Caterpillar.

In addition, Goodyear demanded the right to close plants and issue layoffs as it saw fit. Goodyear coupled the threat to close plants with a negotiating strategy that offered proposals to local unions in plants slated for closing to "save jobs." But the supposed "job security" guarantees the company proposed were bound up with further cost cutting to boost future profitability. In the process of negotiations, both Goodyear and the USWA announced regularly that the goal of each party was to reach an agreement that would "save the North American tire industry" from foreign competition.[62]

Under scrutiny, however, the union's demand to "save the North American tire industry" had nothing to do with saving the jobs and defending the living standards of rubber workers. Instead, it was a call to assist corporate management to cut labor costs and increase productivity to win a greater market at the expense of other rubber workers around the world. Tire production is one of the most globally integrated industries. Goodyear operates in twenty-nine countries and employs 80,000 workers. The world's largest tire maker, France-based Michelin-BF Goodrich, employs 125,000 workers worldwide, while Japan-based Bridgestone/Firestone has thirty-eight facilities in the United States, with divisions on every continent employing 110,000. The response of the USWA and other unions to globalization has been to pit these workforces against one another both nationally and internationally in a futile race to the bottom. The USWA-pattern contracts actually encourage demands for more concessions by rival companies seeking to compete against their international rivals.

After a twelve-week strike, Goodyear workers at ten U.S. plants voted to ratify a three-year contract. The USWA did not release the vote count, but the union indicated that at least one-third of the workers voted against the contract, which accepted the destruction of more than a thousand jobs, reduced wages, and made concessions on benefits. The USWA surrendered its stated goal of preventing further plant closings. The agreement contained no general wage increase, although it did provide for the continuation of cost-of-living adjustments (COLAs).

However, a portion of the inadequate COLA payments were to be diverted to help fund retiree health benefits. Further, the contract established a voluntary employees' beneficiary association (VEBA), which Goodyear agreed to fund with $1 billion in stock and cash, an amount less than the total needed to fully fund retiree benefits. At the same time, the contract allowed Goodyear to cap its obligation for retiree health care. The VEBA, independent of Goodyear, is managed by three USWA trustees and four additional trustees appointed jointly by the company and the union.[63] For the USWA, it provides a new source of potential income and financial leverage that would continue even if Goodyear filed for bankruptcy.

But the likelihood that Goodyear would declare bankruptcy, which during negotiations company management suggested might occur, appears to have been at best a threat and little more than a remote possibility. In 2005, Goodyear had sales of $19.5 billion, boosting its profits 7 percent to $337 million. The company paid CEO Robert Keegan more than $7.7 million in salary and stock options in the same year, including a $2.6 million bonus. Despite increased profits, Keegan and the company's big shareholders demanded more concessions from USWA members in 2006. USWA Executive Vice President Ron Hoover indicated the union was willing to comply when he said, "Our Union has shown that it can be an extremely innovative partner," advocating more labor-management collaboration to secure the "competitiveness" of Goodyear's U.S. operations.[64]

Outsourcing and Offshoring

Record profits and high pay for executives at Goodyear, Caterpillar, and elsewhere combined with workers' concessions in wages and benefits are indications that a transformation in the world of work in the United States is taking place. While unions supply firms with the type of worker required by the new international division of labor in the hope of saving jobs, their actions have done little or nothing to stop other industry cost-saving maneuvers. In recent years, the most widespread practices of companies seeking cheaper labor costs have been outsourcing, the movement of jobs and tasks from within a company to a supplier, and offshoring, the movement of jobs to lower-wage countries.

Most notable among those industries that engage in both outsourcing and offshoring is the majority unionized and heavily government-subsidized aircraft industry. Boeing, the largest corporation in the industry, greatly relies on defense contracts to maintain profit margins. In the era of globalized production, like other aircraft manufacturers, Boeing makes bids to the U.S. government for contracts based upon cost factors that are determined internationally. In the process of securing these bids, Boeing buys finished products from hundreds of suppliers. Regardless of where final assembly is located, Boeing scours the globe for the cheapest and most reliable components. In its dealings with unions over these matters, the IAM and the Society of Professional Engineering Employees in Aerospace (SPEEA), with which Boeing has entered into collective bargaining agreements, the aircraft company has insisted on the right to outsource.

On March 30, 2004, members and officials from the SPEEA and the IAM converged on Chicago at the Boeing Corporation' to protest the aerospace giant's cutting of its U.S. workforce while expanding overseas employment. From 2001 to 2004, Boeing cut more than 35,000 employees from its U.S. workforce. Dozens of protestors in Chicago were members of the Wichita, Kansas, SPEEA local that had recently rejected a contract offer by the company that would have given the employees the lowest wage increases and the highest health care premiums of any group of Boeing employees at the 12,000–employee Wichita plant.

SPEEA member Jennifer MacKay, a manufacturing engineer from Spokane, Washington, protested in Chicago because she saw employees get laid off and have their benefits cut and wages decreased by 3 to 15 percent when her plant was sold to Triumph Composite Systems, Inc. Steffan Gillyard, an engineer from Seattle, Washington, picketed to draw attention to the ongoing transfer of work to a Boeing design center in Moscow, Russia. Others arrived in Chicago to stop Boeing from transferring the engineering and writing of the aircraft maintenance manuals overseas to less experienced and less costly workers in China, Italy, Korea, and other locations.[65]

In the United States, Boeing eventually sold its airframe manufacturing operation in Wichita to investors. The new company now works as a Boeing subcontractor, absorbing costs Boeing once shouldered. "The world has changed, and Boeing has changed with it," said Michael Boyd, president of the Boyd Group, an aviation consulting firm in Evergreen, Colorado. "They've offloaded a lot of production. They are farming out everything to others so they don't have to build it," he said.[66] The Boeing example is proof that even the most complex products must conform to a market driven by low production costs, hyperefficient supply chains, and mass standardization in the era of globalized production.

As the template for globalized production in North America, NAFTA is accelerating the offshoring of jobs in the aircraft and aerospace industries. In 2005 and 2006, Cessna Aircraft, Bombardier Aerospace, and Raytheon Aircraft announced plans to move wire harness production from Wichita, Kansas, to various locations in Mexico. At the same time, Bombardier stated its intention to build major components at its new Mexican facility. The planned moves by the three companies involved the loss of more than three hundred U.S.-based jobs.[67]

In June 2008, in what media outlets described as a move that would send economic shock waves across Kansas for generations, Hawker Beechcraft announced plans to build a tip-to-tail aircraft assembly plant in Chihuahua, Mexico. At the same time, the company stated its long-range goal to move from manufacturing small parts to full aircraft assembly in Mexico after 2012. The relocation plan involves the eventual transfer of more than 4,300 jobs from its Wichita facility to Chihuahua, where Hawker Beechcraft had set up part of its assembly operations years earlier.

In an official union press release commenting on the company's announcement, IAM President Tom Buffenbarger said, "Hawker Beechcraft shows no recognition of the damage they do to our economy, our industrial base or our national security when they transfer sophisticated technology and production to countries that turn around and compete with U.S.-based companies." Buffenbarger added, "Thanks to NAFTA and other job-killing trade deals, we're encountering this phenomenon at every bargaining table in the aerospace industry."[68]

The Wages of Concessionary Bargaining and Declining Unionization

Concessionary bargaining, declining union membership, and fewer strikes have paralleled downward pressure on wages for unionized workers. In this context, the wage premium for union workers versus nonunion workers has been shrinking. In the late 1970s, for example, among wage and salary workers, the union wage premium ranged between 21 and 23 percent. By 2001, it had fallen to 14 percent.[69] Most important, the premium had fallen for virtually all types of workers in the private sector, and those that at one time enjoyed the largest premiums experienced the steepest declines.[70]

The drop in the union wage premium has coincided with another long-term trend: the declining share that wages make up of national income. In 2006, the *New York Times* reported that wages and salaries constituted the lowest share of the nation's gross domestic product since the U.S. government began recording the data in 1947. One reason for this development is that buying power of the minimum wage is at a fifty-year low.[71] The decline in the minimum wage is reflected in part by the overall stagnation of real wages since the 1970s. In 1973, the median hourly wage for American workers in today's dollars was $17.26, while in 2007 it was up less than 1 percent to $17.42.[72] Over the same period, U.S. workers' productivity nearly doubled.[73] For most of the last century, wages and productivity, the key measure of any economy's efficiency, had risen together.[74]

In great part, increases in worker productivity result from American workers putting in more hours than anyone else in the industrialized world. Americans added almost one week of work to their total annual hours worked from 1990 to 2000, increasing from 1,942 hours to 1,978 hours during the decade. This ran counter to trends occurring in other industrialized countries, where the number of annual work hours had actually declined. The average Canadian or Mexican worker was on the job roughly 100 hours less than the average American over the course of a year, or almost two-and-one-half weeks less. And a 2007 study conducted by the International Labour Organization (ILO) indicates that the trend of longer working hours in the United States is continuing.[75] Despite longer hours and resulting higher rates of worker productivity in the NAFTA years, the U.S. manufacturing sector has shed millions of jobs. From 1994 to 2003, more than 525,000 workers qualified for assistance under a U.S. government-sponsored NAFTA Trade Adjustment Program.[76] Between 2001 and 2003 alone, the manufacturing sector in the United States shed 3 million jobs.[77]

The Crisis of American Unions and the Split in the AFL-CIO

The decline in manufacturing employment has adversely affected the financial base of the unions. In July 2005, the erosion of the union's financial base became glaringly evident at the AFL-CIO's fiftieth anniversary convention. The AFL-CIO lost roughly one-quarter of its membership and some $20 million in annual per capita contributions when its two largest unions, the Teamsters and the Service Employees International Union (SEIU), withdrew.

Two other unions, the United Food and Commercial Workers (UFCW) and UNITE/HERE, an organization representing textile and hotel workers, soon afterward joined the Teamsters and the SEIU in splitting from the AFL-CIO, which resulted in the loss of fully one-third of the federation's 13 million members.[78]

The four unions had been members of the Change-to-Win (CTW) coalition that had been formed to press for changes in the AFL-CIO's policies. The CTW also includes the Laborers, Farmworkers, and Carpenters unions. When announcing the split, CTW leaders, Teamsters President James Hoffa and SEIU President Andy Stern, insisted that it opened up a new road for the unions to grow the labor movement. This talk, however, only masked the real reasons for the split, which took place within the context of retrenchment and the allocation of dwindling financial resources. The withdrawal of the Teamsters and the SEIU from the AFL-CIO meant that they would keep the approximately $10 million that each union had previously kicked in annually to the national federation.[79]

Absent in the forty-three pages of resolutions and amendments that the CTW faction submitted to the AFL-CIO convention were any mention of the abandonment of the strike or the practice of concessionary bargaining in pursuit of partnerships with employers that increasingly outsource and offshore union jobs. Thus the CTW unions presented no principle grounds for the organizational break. Disagreements expressed over policy were of an entirely marginal and tactical nature. For the vast majority of American workers, the crisis afflicting AFL-CIO leadership was of little consequence, since at the time of the split the proportion of the U.S. workforce that was unionized had fallen to almost negligible levels. Moreover, the labor officialdom struggle took place behind the backs of the 13 million members of the AFL-CIO, and especially those affiliated with the CTW unions, who were never provided the opportunity to vote on the question.[80]

In his well-publicized 2006 book *Getting America Back on Track: A Country That Works,* as SEIU president and now head of the CTW, Stern makes it clear that the 2005 split means business as usual for American unions as they continue cooperating and pursuing partnership with employers. In his book, Stern defines union-management partnership explicitly when he writes that unions need to "add value" to win the confidence of employers.[81] Although the SEIU represents workers in many jobs not threatened directly by outsourcing or offshoring, its strategy is no different from that of the industrial unions that are more exposed to the globalization of production and finance. Stern writes: "In a fast-paced competitive world, unions need to facilitate competition by leveling the playing field for all employers, not by simply raising the cost of doing business for unionized ones."[82] Stern lamented that many union leaders "just don't get it and still suffer from a lingering class struggle mentality."[83]

But union membership and political influence have both declined even while organized labor has been shedding its "class struggle mentality" through concessionary bargaining and abandoning the strike in the pursuit of partnership with employers. To reverse membership decline, both the CTW and the AFL-CIO have pinned their hopes on the passage of the Employee Free Choice Act. Blocked by Republicans in the Senate after passing the House of Representatives in 2007, the legislation will likely be considered again in 2009 when a new U.S. president takes office. The bill increases penalties against employers for violations of labor laws during union organization campaigns, such as discriminatory firings, and provides binding arbitration in cases where employers fail to negotiate a first contract with a newly formed union. Most important, the bill provides for immediate recognition of a new union if a majority of workers sign authorization cards (card check), without a secret ballot election.[84]

The Employee Free Choice Act reflects the trade unions' view that membership decline is solely the result of employer hostility and manipulation of current labor law that they claim lacks adequate provisions to ensure a fair process. It is well established that union organization efforts generally confront thoroughly antidemocratic attacks by employers, including systematic intimidation of workers to pressure them into voting against the union even after they have signed authorization cards. Half of all union organization drives fail even after winning majority support from the workers in a card check, in part because employer threats sway the outcome of the subsequent balloting.[85]

At the same time, however, the unions have abandoned any pretense of struggle against management and, in fact, collaborate to boost the competitiveness of American corporations versus their overseas rivals in the hope of saving jobs. Despite union no-strike pledges and concessionary bargaining, employers continue outsourcing and offshoring jobs. At the same time, companies downsize their domestic operations while demanding greater concessions in the form of wages and benefits from workers who remain.

Accordingly, even if the Employee Free Choice Act becomes the law of the land and union membership reverses its decline as a result, it does not change the fact that the geoeconomic foundations on which the unions are based have been shattered by the globalization of production and finance.

In this environment, the workers' act of unionizing becomes less significant as a way to win greater security and power. Even where union density is high, such as in the U.S. airline industry, pensions and wages have been cut and hard-won work rules have been abrogated.[86] Accordingly, higher union density does not change the economic and social conditions under which collective bargaining occurs.

Because they are organizations born and nurtured in national soil and welded to the success of the economies and industries of the countries in which they are based, the unions must deliver the type of worker needed by companies to compete globally against their rivals. Failure to do so means the possibility of not only company bankruptcies and lost jobs but also the unions running the risk of going out of business themselves. Moreover, the foundation on which the Employee Free Choice Act is built (card check and first-contract arbitration) has been a feature of labor landscape in Canada. Yet Canadian union membership has stagnated from its historic highs recorded in the 1980s, challenging the notion that a legal change in the rules governing organizing would automatically result in greater levels of union density.[87]

Canada: A Friendlier Labor Environment?

Reflecting on labor and the economy in Canada in the 1990s, Canadian Labor Congress President Ken Georgetti called it "the worst decade for Canadians in our history, as bad as the Great Depression decade of the 1930s."[88] He pointed to the stagnation in real wages, unemployment, the steady growth of poorly paid part-time and short-contract employment, rising inequality and poverty, cuts in social programs, longer working hours, and the greater intensity of work due to downsizing and contracting out.[89] Georgetti added that under both the Canada-United States Free Trade Agreement (CUFTA) and NAFTA, the market economy had failed to deliver rising living standards through higher earnings. Instead, it had produced insecurity and stagnant incomes for the great majority.[90]

Although Georgetti's attention focused on the 1990s, Canadian workers began to experience wage stagnation and job security in the 1970s. As in the United States and in the rest of the industrialized world, stagflation hit the Canadian economy hard. This placed pressure on Canada's "social wage" programs and the factory-to-factory rounds of collective bargaining. Canadian labor historian Craig Heron explains that in Canada's decentralized collective bargaining system, employers seeking to control inflation and reverse falling profit margins attempted to pit workers in the same industry against one another. Employers demanded work speedups and minimal or no wage increases, citing the necessity for workers in one factory to compete against the others to save jobs. This practice, called whipsawing, precipitated a wave of strikes.[91]

In 1975, under pressure from the business sector to put workers' wage demands in check and halt the wave of strikes, the Liberal government of Pierre Trudeau established Canada's first peacetime wage- and price-control program. In effect, the program was fundamentally a wage restraint measure. And while the program did control price increases for a time, by the end of the 1970s inflation had returned to annual double-digit growth. Governments at both the federal and provincial levels reacted by cutting spending for social services. The postwar Canadian government policy of maintaining relatively full employment and steadily rising incomes had come to an end. At the same time, the Canadian state began its efforts to recast the country's union-management relations system in favor of placing checks on increases in workers' income. This trend gained momentum in the early 1980s when the economy had its most severe recession since the 1930s.[92]

The Liberal government's attacks on the unions and workers' wages occurred within the context of a deepening Canadian nationalism. In the midst of the 1970s and early 1980s economic malaise, Canada sought to diversify its economic partners in order to reduce its dependence on the United States. At the same time, Canada would reduce its integration in the U.S. economy and become a more nationally integrated economy. The government obliged foreign companies to negotiate performance goals in order to give greater benefits of foreign investment to the national economy.[93] Sacrifices made by workers and unions in this period were cast and justified in this nationalist mold.

The nationalism of these years, however, faced stiff headwinds. As in the United States, the economy in Canada experienced recession in the early 1980s. In 1983, unemployment rose to 11.8 percent.[94] In 1984, the economic hard times helped usher in a neoliberal reign in Canada under the newly elected prime minister, Brian Mulroney. The Mulroney government brought in significant privatization and deregulation measures during its first term of office. These included the deregulation of the energy, financial, transportation, and foreign investment sectors and the privatization of public airline, oil, aircraft, telecommunications, and satellite companies. The economy opened wide to foreign investment. In 1986, when the Canadian government began negotiations for a free-trade agreement with the United States (CUFTA), fifty large corporations (mainly American owned) accounted for 70 percent of United States-Canada trade.[95]

In 1989, when CUFTA went into affect, the largest wave of corporate restructuring in Canada took off. From 1989 to 1993, in Ontario alone, which contains 40 percent of Canada's manufacturing capacity, 452 major manufacturing firms closed their facilities. Companies blamed the closures on increased competition. For workers who remained, employers demanded concessions in wages and benefits and in work organization, all in an attempt to lower costs. Firms also increased their use of part-time, temporary, and contract workers and started outsourcing to nonunion firms in low-wage jurisdictions. When Canada entered NAFTA in 1994, these practices expanded.[96]

At the end of the 1990s, the Canadian government's Workplace Information Directorate of Human Resources Development Canada (HRDC) published the results of a series of surveys covering workplace conditions during the CUFTA and NAFTA years. The surveys' findings, at least in the context of union-management relations, showed that trends begun in the 1970s and continued throughout the 1980s also were apparent in the 1990s. More specifically, the surveys attempted to identify the unions' overall organizational and bargaining priorities, their strategies, and their support systems to facilitate workplace change that benefits membership and strengthen their influence in the workplace. The design, execution, and analysis of the survey were done through a partnership between university researchers and the HRDC.

The results of the surveys showed that Canadian unions had experienced increasing downward pressure on employment, particularly full-time employment, and that it had translated into membership decline. The majority (88.5 percent) of survey respondents reported an increase in domestic and international competition manifested in management strategies to reduce costs. Nearly three-quarters of union respondents reported plant closures and company mergers, downsizing, outsourcing, and contracting out. Two-thirds of the unions responded that management increasingly utilized temporary and part-time workers. Surveys also found that these trends were more systematic in the public sector than in the private sector. Almost 58 percent reported from the public sector that their agencies had undergone privatization as a result of cuts in government spending for social programs. Nearly an average of 50 percent of survey respondents in both the public and private sector pointed to longer hours, increased workloads, and concerns over health and safety and job security.[97]

The surveys also found that more than three-quarters of union respondents reported increases in employer demands for wage and work rule concessions and that they were more prevalent in the public sector. Moreover, nearly half of the respondent unions (45.2 percent) reported that they were often asked for wage or other concessions during the term of an agreement. Two-thirds of union respondents (66.3 percent) said that employer bargaining power had increased to the detriment of union bargaining power, while nearly 60 percent reported a decrease in union bargaining power.[98]

In 2000 and 2001, the HRDC Workplace Information Directorate and academic experts conducted another survey of innovation and change in labor organizations. In all categories of questions, unions reported an acceleration of trends revealed in previous surveys. More than three-fourths of respondents reported modest to significant increases in management emphasis on cost reduction, while nearly half (46.5 percent) indicated an increase in downsizing and layoffs. In the areas of outsourcing and contracting out, 47.3 percent of union respondents reported increases in these management practices, while 60 percent indicated increases in workplace closures and company mergers.[99]

Union respondents also reported modest or significant increases in employer demands for concessions in wages and benefits (42.6 percent) as well as work rules (51.5 percent).[100] In all cases, less than one-third of all union respondents reported success in restricting the continuing management practices of contracting out or outsourcing and increasing workloads. Around 20 percent of union respondents indicated success in obtaining layoff protections and improving pensions and early retirement provisions.[101]

These government-sponsored surveys on union-management relations conducted from the mid-1990s through 2000–2001 demonstrate that globalization and NAFTA have strengthened the relative bargaining power of employers.

In Canada, as the survey results show, these forces also have influenced union-management relations in the public sector. In all NAFTA countries, however, the globalization of finance capital increasingly empowers market forces in government decision making regarding social policy. Competition for business investment and the jobs it creates is having a significant affect on the size and function of the public sector, and this has had a profound impact on union-management relations.[102] Speaking to these realities in June 2008, Ed Ott, the executive director of the New York City Central Labor Council, made up largely of public sector unions, said, "Every time you go to the bargaining table now, there's downward pressure." He added, "Even in the public sector, it's any improvement you want; you have to pay for with concessions."[103]

Although union density remains high in the Canadian public sector, employment structure continues to shift toward private services, challenging unions to formulate new strategies to adapt to these changes.[104] In the private sector, however, union density has begun to show signs of a declining trend, especially in manufacturing and natural resources, industries that have been most susceptible to increased market pressures, finance liberalization, and the relaxation of trade barriers, beginning in the early 1980s.[105]

In 1952, almost 50 percent of Canadian union members were employed in manufacturing, while around 40 percent of all manufacturing workers belonged to unions.[106] In 2001, the union membership rate among manufacturing workers was at 30.3 percent, compared to 36.2 percent in 1991 and 44.3 percent in 1982.[107] Union density in Canada averaged in the mid-30–percent range between 1980 and 1995, before declining to 31.9 percent in 2002. Private-sector union membership fell from an estimated 21 percent in the mid-1980s to 19 percent in 1997 and 18 percent in 2002.[108]

The decline in union density, especially in the private sector, has paralleled the decentralizing of bargaining and has disrupted pattern bargaining. Industry-wide bargaining, particularly in manufacturing, has moved increasingly toward the plant level, where employers make demands on unions for flexibility in setting conditions of employment. This generally involves linking pay to performance through increasing the pace of work with the objective of achieving higher levels of productivity. These schemes, called variable pay systems, deviate from traditional wages and pay. In Canada, although the number of firms using performance-based pay has increased since the 1980s, it is still far from an organizational norm, as traditional pay systems still prevail.[109]

But skill-based pay, wage incentive plans, such as piece rate, group incentives, gain sharing, and profit sharing are found more often in manufacturing. Piece rate pay, which is based on individual incentives, usually results in a bonus payment for output in excess of a base production rate. Piece rate pay in recent years has been on the decline. The drop has been the result of the implementation of group incentives that pay on the output of the group as a whole. In manufacturing, the group may include sections of a plant or an entire plant.

While the incidence of group incentive plans increased only slightly between 1988 and 1998 (nine in 1988 to twelve in 1998), the actual number of employees participating in this plan more than tripled, from around 9,000 workers to more than 32,000. Gain sharing also increased in use as a pay structure in collective agreements between 1988 and 1998. Gain sharing is measured by a predetermined performance formula and is applicable either to a group of employees to whom bonuses are paid according to the group's performance or to overall enterprise performance. In Canada, gain sharing plans reported in 1998 were twenty-five, a jump from twenty ten years earlier. Overall, employee coverage in gain sharing plans also shot up from 22,400 to 32,600.[110]

Profit sharing programs, which also provide a bonus payment, usually based upon a percentage of the company profits in excess of a previously agreed base, also increased between 1988 and 1998. Manufacturing witnessed the biggest increase from three to fifteen, while the transportation industry recorded eleven in 1998, a 100 percent increase from 1988. Employee coverage also jumped significantly over the ten-year period from 5,300 to more than 56,000. In 1998, Canada recorded a total of 148 pay incentive plans identified in collective agreements, and coverage rose by 12 percent from 1988 to include some 203,880 employees.[111]

By way of comparison, variable pay structures in the United States are found in about one-third of collective bargaining agreements. Group incentive programs are in 16 percent of those agreements, a reflection of an increasing emphasis on teamwork and new forms of work organization that sometimes are indicated by the presence of variable pay structures.[112] As in Canada, group incentive pay plans are favored most by manufacturing firms, since production levels are more easily measured in manufacturing compared to other economic sectors.[113] In 2002, 53 percent of manufacturers had contractual compensation plans based on production and profit, to only 18 percent of establishments outside of manufacturing.[114]

Outside of manufacturing, variable pay systems in the United States are particularly prevalent among producers of basic goods (e.g., primary metals, paper). In those branches of industry, 73 percent of contracts in 2002 provided for gain sharing or some form of group incentives.[115] In contrast, only about one of ten contracts has provisions for individual incentives and profit sharing.[116] The growing prevalence of pay-for-performance provisions and variable pay structures in collective agreements shows that the globalization of production and finance has made human resource management and team-based employment relations strategies part of the union-management relations template.

In Canada, as in the United States, the changes described in union-management relations have resulted in fewer strikes. Strikes and lockouts in Canada fell from an annual average of 754 in the 1980s, to 394 in the 1990s, to 319 in the 2000s. The time-loss ratio, which controls for the rise in employee numbers, also reveals an overall declining trend: from an annual average of 541 workdays lost per 1,000 employees in the 1980s, to 233 in the 1990s, to 203 in the 2000s. In the 1990s, strikes involved an average of 195,000 workers each year and an annual average of about 2.3 million working days lost. Working time lost due to strikes as a percentage of total estimated working time averaged 0.07 percent in the 1990s. In the four years beginning the decade of the 2000s, the number of workers involved in strikes came in at an annual average of 174,000, with almost 2.4 million working days lost. Working time lost due to strikes and lockouts as a percentage of total estimated working time averaged just 0.1 percent.[117]

In 2004, however, this trend began reversing itself. In just the first six months of that year, 177 strikes took place, and they involved more than 100,000 workers, exceeding the total number of affected workers for the previous year.[118] The surge in strike activity resulted from increasing contentious labor relations in the Canadian public sector, especially in the areas of administration, health care, and education, where fiscal restraint and downsizing have created more adversarial collective bargaining climates.

The growing adversarial climate in Canadian union-management relations resulted in 261 strikes in 2005, compared with 221 in 2003. The 2005 strikes and lockouts involved 429,000 workers (a fivefold jump from 2003) and cost 4.1 million working days (almost two-and-a-half times the 2003 figure). Similarly, the time-loss ratio of 301 in 2005 was more than twice the 2003 level. Quebec posted the largest share of strikes and lockouts (336, or 45 percent). Approximately 29 percent of the strikes and lockouts occurred in manufacturing, the sector of the Canadian economy affected most by globalization, followed by education, health, and social services (21 percent).[119]

Despite increases in work stoppages and the number of workers involved in them as well as the percentage of work time lost due to strikes, the figures are low by historical standards. In a 2006 report issued by the Organisation for Economic Cooperation and Development (OECD), the principal reason given for the long-term decline in strikes in member countries are the changes in the structure of employment by industry. While noting that there has been a marked shift away from manufacturing employment toward services, the report points out that strike rates are usually twice as high in industry (mining, manufacturing, electricity, utilities, and construction) than in the service sector (with the exception of transportation). But this only partially explains the decline in strike activity, because in most OECD countries, strike rates have declined since the late 1990s in both the industry and service sectors.[120]

In Canada, however, management has been especially determined in holding their positions during negotiations. According to Prem Benimadhu, a vice president at the probusiness Conference Board of Canada, the employer hard line takes place in the context of extensive government reliance on back-to-work legislation, which has tilted the balance of the Canadian industrial relations system decisively in favor of management. Benimadhu suggests that growing global competition is to blame for this sudden turn in Canadian industrial relations, particularly in the heavily unionized manufacturing sector that has faced stiff headwinds.[121]

In 2007, the conservative Toronto daily newspaper the *Globe and Mail* reported on the affects of increased global competitiveness in the manufacturing sector on wages. The share of wages as national income in Canada has fallen steadily since the early 1990s, the daily paper noted. At the same time, corporate profits, as a share of gross domestic product, are running at all-time highs, while wages adjusted for inflation are flat and have been since the late 1980s.[122] Confirming this trend was a 2008 Canadian government study that indicated, from 1997 to 2007, blue-collar workers in manufacturing experienced virtually no earnings growth.[123]

Another Canadian government study connected declining rates of unionization to stagnant earnings growth and decreases in pension coverage.[124] In Canada, as in the United States and Mexico, the union-nonunion wage differential (union wage premium) has been narrowing substantially since the 1970s. The Canadian union-wage premium stood at 10 percent in the 1980s, a decline from the 15 to 25 percent range that fluctuated throughout the decade of the 1970s. By the late 1990s, the difference that union workers enjoyed versus their nonunion counterparts had been reduced to less than 8 percent.[125]

The shrinking of the union-wage premium in North America and its connection to the advent of globalized production and finance have weighed heavily on the program of national reformism in which unions have traditionally sought to maintain and improve the social position of the working class, especially in developed, industrialized countries. Since the mid-1980s, the share of national income for labor in all advanced countries has declined by 7 percent, reflecting the growing inability of nationally based labor organizations to mount serious challenges to internationally organized corporations.[126]

In sum, both NAFTA and globalization have placed increasing demands on workers and unions to subordinate the defense of jobs, wages, pensions, and working conditions to the requirements of the capitalist market and the profit demands of business. Labor organizations not only have failed to muster a fight against the giant transnational corporations that shift production all over the globe, but they also have in fact collaborated with these enterprises in the restructuring of basic industries at the expense of their membership and the entire working class.

In their pursuit of partnership with the transnationals, the unions have assisted employers in the slashing of wages, the imposition of speedup, and the elimination of millions of jobs. These actions are justified on the grounds that sacrifices by workers are necessary to help their "national" businesses make profits and compete with foreign rivals. Although these conditions are prevalent throughout North America, they are most evident in the United States, where concessionary bargaining and the abandonment of the strike have been the hallmarks of union-management relations since the 1970s.

Implemented more than a quarter century ago under the rationale that it would save jobs and preserve organizational density, these strategies were and remain the unions' answer to globalization and NAFTA. Rather than achieving their stated objectives, however, they have instead been accompanied by industry downsizing and a significant drop in union membership, which has placed enormous pressure on the financial base of the trade unions. While dues increases, union mergers, and consolidations masked these financial problems for a period of time, they have boiled over to form the backdrop for union fracturing and waning political influence, reflected by the 2005 breakup of the AFL-CIO.

The crisis unions are facing as a result of globalization and NAFTA is most apparent in the auto industry. While blaming the ability of employers to drive down wages and the loss of membership on "foreign competition," the unions argue that for workers there is no alternative but to embrace partnership with their employers in order to make "national" industries globally competitive.[127] What follows is a closer examination of this outlook and the outcomes it has produced in terms of job security, wages, benefits, and quality of work life for autoworkers in North America.

6

The North American Auto Industry: The Apex of Concessionary Bargaining

The real story is that we've become partners
in some of the most profitable companies in the world,
DaimlerChrysler, Ford, and General Motors.[1]
—UAW President Stephen Yokich (1999)

Nowhere have the pressures associated with globalization and NAFTA been more evident than in U.S.-based auto manufacturing, once considered the world's undisputed titan of the industry. For more than a century, the auto industry had been an anchor for the U.S. economy, a trendsetter for both corporate America and the trade unions. Following World War II, the United Auto Workers (UAW) and auto management negotiated agreements that provided the industry's workforce with wages, health benefits, and pensions that set standards for unions in steel, mining, rubber, trucking, construction, telecommunications, and other industries. The pattern of steady wage increases together with increasingly stronger health and retirement benefit packages stretched well beyond heavily unionized industries, setting benchmarks for all the nation's employers, union and nonunion alike.[2]

As late as 2005, automobile manufacturing remained one of the U.S. economy's best-paying industries, with production workers earning an average hourly wage of $29.91 (excluding benefits). Wages in the auto sector were 79 percent greater than the national average for all manufacturing industries.[3] But over the last few decades, the hegemony of the U.S. auto industry has been increasingly challenged by foreign competition as a result of an ever more integrated global economy. In recent years, this trend has intensified, as American-based auto companies have lost market share both globally and within the United States.[4]

In November 2005, the severity of the crisis for the auto industry and its broader implications for the American economy became apparent when Delphi Automotive filed for bankruptcy, the largest industrial enterprise to do so in the entire history of the United States. While announcing the company's bankruptcy, Delphi's chief executive officer (CEO), Steve Miller, signaled what was at stake: "I want you to view what is happening at Delphi as a flash point, a test case, for all the economic and social trends that are on a collision course in our country and around the globe."[5] Miller emphasized that a successful course of action to avert catastrophe lay exclusively with Delphi's union members who needed to "sacrifice" in order to "save" the industry.[6]

On the heels of the Delphi bankruptcy filing, General Motors (GM) announced plans to close or eliminate shifts at nine of its assembly plants and cut 30,000 hourly workers' jobs in the United States and Canada by the end of 2008. The elimination of 22 percent of the North American workforce was part of a major restructuring plan designed to boost profits and raise share values for the company's stockholders. In the months leading up to the announcement, Wall Street investors had driven GM share values to the lowest point in eighteen years, and the company's credit rating had dropped to junk status. With losses of $5 billion in 2005, some analysts had predicted that the company would file for bankruptcy before 2008.[7]

When announcing the massive job-cutting program, company CEO Rick Wagoner said the objective was to reduce structural costs by $6 billion and bring the company's expenditures "in line with our major global competitors." He continued: "In short, they are an essential part of our plan to return our North American operations to profitability as soon as possible."[8] The downsizing measures represented the most extensive since the early 1990s when GM closed twenty-one assembly plants and manufacturing operations and cut 74,000 hourly and salaried jobs in just a few years. The new round of cuts sought to reduce the U.S. GM blue-collar workforce to 86,000 by the end of 2008.[9] At its peak in the early 1970s, GM employed more than 600,000 American workers. By 1978, GM employed 466,000 hourly workers, and by 1993 the numbers had been reduced to 233,000 blue-collar employees. GM's hourly U.S. workforce shrank by more than half, or 114,800 workers, between 1994 and 2004. In 2005, only 35 percent of workers in all auto companies and suppliers were unionized, down from nearly 65 percent in the mid-1970s.[10]

The downsizing at GM and the drop in union membership reflected the general decline in the position of U.S. industry in the world market. Founded in 1908, GM grew to become the world's largest industrial concern, dominating the global auto market in the 1950s and 1960s. In the 1970s, however,

Asian and European competitors challenged GM and other U.S. automakers, not only on the world market but also within the United States itself. In the 1980s, the Big Three (GM, Chrysler, and Ford) and the UAW reacted to the intensification of competition from imports by getting the U.S. Congress and the Ronald Reagan administration to negotiate a "voluntary export restraint" on the part of Japan. In 1995, these restraints lapsed when the United States and its trading partners agreed to eliminate trade quotas of this type in creating the World Trade Organization (WTO).[11] In 2005, GM, which once sold half of all vehicles bought in the United States, controlled less than 25 percent of the U.S. market, and its world market share had fallen to 15 percent.[12] For workers in the industry, the message delivered by auto executives was clear. They must make sacrifices to restore the global competitiveness of the U.S.-based car companies.

A January 16, 2007, front-page article in the *Detroit News* entitled "UAW: Expect Sacrifice" captured the tenor and the thrust of the new era of union-management relations in the auto industry. The hard-line rhetoric of the UAW that had characterized past negotiations was over, the paper reported, and instead, union leaders are using the language of sacrifice and the need to help GM, Ford, and Chrysler restore competitiveness. While UAW Vice President Cal Rapson toured GM plants around the country telling members, "The way we conducted business in the past when General Motors was very profitable, would have to change." James Kaster, president of UAW Local 1714 at GM's Lordstown, Ohio, plant explained to his constituency that "if we don't make a profit, we don't have a plant." Kaster added that his local union "already had a program in place to 'educate' workers on why GM's financial success should matter to them."[13]

Union leadership at Ford locals used the same approach to convince members that sacrifice was necessary on their part to save both the company and jobs. In 2006, Ford reported a record loss of $12.7 billion and announced the shutting of sixteen plants and the shedding of more than 40,000 hourly and salaried workers. Jim Stoufer, president of UAW Local 249 at Ford's suburban St. Louis plant, explained, "Common sense tells you this is going to be rough. We are going to have to play ball with Ford and keep them competitive."[14] Summarizing the approach of the UAW in the 2007 contract talks with the auto companies, international union Vice President Bob King said, "We have made a conscious choice to put aside the adversarial approach."[15]

The "nonadversarial" approach remained in place even while Ford increased bonuses for its executives. In 2006, Ford Motor Company's new CEO, Alan Mulally, earned $39.1 million for his four months of work. Ford Division of the Americas President Mark Fields received a total of $10.86 million in 2006, including a salary of $1.25 million. Ford awarded its chief financial officer, Don Leclair, $7.99 million, $1 million of which was salary. William Clay Ford Jr., great-grandson of the company's founder, executive chairman, and former chief executive, received "no cash salary, bonus or other awards" for 2006, the auto firm grandly announced. According to the company, his "sacrifice" was part of an arrangement to forego any new compensation until the company's automotive sector returns to profitability. However, his 2006 compensation still totaled $10,497,292, related to his previous options and other stock-based awards.[16]

UAW President Ron Gettelfinger responded to the news that Ford executive salaries had increased by saying, "UAW members have made significant sacrifices to help auto industry employers get back on track and remain competitive." He went on to add, "During a period of plant closings, employment reductions, and other painful changes for workers and communities, it's fair to ask whether executives are truly adding value in proportion to any compensation increases they have received."[17] Gettelfinger himself made $208,000 in salary, benefits, and expenses in 2005, according to the most recent publicly available IRS filing for the UAW, a sum of money that did not exactly place him in the category of UAW members who were experiencing what he called "painful changes."[18]

Like Gettelfinger, Ford CEO Mulally acknowledged in a *Detroit News* interview that it was a tough time for Ford employees. "There've been a lot of tears," he said, adding that it is also "a pretty exciting time at Ford because the employees who remain have the opportunity to be part of a historic transformation that will have far-reaching consequences for the automotive industry and Detroit as a whole."[19] In this context, Mulally offered that he "couldn't be more pleased with the thoughtfulness and thoroughness" of UAW officials in considering Ford's labor costs.[20]

Mulally praised Gettelfinger as a "realist," someone who understood the difficult balancing act a labor leader must perform. "Gettelfinger has seen Ford's books, and he knows just how serious the automaker's problems are and comprehends the magnitude of the concessions necessary to make Ford competitive again," Mulally added.[21] He concluded by noting that the many operating agreements Ford had negotiated with UAW locals over the past year had already made the company more competitive. In so many words, according to Mulally, the days of an "adversarial approach" in auto union-management relations had passed.[22]

However, an examination of the history of UAW-management relations over the last three decades reveals that the union abandoned any adversarial approach long ago. For more than thirty years, the UAW has officially subscribed to the corporatist policy of "labor-management partnership," which accepts the premise that rank-and-file workers must pay for a crisis not of their making. Instead of blaming millionaire company executives and wealthy investors who sacrificed the long-term health of these enterprises to maximizing immediate financial gains, UAW leaders promoted nationalism and the need to compete against foreign rivals as a means to justify productivity increases, work organization restructuring, lower pay, and a loss of shop-floor autonomy.

A major driving force behind the adoption of this approach is an enormous crisis of overcapacity in the auto industry. The vast gains in labor productivity that have resulted from speedup and the introduction of modern production methods have adversely affected workers. Rival car companies push to manufacture far more than they, in their totality, can possibly sell at a profit. According to a 2008 International Labour Organization (ILO) report, almost 1.3 billion workers, or 43.5 percent, still live below the U.S. $2 per day threshold, hardly a burgeoning consumer market for the purchase of automobiles.[23] The system dictates as a solution to this crisis the elimination of plants, machines, and hundreds of thousands of jobs.

For its part, the UAW has demonstrated that it is neither willing nor able to resist the auto industry's downsizing of the workforce or the downgrading of jobs that remain. The reasons for this go beyond personal cowardice, corruption, or the bad leadership of individual union officials. They are rooted in the basic political outlook of the union apparatus and the social interests of the labor officialdom. This outlook defends GM and its right to make profit through stepped up methods of production. Saving workers' jobs depends on whether workers can effectively subordinate their interests to the requirements of the market. In this role, the union needs to convince the company that it can extract greater profits by assisting management in introducing cost-cutting measures at its existing plants, rather than shifting production elsewhere.

The UAW's nationalist orientation is incompatible with modern industry and economic life that are increasingly international in their scope. Transnational corporations proceed from a world strategy and the need to organize production systems on a global scale. In order to construct a viable defense of their interests, workers need to do the same. Yet the UAW outlook suggests that workers in the United States should defend their jobs by pitting themselves against workers in Germany, Australia, Canada, Mexico, and

Latin America. In practice, the UAW nationalist perspective underscores the industry's strategy to divide workers across national borders as well as within the United States and inside other nations.

North American Auto Production and the Fracturing of Trade Unions

The earliest sign of the impact of global competitive pressures on the auto unions in North America occurred in the mid-1980s when the Canadian section of the UAW split off and formed the Canadian Auto Workers (CAW). Although minor tensions always had existed between the U.S. and Canadian sections of the UAW, they surfaced in more serious forms over the issue of concessionary bargaining with GM. In 1984, Canadians learned that then UAW President Owen Bieber had actively prevented their attempts to resist company proposals that already had been accepted by the union in the United States.

Specifically, GM (and the UAW) wanted workers to accept lump-sum payments and profit sharing while the Canadians insisted on annual wage increases. In Canada, the dispute evolved into a strike that quickly affected jobs and production in the United States. Bieber then threatened to withdraw strike authorization, which also would have suspended strike pay for the 36,000 Canadian GM workers. But the Canadian section continued to strike for thirteen days in defiance of the company and its own union leadership. After winning their demands, the Canadian section, led by Bob White, sought greater autonomy within the International Union by petitioning the International Executive Board to limit U.S. interference in future Canadian bargaining. When the board rejected White's bid for greater autonomy by a vote of 24–1, the Canadian UAW was on its way to independence.[24]

The 1985 establishment of the CAW paralleled the advancing integration of the auto industry in North America, which received a significant boost in 1965 when the United States and Canada signed the auto pact. The agreement established a continental-wide free-trade zone in auto parts and gave the Canadians production guarantees and content requirements that specified that all auto product imports south of their border would come from Canada. The emergence of a regional system of automotive production resulted, which facilitated the U.S.-based companies in the planning of strategies to achieve higher levels of productivity and efficiency designed to challenge the growing market share of their Japanese rivals.[25]

Today, the North American automotive industry is more integrated than any other sector of the regional economy. Motor vehicles and parts account for a larger share of intraregional trade in North America than any product sector. Three-way auto trade in 2003 was $125 billion, representing 20 percent of total trade between NAFTA partners. Between 1993 and 2003, the volume of NAFTA auto trade almost doubled, accounting for 18 percent of the total growth in NAFTA trade over this period.[26]

In the process of developing this economic dynamism, a central component of this corporate strategy included an effort to extract concessions from the industry's unionized workforce. By splitting the unity of North American autoworkers, the Big Three opened the way for a whole wave of further concessions in the United States, and it increasingly pitted Canadian and American workers against one another in a series of whipsaw threats to close plants and cut wages. In fact, the Canadian UAW leadership successfully avoided the givebacks arranged by UAW President Bieber in the years immediately prior to the split, largely because of the existence of an $8–per–hour advantage in labor costs due to the lower value of the Canadian dollar and the publicly funded Canadian national health care system. For more than twenty years, these factors allowed the CAW to maneuver its bargaining by claiming that it provided incentives for the auto companies to invest in new plants in Canada and to keep jobs there instead of in the United States, where production costs are higher.

This strategy, however, has proved futile. First, when the Canada-United States Free Trade Agreement (CUFTA) went into effect in 1989, the penalties imposed by the Canadian Auto Pact expired. The recent rise in the value of the Canadian dollar and the loss of Canadian manufacturing jobs resulting from it have prompted the CAW to openly call for protectionist measures to save Canadian jobs. At the same time, the CAW has launched a "buy Canadian" campaign, further driving a wedge between autoworkers in North America.[27] Moreover, these new tactical measures run straight into the reality that the North American automotive industry is a continental system that also includes Mexico, where the relocation of automobile and parts production has been by far the more significant trend. Mexico's integration into Ford, GM, and Chrysler transnational production systems started in the mid-1970s, and its importance has grown over time.

For example, engine exports from Mexico to Canada and the United States were 400,000 per year in the early 1980s and increased to 1.3 million between 1985 and 1989.[28] Vehicle exports grew from 14,000 to 186,000 between 1981 and 1989 and over the next three years more than doubled, reaching a figure of 393,000 in 1992.[29] NAFTA also eliminated a previous rule that had established an export minimum for maquiladora facilities in the production of auto parts. Under NAFTA origin rules, any product now manufactured in Mexico enters the United States duty-free. The result in Mexico has been a sharp increase in auto sector employment. The industry as a whole accounts for 13.4 percent of all manufacturing jobs inside the country, and in the parts sector alone, employment more than doubled from 200,000 to 470,000 from 1998 to 2007. In 2007, Mexico sold 80 percent of new cars abroad, compared with 41 percent in 1988.[30]

Reflecting these developments, in June 2007, immediately following the Cerberus Capital Management Group's acquisition of Chrysler from Daimler, the company announced its intention to build a state-of-the-art engine plant in Saltillo, Mexico, rather than in Canada or the United States. The news came on the heels of announcements by both GM and Ford that they, too, would invest more in Mexico.[31]

The most important reason for the growth in Mexican production is the lure of lower wages. In 2005, hourly compensation costs for motor vehicle and parts manufacturing production workers in Mexico were 10 percent of what they were in the United States and 24 percent of the wages paid in Canada.[32] Although advanced production technologies reduce the amount of labor required for production, reducing wages still remains of fundamental importance for auto production because labor costs represent approximately 20 percent of total costs.[33] In addition, Mexican unions have been quicker in conceding to auto management absolute authority on the shop floor, and the length of a regular workday is nine-and-one-half hours, versus the standard eight-hour shift in the United States and Canada.[34] In 2000, Mexican government surveys indicated that 73.9 percent of manufacturing workers reported an average workweek of more than forty hours.[35]

Thus, in the whipsaw battles taking place across North America in the auto industry, Mexican unions provide employers with employees who not only earn lower wages but also work longer hours. The whipsaw effect has intensified the ever-growing subordination of union members' interests to the dictates of these giant transnational corporations. Precisely at the time when the auto industry accelerated the trend toward regional and globalized production, the unions representing the workforce fragmented along national lines and increasingly embraced the corporate program of "international competitiveness."

Representative of the nationalist and chauvinist approach was a 2005 demonstration carried out by the UAW at Ford headquarters in Dearborn,

Michigan. Protesting the transfer of operations to Mexico, participants with bullhorns chanted slogans like "Hey, hey, ho, ho, we want jobs not Mexico" and "No Lincolns built in Mexico, hell no!" Comments made by UAW Local 36 President Dave Berry reflected the nationalist and chauvinist tone of the protest when he said, "We need to save American jobs. Our goal is to keep the American jobs here."[36] But instead of achieving the intended goals of "saving jobs" and increasing membership, the corporatist and nationalist approach pursued by the UAW has resulted in a precipitous drop in membership, from more than 1.5 million members in 1979 to less than 500,000 in 2007. How did the UAW transform itself from a militant mass movement into an "asset" of management, willing to act in partnership with employers who are increasingly hostile to the workers whose interests the union ostensibly represents?

The Chrysler Bailout and Its Impact

The UAW transformation from an adversary of management to one of partner with management began in the mid-1970s when the United States went into its biggest economic slump since the Great Depression. The economic downturn hit the auto industry hard, as the Arab oil embargo, rising fuel prices, and falling sales of full-size vehicles took their toll on company profits. The 1974–75 recession revealed not only the crisis of the auto industry but also a dramatic decline in the international position of the U.S. economy as a whole. American corporate profits had badly stagnated, and by the end of the decade the U.S. economy was experiencing runaway inflation.[37]

In 1978, Chrysler Corporation, the weakest of the U.S. Big Three automakers, which had barely escaped bankruptcy in 1975, lost $500 million. In 1979, the company began losing $6 million to $8 million per day and headed toward an eventual total loss of $1.1 billion, the largest amount in U.S. corporate history. Chrysler management reacted by selling off its overseas operations and other assets, while announcing the closing of several factories. Facing imminent bankruptcy, the company turned to the Jimmy Carter administration, appealing for a federal bailout, much like the government had organized earlier in the decade with Penn Central Railroad, Lockheed, and New York City.[38]

After sharp debate within business and government circles, a consensus emerged that called for the federal government to provide Chrysler with loan guarantees, under the condition that the UAW demonstrate a commitment to work with the company to close factories, slash the workforce, and agree to hundreds of millions of dollars in wage and benefit concessions for its members. In October 1979, the UAW complied by ending its long-standing tradition of industry-wide contracts by signing a separate agreement with Chrysler, giving up more than $200 million in wages and benefits. In return for these concessions, Chrysler Chairman Lee Iacocca appointed then UAW President Douglas Fraser to the company's board of directors. With the UAW on board to close plants, destroy jobs, and make concessions, in December 1979 Congress approved the Loan Guarantee Act, which demanded that UAW members give $250 million more in concessions, in addition to the $203 million it had already made.[39]

Over the next few years, Chrysler closed nearly thirty factories throughout the United States and reduced its unionized blue-collar workforce from 98,000 to 45,000, while downsizing the number of white-collar employees from 40,000 to 22,000. By 1982, the UAW had handed over to Chrysler a total of $1.1 billion in concessions, nearly $10,000 per worker. The UAW also engineered givebacks to Ford and GM, ostensibly to make them competitive. In national contracts after 1980, the UAW negotiated wage increases with Chrysler, GM, and Ford that were smaller than the 3 percent annual improvement factor plus cost-of-living increases common in contracts from 1948 through 1979. These pay concessions were accompanied by the introduction of profit-sharing and job security programs.[40]

In 1983, at the UAW Constitutional Convention, the union officially adopted corporatism as its guiding principle.[41] According to this outlook, the UAW and its members have no interests that are divergent or distinct from those of the corporations. Essentially, the union's traditional role in labor-management relations was constitutionally redefined. Rather than based on the protection of workers' rights and the time-honored principle of international worker solidarity—that is, "an injury to one is an injury to all"—the union's primary mission changed to one of collaboration with management to boost productivity and cut labor costs in order to help U.S. companies compete against Japanese and European auto companies.[42]

The so-called partnership forged between the UAW and the auto companies initiated a whole series of joint union-management programs, which, among other things, were designed to increase productivity, improve work quality, and reduce absenteeism. Workers' wages and living standards were tied to the profitability of the auto companies and not to the granting of annual wage improvements. The proliferation of labor-management committees and structures appeared at every level: national, regional, and within the factory.[43] They served to eradicate the militant traditions of the past and remove any residual class consciousness generated during the heroic struggles of the 1930s, which gave birth not only to the UAW but also to industrial unionism overall.

More specifically, in the 1980s, labor-management committees and the perks resulting from them for some union members helped neutralize a serious rank-and-file challenge to the UAW officialdom. In 1985 in the UAW southwestern region, headquartered in St. Louis, several local leaders launched an insurgency called the New Directions Movement. Led by Jerry Tucker, the region's assistant director, New Directions sought to reverse the trend of what they called union givebacks and the new framework of relations with the automakers referred to as "jointness." As Tucker criticized the union's move toward "cooperation" as a one-way street, his popularity grew. In 1986, Tucker decided to run against the incumbent regional director. Dismissed from his position by the UAW hierarchy, Tucker narrowly lost the election. While he later unsuccessfully challenged his dismissal and election results in court, UAW members ratified contracts at Ford by a 72 percent margin and at GM by 81 percent. Workers voted in the affirmative because cooperation expanded perks. For example, the GM contract with the UAW called for the company to spend $300 million a year on joint activities like job retraining and substance abuse programs.[44]

At the same time, joint investment, educational funds, and other programs provided UAW officials new sources of income designed to offset the loss of dues money from a dwindling membership. In return for keeping rank-and-file demands in check and implementing industry schemes to reorganize and accelerate the pace of work, management guaranteed union officials a certain level of perks and privileges. Over the years, the corporate-UAW relationship has grown as a result, and it features an abundance of jointly administered programs staffed by a layer of middle managers of both company and union officials. All of these programs are funded from union members' labor.[45] In place for more than a quarter century, these types of programs constitute the real legacy of the Chrysler bailout, which today conflicts with the UAW officialdom's duty to represent union members.

The development of the Joint Funds and the growth of the union-corporate partnership have aided the UAW in justifying its collaboration with management and acceptance of new concessions that are routinely rationalized by the claim that only by making such sacrifices could workers achieve job security. While so-called iron-clad guarantees, including various schemes such as jobs banks and moratoriums on plant closings, consistently have appeared in contract language over the years, those same provisions also have contained loopholes permitting management to shut factories and lay off workers for economic reasons. Under a 1982–2000 series of agreements called "job security" contracts, UAW leadership also consented to attrition clauses that reduced the labor force in the Big Three auto plants by 156,000.[46]

Concessionary Bargaining and the Coming of the Delphi Bankruptcy

Since 2000, UAW-management collaboration has reached new heights, which have paralleled the battering of the U.S. auto industry by increasing foreign competition, overcapacity in the global market, and a resulting decline in profits. As U.S. market share has fallen below 50 percent and Asian manufacturers such as Toyota have gained ground, auto companies and the UAW have collaborated in several rounds of job cuts and downsizing in an attempt to offset this trend. Since 2000, GM, Ford, and Chrysler have cut or have announced plans to slash 175,000 jobs, more than one-third of their entire North American workforce.[47]

These job losses, however, represent only the tip of the iceberg on a list of wholesale union concessions to the automakers. At Delphi in 2003 and again in 2006, the UAW accepted the reduction of hourly wages from $27 to $14, and at several Chrysler plants the union allowed the hiring of temporary workers, who, while earning $18 per hour, receive no paid benefits such as health insurance or pensions. Additionally, new contract provisions include not only further rollbacks in wages but also gain sharing, a provision that would provide pay increases only when profits and productivity go up.[48]

While agreeing to slash wages and benefits for employees, the UAW also accepted midcontract concessions that for the first time made GM and Ford retirees responsible for paying a significant part of their health care costs. The agreement also forced active workers to subsidize the companies' pension and health funds by deferring future wage increases.[49] In order to impose these concessions, worth billions, the UAW prevented retirees from voting on the givebacks and then went to court to prevent suing to protect their benefits.[50] In addition, the union discussed the possibility of negotiating the termination of the so-called jobs bank, which compensated laid-off workers for the length of the contract while they remain unemployed.[51] Addressing the June 2006 UAW convention, President Ron Gettelfinger signaled the union's willingness to make further concessions when he said, "Our challenges are unlike any we've faced in the past, largely due to globalization."

He then added, "Like it or not, these challenges aren't the kind that can be ridden out. They demand farsighted solutions, and we must be an integral part of developing those solutions."[52]

How the UAW and other unions representing autoworkers would face the challenges and develop "farsighted solutions" to confront them was answered in June 2007 when the union officially accepted and the rank and file ratified the demands made by Delphi at the time of the bankruptcy filing. Affecting more than 33,000 production workers, the UAW's ultimate acceptance of Delphi's demands set into motion a process by which workers and their organizations would agree to roll back wages and set new benchmarks for the drastic lowering of living standards for workers not only in the auto industry but also throughout the entire U.S. economy.

Spun off from General Motors in 1999, Delphi demanded from the UAW that it accept wage cuts of up to 60 percent, along with massive job reductions and huge concessions in health and pension benefits.[53] At the time of the bankruptcy filing, Delphi CEO Robert "Steve" Miller also announced his intention to shut down or sell off a "significant" number of the company's thirty-one U.S. plants.[54] The Delphi demands also extended to the International Union of Electrical Workers-Communications Workers of America (IUE-CWA), the company's second largest union. Through plant closings, retirements, and layoffs, the IUE-CWA faced the prospect of losing 5,500 of the 8,500 workers it represented.[55]

For those who remained, Miller also announced company intentions to reduce hourly wages to "more competitive" levels, adding that he hoped to get cooperation from both the UAW and the IUE-CWA because the labor agreements it had inherited from GM made it impossible to do business in North America.[56] Miller expressed confidence that the unions would cooperate when he said, "The unions are being realistic. They know life has to change and that we can't go on as usual."[57] UAW President Gettelfinger responded by stating that the union had "been engaged in discussions with Delphi to craft a mutually agreeable approach to the company's financial problems" and that he had made clear his willingness to "continue discussions and consider a wide range of options."[58]

At the same time, while it was seeking to slash wages, benefits, and pensions, Delphi looked to reward hundreds of top executives and managers who remained with the company through its financial reorganization with up to 10 percent of Delphi's stock and bonuses, representing around 250 percent of their annual salary. In so doing, Delphi filed documents with the U.S. Securities and Exchange Commission that stated that it had improved the severance pay of twenty-one top managers, claiming that a more "competitive" package was required to retain the "best" executives. In so doing, Delphi asked the bankruptcy judge to approve a Key Employee Compensation Program that would provide 600 corporate executives with more than $400 million in cash and other perks.[59]

At this point, Gettelfinger charged Delphi CEO Robert Miller with seeking to create a country "sharply divided between the super-rich elite and the working poor." With their wages cut to $10.00 an hour, the UAW president said it would take a Delphi worker 171 years to match the $3.75 million Miller has pocketed since signing on as CEO six months before.[60] Miller's gains, combined with the company's desire to downsize the workforce, were consistent with trends in the U.S. auto industry, which had shed more than a quarter-million jobs since the late 1970s. At the same time, top executives' pay had risen 109 percent. Meanwhile, real wages for production workers had stagnated. In 2002, for example, average salary, bonus, and other compensation for the top five executives at Delphi, Ford, General Motors, and Visteon was more than $1.5 million. Between 1992 and 2002, the annual average of inflation-adjusted real wages for UAW-represented autoworkers increased by a paltry 1.28 percent.[61]

Instead of looking at disparities in pay between production workers and executives in the United States, for years Wall Street analysts had been pointing to wages in Mexico and China as the benchmarks for labor costs. In Mexico, where Delphi employs around 70,000 workers and is the nation's second-largest employer in the private sector behind Wal-Mart, workers earn about $1.45 per hour, around 15 percent of what Delphi workers in the United States are paid. Even at this low rate, Delphi had closed several of its Mexican plants, sacking nearly 8,000 Mexican workers, and shifted production to China, where auto parts workers earn 59 cents per hour. Of the $650 million of components Delphi produced in China in 2003, the company shipped roughly 20 percent outside of China to North America and other destinations around the globe, a number that analysts expect to grow significantly in the future.[62]

Despite making statements about the unfairness of Delphi executive pay, the UAW presented a very different rationale to the bankruptcy court when it entered a plea for opposing the hefty hike in executive pay. In a legal submission filed on November 22, 2005, lawyers for the UAW argued that Delphi Corporation's plans to reward top executives with huge bonuses stymied union efforts to help impose wage and benefit cuts demanded by the bankrupt auto parts supplier. The UAW legal team complained that Delphi's executive compensation plan would "unduly and unnecessarily complicate an already difficult reorganization by impeding the union's ability to reach a consensual restructuring agreement with Delphi."[63] UAW lawyers argued that the company could not have picked a less hospitable time to seek approval of a rich payment package for its executives because any negotiated modifications to the UAW labor agreements would require membership ratification. The UAW legal team claimed that it was unlikely that the union could garner the necessary support among its membership for a negotiated agreement if the employees viewed the process as tainted by large awards for a select few while they bear the brunt of the cost cutting.[64]

Delphi's executive compensation plan sent the "wrong message," the UAW told the court, because it "destroys any notion that Delphi's bankruptcy will require shared sacrifice," in effect arguing that Delphi's insistence on exorbitant bonus pay for its executives subverted its work in pitching to its members the idea of partnership. The union complained that top management was "apparently tone deaf" to the rage its compensation program was provoking and warned that the windfalls to executives would further incite an "already volatile" workforce. At a time when Delphi was proposing deep cuts in wages and benefits and contemplating a severe contraction of its domestic operations that could leave tens of thousands (both hourly and salaried) without jobs, deep resentment and anger over a program valued at more than $500 million could neither be understated nor should it be ignored, the union argued.[65]

The lawyers for the union boasted that the UAW had actively participated in the restructuring of more than a dozen bankrupt auto supply companies in recent years, such as American Axle Corporation, where two-tier wage systems had been put in place.[66] "Delphi is critically dependent on the participation of the UAW and its union-represented employees for the success of its reorganization," the lawyers wrote in their brief. They also argued that because of the damage to employee morale and that it would hinder the ability of the UAW to achieve a resolution with Delphi, the court should reject the executive compensation plan.[67]

Essentially, through its court filing and its ongoing negotiations with Delphi, the UAW made clear it had no intention of opposing the plant closings as well as the massive wage and benefit cuts. In fact, the union had long collaborated with the Big Three automakers to keep labor costs low in the auto parts sector. In 1980, an auto parts worker earned 15 percent lower wages than a worker at a Big Three assembly plant. By 2000, the differential had risen to 31 percent.[68] The UAW sanctioned this wage disparity to lower costs for GM, Ford, and Chrysler in order to boost competitiveness versus their Japanese and German rivals.

By the time GM and Ford had spun off their parts operations in the late 1990s, the bulk of U.S. auto parts rolled out of nonunion plants or in lower-wage countries, putting downward pressure on wages at the new spin-offs, Delphi and Visteon. By 2001, the UAW represented only 23 percent of workers in auto parts factories, down from 51 percent in 1981.[69] Despite this downward trend in the wages of auto parts workers, in February 2007 Judge Robert Drain approved Delphi's executive pay plan. Although acknowledging the difficulty union workers would have in accepting lucrative executive bonuses while they faced deep wage cuts, the judge asserted that both were necessary to make Delphi "competitive."[70]

Judge Drain's decision was consistent in upholding the notion that hefty executive salaries and bonuses were healthy for the auto industry. Visteon and Ford already had announced large executive bonuses, even as the company announced a $1.5 billion loss for 2004. While slashing thousands of jobs and spinning off two dozen plants to its former parent company Ford, Visteon gave its executives bonuses between 50 and 130 percent of their base salaries. In addition, the company announced larger long-term incentive awards that ranged between 120 and 475 percent of executive base salaries. Visteon said the bonuses were part of a plan called "retention awards" to ensure that "select key employees" remain with the company.[71]

In March 2006, the UAW concluded a deal with GM and its former parts company Delphi Corporation that paved the way for the major downsizing of the U.S. auto industry through the elimination of tens of thousands of permanent jobs. The Special Attrition Program, as it was called, provided retirement incentives and buyouts aimed at moving an older generation of autoworkers who over the years had obtained wage levels, benefits, and working conditions that Wall Street and auto executives considered "noncompetitive." The industry's goal was to create a leaner, younger, and more productive workforce, earning significantly lower pay and receiving no employer-paid medical benefits or guarantee of a pension.

Opting not to wage any serious fight against the destruction of jobs at both Delphi and GM, the union allowed GM to replace union employees lost to buyouts and retirements with temporary workers. The hiring of replacements, the UAW and GM management claimed, would help the automaker close nine factories and three parts depots by 2008 because the new workers would make $18 to $19 per hour, or 30 percent less than an average UAW assembly worker's pay.[72] The UAW action was consistent with the union's record of helping with the imposition of downsizing and cost cutting demanded by the auto companies. By its total embrace of partnership with management and its steadfast refusal to even consider collective action to defend members' jobs and living standards, the UAW dropped any pretense of solidarity, for which its newspaper and international headquarters in Detroit are named.

Former UAW President Douglas Fraser reflected the UAW perfection of the corporatist model in the union's engineering of the buyout program when he said, "The union is wise not to push its members either way. After all, putting the onus of a decision entirely on workers allows the union and president Gettelfinger to avoid the appearance that they are working hand in glove with the company." Fraser added, "The beauty of the buyout is that it is an individual decision, and individuals are motivated by different reasons."[73]

But the 2006 deal with management went far beyond what the earlier episodes had produced. *The New York Times* noted, "The agreement marks unprecedented cooperation by the union, which has been put in the position of convincing its members to give up jobs that the UAW has fought for decades to protect." In a statement, Delphi management praised the UAW and the new deal as a "critical milestone in its restructuring that enables a more rapid transformation to a reduced labor cost structure across Delphi's U.S. manufacturing operations."[74] It is reasonable to assume that rank-and-file experience regarding the UAW officialdom's collaboration with GM in the recent past factored in to the June 2006 decision of 47,600 autoworkers to accept the buyout offer.[75]

The UAW fear of bankruptcy stemmed primarily from a desire to protect the financial base of its respective unions. The union has involved itself in scores of labor-management structures that provide lucrative sources of income in exchange for cooperation in reducing costs, boosting productivity, and managing worker resistance on the shop floor. Bankruptcy proceedings always threaten these relationships because they can potentially allow management to tear up all existing agreements. Moreover, those agreements compel employees to join the union and pay dues through automatic payroll deductions. Because union dues have declined in recent years and the outlook for a continuing drop in the future is all but certain, UAW officials searched for measures to keep revenue streaming in to support salaries and perks.

Measures adopted at the June 2006 UAW Constitutional Convention reflected union leadership desire to maintain the organization's financial base. One initiative, presented by the leadership as a move to increase funding for union organizing drives, actually works to siphon money from the strike fund to sustain the salaries and perks of the officialdom. Although illegal to use strike funds directly for salaries, benefits, and expense accounts, shifting these monies to the union's general fund and to other funds, such as member education and advertising, is permissible.[76]

The practice of giving rebates to locals started in the 1980s when the UAW began collaborating with auto management in closing plants, laying off workers, and engaging in concessionary bargaining. In the process, the union altered its constitution to provide rebates to locals affected by these measures. Taken from the strike fund, the rebates provided infusions of cash to locals strapped for funds resulting from sharp declines in dues revenues. Locals engaged in plant bargaining, unlike the UAW international organization, under the arrangement could use rebate money from the strike fund to pay staff salaries, benefits, and expenses. There was further incentive to abandon the strike completely because rebates were available only to locals as long as the strike fund remained greater than $500 million.[77]

As plant closings and layoffs have affected local unions adversely for the last three decades with regard to dues revenue and financial base, the rebate system has provided a powerful cash incentive for leaders not to call strikes and support the international's no-strike bargaining position. In the process of downsizing their operations over the years, the auto companies identified "underperforming" plants, while they demanded that bargaining take place over local issues and be carried out exclusively at the plant level. In the name of making the companies profitable, UAW local officers opted for concessionary bargaining rather than striking.[78]

The UAW general fund, which finances the day-to-day activities and salaries of union officers and staff, has dropped dramatically as a result of the decline in dues revenues. The strike fund, however, which is less dependent on dues income, has ballooned to almost $1 billion.[79] The growth of the strike fund, in the midst of such an unprecedented attack on the jobs and conditions of autoworkers, is itself a testament to the fact that there has not been a national strike of any real significance against one of the Big Three American automakers in decades, and local strikes have all but disappeared. Instead, the strike fund has been transformed into a giant insurance fund to protect the perks and privileges of the UAW officialdom.

Nowhere has this development been more apparent in recent years than in the auto parts industry, and especially at Delphi. In March 1996, members of UAW Local 696 struck two Delphi brake plants in Dayton, Ohio, for seventeen days, resulting in the shutdown of twenty-six of the company's twenty-nine assembly plants across North America, idling 180,000 autoworkers. When the strike ended, the new bargaining agreement included $5.6 million in grievance payments and commitments by Delphi to replace jobs lost to outsourcing. Although officially a local strike, both GM and the UAW attempted to win precontract concessions from each other. GM had hoped to establish outsourcing as an acceptable means of eliminating jobs, while the UAW leadership wished to at least slow down the pace of outsourcing, which had been accelerating at a rapid pace, affecting dues income resulting from declining membership.[80]

Although the UAW claimed victory after signing the four-year agreement, almost immediately pressures to overturn the agreement mounted. GM put both factories on its list of "underperforming plants," facilities that GM could close or sell because of falling profits. Within one year, the local union leadership reopened provisions of the contract regarding productivity and job classifications. As the pace of work speeded up, shop-floor grievances multiplied. In June 1998, GM informed UAW Local 696 of its intentions to reduce the workforce from 3,000 to 1,500 by the end of 1999. Acting under pressure from members, UAW Local 696 leadership had no choice but to seek strike authorization, claiming that management's previous commitments to partnership with the union "lacked integrity and credibility." Instead of striking, however, UAW leadership agreed in July 1998 to workforce reduction and increased flexibility of shop-floor rules that meant a substantial increase in the pace of work.[81]

The agreement also established an attrition program with incentive retirement bonuses in which more than 1,700 jobs were destroyed during its duration. At the same time, both parties agreed to extend the life of the memorandum agreement until September 2002, and management consented not to close or sell the Dayton Delphi brake plants in exchange for a no-strike pledge. Additionally, the union committed to help Delphi break even by the year 2000 and attain a 5 percent net profit by 2003. In order to help achieve that goal, the union allowed for the replacement of retirees with the hiring of hundreds of workers who earned less and produced more. While some were permanent workers who earned two-thirds less than senior workers at the top tier of the wage scale, the majority were temporary workers who earned $15 per hour with no benefits or job security, more than $13 below that of what Delphi paid permanent workers at the time.[82]

The events at Dayton set new benchmarks for concessions throughout GM. They provided a major step toward GM's plans to spin off its Delphi Automotive parts division. An analyst for the Wall Street investment house

Merrill Lynch praised the job cuts by saying, "Hopefully this is going to be the model for future agreements."[83] The results of two 1999 strikes at Flint, Michigan, for fifty-four days over issues such as outsourcing to Mexico, where workers received just $8 per day, reflected the auto industry's increasing success in dictating terms and conditions of employment regarding production, downsizing, multitier wage systems, and the hiring of temporary workers. The walkouts in Flint ended with the UAW pledging to suspend local strikes and giving management the green light to ax tens of thousands of jobs.[84] While the dismantling of what was left of decent wages, work rules, job security, and benefits occurred, local union officials, with rebates from the UAW parent organization and concessions made at the bargaining table, maintained their perks and privileges. They did so by splitting the workforce into an ever-shrinking core of higher-paid senior workers and underpaid lower-seniority and temporary workers, all of whom paid union dues.

It is precisely under these conditions by which rank-and-file Delphi union members ratified the June 2007 contract that rolled back wages, benefits, and working conditions to an era that predated the auto industry's unionization. The new Delphi contract surrendered virtually all the gains made by autoworkers over the past seventy years. Among other things, the contract imposed pay cuts of up to 50 percent for current employees by slashing top rates from $27 to $14 per hour and the hiring of new, temporary workers for as low as $10 per hour. Under the new deal, senior workers who decided to remain with Delphi were required to pay the higher deductibles and co-payments paid by workers brought in under the two-tier wage structure. The new contract also terminated the existing defined benefit pension plan and replaced it with a 401(k) plan.[85]

It also included elimination of the jobs bank, a program that allowed laid-off workers to continue receiving 95 percent of their previous wages until they were rehired. In an attempt to win support for the contract from new hires not eligible for the jobs bank until accruing three years of seniority, the company offered severance pay of $1,500 for every month of service up to a maximum of $40,000. Further, the contract implemented "competitive operating agreements" by ripping up existing work rules and combining job classifications that paved the way for speedup and more job cuts. The agreement also stipulated that to achieve cost savings, "the local parties would not be constrained by existing agreements/past practices."

The Delphi contract also offered senior workers so-called buy-downs, lump-sum payments of up to $105,000 apiece over the next three years to offset the pay cuts over that period. The buy-downs were part of the long-established strategy employed by the UAW to obtain ratification of concessions by dividing the workforce. After Delphi declared bankruptcy, the union signed an agreement with the company on a package of buyouts to encourage senior workers to leave, opening the way for management to increase the number of new hires at the lower pay rate. The union also allowed the company to hire large numbers of part-time workers.

Of the 33,000 full-time Delphi workforce employed in November 2005, only 17,000 workers remained by June 2007, and more than 13,000 were new hires earning $14 per hour or less and receiving reduced health benefits.[86] Given this lopsided majority and the fact that, for these temporary workers, voting yes for the contract made their jobs both full-time and permanent, seven locals overwhelmingly approved the contract. But the Lockport, New York, local, which still had a large majority of the workers at the higher pay scale, voted down the contract 1,107 to 274. Commenting on the negative vote, UAW Local 467 President Jim Hurren said, "There are a few disgruntled people out there, but they're not living in the real world."[87] The real world for the UAW was that, after full implementation of the downsizing provisions in the new agreement, the union would end up representing about 2,300 members at Delphi by 2012, less than one-tenth of what the company employed in 2005 when it filed for bankruptcy.[88]

In August 2007, IUE-CWA members voted to ratify the new four-year contract with Delphi. Seventy-five percent of the 2,000 members eligible to cast ballots approved the deal, which was identical to the UAW-Delphi settlement. Consistent with the union's corporatist approach, IUE-CWA President Jim Clark praised the agreement as a historic opportunity for Delphi workers. "This vote gives members options about their future on the job and allows the union to start the rebuilding process," Clark stated. He went on to add that "Delphi is now more competitive than ever thanks to the sacrifices of our members."[89]

The agreement called for the slashing of hundreds of jobs at plants in Warren, Ohio, and Brookhaven, Mississippi, while putting plants in Gadsden, Alabama, and Kettering, Ohio, up for sale and closing its plant in Moraine, Ohio.[90] The IUE-CWA agreement and the ratification of the same by members of the United Steelworkers of America (USWA), which closed a Dayton, Ohio, Delphi plant employing some 700 workers, also allowed the company to exit bankruptcy. After full implementation of the new four-year contracts, the IUE-CWA and the USWA would together represent fewer than 800 Delphi workers.[91]

For both the UAW and the USWA, the downsizing at Delphi accelerated their protracted membership decline, and the loss of dues threatened their respective financial bases. While the outlook remained bleak in terms of reversing membership decline, both unions, and in particular the UAW, soon found a new stream of income to possibly offset the financial woes resulting from the loss of dues. In early July 2007, the UAW and the USWA reached four-year agreements with the Dana Corporation, one of the biggest auto parts companies in the United States, which, like Delphi, had been operating under bankruptcy protection.

The deals with the unions, which covered about 8,000 workers, allowed Dana to shift its liability for retiree health care and long-term disability coverage for other workers to a trust, called a Voluntary Employee Benefit Association (VEBA), moving the obligation off its books, thus helping the company reorganize and exit bankruptcy protection. Dana contributed about $700 million in cash immediately to the trust, and after reorganization the agreement called for an additional $80 million contribution in stock to the trust, which the unions would administer. The agreement also created a new two-tier wage structure, allowing Dana to hire new workers at significantly lower rates than older workers, and outlined changes to reduce the payment of disability benefits.[92]

As regard the UAW, the deal with Dana highlighted the growing collaboration between the union officialdom and various private equity groups that bought up auto suppliers and auto companies. These firms specialize in cutting costs by slashing wages and downsizing operations. A key player in the Dana-UAW settlement was the New York–based private equity firm Centerbridge, which agreed to invest $500 million in Dana once it had emerged from bankruptcy protection and to line up an additional $250 million from outside investors. Because these funds supplied the necessary resources to cover the cash contribution to the UAW and USWA-controlled VEBAs, Centerbridge would ultimately own close to one-half of the business.

For his part, UAW President Ron Gettelfinger, consistent with the union's corporatist outlook, praised Centerbridge. "This settlement would not have been possible without the involvement of Centerbridge Partners," he said. Gettelfinger added, "They're going to play a key role in the future of Dana, and we look forward to working with them to help this company succeed in the marketplace." The UAW cut the Dana deal with Centerbridge on retiree health care despite the fact that previous experiments in this area with Caterpillar and Detroit Diesel failed when funding for their respective VEBA programs ran dry just a few years after their inception.[93]

The UAW embrace of Centerbridge, a firm notorious for realizing huge profits by slashing jobs and wages and selling off corporate assets, was a move to offload the U.S. automakers' retiree health care liabilities to a new UAW-controlled company. For union officials, the decision to go into the health care business is a logical outgrowth of the policies they have pursued since the late 1970s, which have occurred in tandem with the decline of the global market position of the U.S. automakers. During that time, the UAW officialdom has sought ways and means to distance its own fate from that of the autoworkers it nominally represents.

Wholly supportive of the idea that companies needed to make profits at any costs, the UAW adopted a nationalist perspective while refusing to advance any independent social and political perspective to defend the interests of autoworkers. Inevitably, the size and industrial power of the union underwent a precipitous decline, and its efforts to reverse these trends have failed. UAW President Gettelfinger, writing in the *Detroit News,* ironically summed up best the union's recent bargaining record when he criticized the United States–South Korea Free Trade Agreement: "Once again, U.S. trade officials have gone to the negotiating table and reached a terrific deal, for the other side."[94]

The UAW's inability to reverse the trend in membership hemorrhaging at the bargaining table is paralleled by its failed attempts to organize workers at the growing number of foreign-owned transplants in the United States as market share for the American-based industry has continued to shrink.[95] The results of those efforts have been disastrous for the UAW. In October 2001, workers at Nissan Motor Company's Smyrna, Tennessee, complex voted two to one against joining the UAW following the union's fourth run at the factory in twelve years. By 2005, the UAW had organized only 3,100 Mitsubishi workers of 57,045 workers employed at all foreign-owned transplants. The UAW blamed Nissan and other companies for suggesting that factories could close or move to Mexico if labor costs got too high.[96]

It is difficult to avoid thinking that the anti-Japanese hysteria promoted by the UAW during the 1980s is at least partially to blame for the union's failure to organize workers at the foreign-owned plants. In what is perhaps the best example to illustrate organized labor's nationalist orientation, the UAW opened the box of World War II symbols, since it resonated across several layers of public sentiment. In the 1980s, two incidents in particular marked the extent to which UAW leaders and some of its members were willing to blame economic frustrations on Japan. At a union picnic, UAW members took turns smashing a Toyota with a sledgehammer, fully reveling in the mass publicity.

And in 1982, the ugliest incident to mark the era of blaming America's economic woes on Japan occurred when two laid-off GM workers in Detroit battered to death an Asian American, who turned out to be an American of Chinese ancestry named Vincent Chin. Despite the public outcry against these incidents, much of the catharsis went unchecked. UAW bumper-sticker politics included several themes and variations on the especially enduring slogan "Buy American: The Job You Save May Be Your Own." The UAW's parking lot in Detroit featured the sign "UAW Parking Reserved for U.S. and Canadian Vehicles Only: Please Park Imports Elsewhere." Meanwhile, a GM worker set fire to a Japanese flag in a New Jersey plant while blaring Bruce Springsteen's "Born in the USA."[97]

The UAW twin strategies of concessionary bargaining and economic nationalism have not saved jobs. The Dana agreement not only established the union in the health care business, but it also resulted in the UAW controlling large portions of company stock, which provides the officialdom with a direct economic incentive to continue to place downward pressure on the wages and benefits of their members and reorganize work to maximize worker productivity in the factories.

Prior to the opening of negotiations with the Big Three automakers in July 2007, UAW President Gettelfinger outlined the continuation of the union's nationalist strategy and partnership with employers. In a speech delivered to Michigan business leaders, Gettelfinger proposed a business and labor front to promote legislative protectionist measures. In so doing, Gettelfinger said, "We have no interest in tearing down employers, and we want employers to succeed, so that workers have a chance to share in that success."[98] This corporatist approach reached its peak in 2007 with the agreements it made with the Big Three automakers.

7

VEBA Las Vegas! Unions Play
Casino Capitalism: Autoworkers Lose

The 2007 United Auto Workers (UAW) agreements with the Big Three automakers (GM, Chrysler, and Ford) represent the capstone of a three-decade-long transformation of the union. The UAW is now a business enterprise, ever more so closely integrated with Big Three management, directly profiting from the labor of the workers it ostensibly represents. The contracts that cover more than 175,000 workers effectively eradicate many of the gains made by autoworkers during the last fifty years. Once the home of the highest-paid industrial workers in the world, the U.S. auto industry is now a place where workers earn near-poverty-level wages and toil in conditions that resemble the sweatshops of earlier periods. Benefits of the job such as employer-paid health care and pensions have been either drastically reduced or entirely eliminated.

With the introduction of a two-tier wage and benefit structure, newly hired workers earn $14.20 per hour instead of $28.75, and they receive fewer and reduced benefits. Following the agreements have been buyout offers to senior workers that the Big Three hope will clear the decks for the entry of tens of thousands of workers paid at the lower rate. At the same time, the auto companies offloaded their obligation to pay $100 billion in retiree health care benefits. In shifting the liabilities to a union-controlled Voluntary Employee Benefit Association (VEBA) retiree health care trust, a large portion of VEBA obligations are funded with notes convertible to stock. The result is that at publicly owned GM and Ford, the UAW is now one of the largest shareholders.[1] The financial incentive for the union is now to help the companies slash the jobs, wages, and benefits of its dues-paying members.

The contracts also froze base pay for all workers (current and new hires). Won by the UAW in 1949, the cost-of-living adjustment (COLA) is now diverted into the VEBA to help defray company health costs for current workers.[2] As in all agreements negotiated with the Big Three over the last thirty years, the 2007 contracts make room for a COLA at local plants. These agreements are designed as an incentive to impose speedup, forced overtime, and other "flexible" work rules that serve to pit one group of workers against the other for jobs downgraded to sweatshop status.

The transformation in the U.S. auto industry also has affected autoworkers in Canada and Mexico. The concessionary character of the Big Three contracts forced the Canadian Auto Workers (CAW) to open negotiations one year early. As in the United States, the CAW made concessions to "save jobs." The long-term CAW strategy of trying to convince automakers to invest in Canada has backfired. CAW arguments that production in Canada was affordable because the national government provided health insurance through a taxpayer-paid plan now have no merit. The advent of VEBA and the claims that a cheaper national currency provides a Canadian advantage for production costs have been shattered with the protracted depreciation of the U.S. dollar. In Mexico, auto unions already are accepting lower wages and other concessions to remain "competitive." The globalization of production has seriously undermined the UAW, CAW, and Mexican unions, whose previous leverage had been bound up with their ability to influence their respective national labor markets.

The Genesis of the 2007 Contract Negotiations and Ratification: The GM Case

Decades ago, gains made by the UAW generally set a precedent for improvements in conditions for those working in all industries and other sectors of the economy. In the 1950s and 1960s, for example, agreements between the union and the Big Three established the first employer-paid pensions and medical benefits for industrial workers. In recent rounds of negotiations, the UAW and the automakers have maneuvered together to roll back the gains workers made in earlier periods. In the process, the Big Three workforce has been downsized from 750,000 in 1979 to 177,000, or by a stunning 76 percent.[3]

Upon entering the 2007 negotiations, the auto companies sought to reduce the $25– to $30–per-hour wage advantage Japanese and European automakers enjoyed at their nonunion plants in the United States. Those plants now build more than half of all motor vehicles sold across the United States.[4] For its part, the UAW agreed in principle that its members were to pay for the falling profits of the Big Three and the loss of market share to their Japanese and European competitors. The union's primary concern was survival as an organization and what it would receive in return for its collaboration.

This came to light when news of a settlement reached the picket lines where workers had been on strike against GM for forty-eight hours. While most workers were relieved the strike was over, some wondered why the union ever called a work stoppage. Others were angry about being kept in the dark about the status of negotiations. James Stewart, a thirty-one-year GM veteran and a quality inspector at the Detroit-Hamtramck plant, expressed his frustration with the secrecy of the negotiations. "A lot of people I know were really disgruntled about that," he said. "If I'm at their mercy, I'd like to at least know what's going on. Mr. Gettelfinger, you should've kept us better informed," said Stewart.[5] A thirty-one-year veteran worker at GM's Janesville, Wisconsin, SUV assembly plant said, "This whole thing's a farce. In the past, we always got updates on contract talks, points of interest from our local union. This time, we're being told nothing."[6]

The *Detroit Free Press* reported that "lots of the poor souls out there on picket lines are completely mystified, because they've been told virtually nothing by Solidarity House or GM about the bargaining details as talks progressed."[7] While some workers said they believed the strike worked in their favor and showed the company how much they valued their jobs, others like Kim Burleigh, a forty-one-year-old worker at the GM power train facility in Pontiac, said, "It makes you wonder what they agreed on."[8]

Although striking workers complained about the dearth of details, President Ron Gettelfinger made the UAW objectives clear when he issued a public statement as the work stoppage began: "We're shocked and disappointed that General Motors has failed to recognize and appreciate what our membership has contributed during the past four years."[9] He added, "Since 2003 our members have made extraordinary efforts every time the company came to us with a problem: the corporate restructuring, the attrition plan, the Delphi bankruptcy, the 2005 health care agreement. In every case, our members went the extra mile to find reasonable solutions."[10]

When the UAW and GM released preliminary details of the agreement, it was clear that the union had gone beyond the customary extra mile. GM immediately expressed its satisfaction with the agreement. Chairman and Chief Executive Officer (CEO) Rick Wagoner praised the agreement for helping the company close the fundamental competitive gaps with its competitors.

He also thanked the UAW bargaining for its hard work in bringing about such a deal.[11]

Industry analysts calculated that the establishment of VEBA and a two-tier wage system in GM's American plants would reduce by as much as 80 percent the $25–per-hour gap in labor costs between Detroit's Big Three automakers and Japanese manufacturers. Under a new two-tier wage and benefit structure, new workers will be paid less than those working at Asian factories in North America. According to the UAW Web site, starting wages for those workers are at $19.62 per hour, while new hires at the Big Three will earn $14.20 and receive substandard benefits.[12] Wall Street roared its approval for the agreement by boosting the price of GM stock by $3.22 per share. Brad Rubin, an analyst with the investment firm BNP Paribus, said, "This is exactly what we were hoping for. We're content that GM got what they intended to get."[13]

What the UAW received for delivering to GM a labor force with lower pay and fewer benefits was control over an investment fund worth more than $60 billion, equal to the twentieth-largest pension fund in the United States. Followers of the negotiations quickly noted the fact that the union had now emerged as a business enterprise. Harley Shaiken, director of the University of California at Berkeley's labor studies program, said, "Rather than rail against the union for hamstringing the domestic automakers, major investment firms will do their best to win the union's business." Shaiken added, "When the UAW talks, Wall Street will listen."[14]

Wall Street was listening when it was revealed that the agreement diverted the first 10 cents of quarterly COLA increases, amounting to $180 million over the life of the contract, to both bolster the VEBA and defray company health costs for current workers. Industry analysts figured that, over four years, the diversions would total around $6,240 per worker.[15] Additionally, instead of participating in a defined-benefit pension plan, new hires would get a 401(k) in which GM deposits 6.4 percent of workers' wages. Also vanished by the agreement was worker retirement health care coverage from the company and employer-paid coverage for survivors. By 2011, GM said that 56,000 of 74,500 blue-collar workers could retire or accept buyouts. The GM goal was the creation of a new workforce, one in which 75 percent would be earning the lower wage and receiving reduced benefits.[16] In effect, a generation of autoworkers who started with the company in the 1970s and 1980s when the mood of GM employees was much more confrontational would be gone.

Gary Chaison, an industrial relations professor at Clark University, expanded on the significance of the contract's transformational character. He said, "It's going to mark the beginning of the end for the concept of good, high-paying manufacturing jobs with job security."[17] Auto industry analysts concurred. In the *Wall Street Journal* they wrote, "For much of the past half century, Detroit's Big Three auto makers had collaborated with the UAW to create an industrial aristocracy of blue-collar workers whose pay and benefits set the standard for the American middle class."[18] If the GM contract is duplicated at Ford and Chrysler LLC, they added, that era in American industrial history may be over.[19]

The UAW officialdom, however, still had the task of selling the agreement to the rank and file. In so doing, the UAW pinned its hopes on selling the agreement as a guarantor of job security. Although the union claimed it had made job security a top priority during negotiations, the settlement contained no such provisions. Essentially, GM stopped short of guaranteeing that specific new products would be assigned to union-staffed plants. While CEO Wagoner made statements that the contract had allowed GM to "maintain a strong manufacturing presence in the United States along with significant future investments," he also made it clear that the union had to agree to flexible work rules in local plant-level negotiations to save jobs at GM.[20]

Local leaders all but ignored contract language that stipulated conditions "beyond the control of the Corporation," such as market-related volume decline that would let the company off the hook for any future product commitments at plants. In the early ratification voting, local union leaders claimed that the deal promised to permanently hire thousands of temporary workers and made dozens of commitments to keep plants open.[21]

In the context of a downward-spiraling Michigan economy, the rank and file ratified the contract. Curt Bailey, Local 653 financial secretary at the Pontiac, Michigan, stamping plant, assessed the contract voting by saying, "It means different things to different people. For the temps, it gives them a permanent job. For some people, it was the $3,000 signing bonus. It touched them in a lot of different ways."[22] One worker who voted for the deal probably summed up widespread sentiment by saying that the deal brought relief, at least for now. "We had to give up a lot this time, but I'm still employed. A lot of people in Michigan can't say that," said Darrell Clank, a line worker at GM's Detroit-Hamtramck Assembly facility. He then added, "But what about next time? Will we have to give even more?"[23]

But nearly one-third of the two-thirds who were eligible to cast ballots ended up voting no on the contract, and rejections included workers at two major plants that had been promised work. Typical of views from rank-and-file members planning to vote against the agreement were those expressed by Leslie Harmon, a fifty-five-year-old machine tech at the GM power train plant in Ypsilanti, Michigan. Harmon was upset at not getting a pay raise for the life of the contract. He said, "No matter how you look at it, we had to give up a lot. If we give up raises and see management get bonuses down the line, that's a problem."[24] Weighing on the minds of Harmon and other GM workers was a recent court decision allowing Delphi to pay its executives more than $37 million in bonuses after UAW members had sacrificed jobs, pay, and benefits.[25]

Workers at the Romulus, Michigan, engine plant and the Wentzville, Missouri, assembly plant rejected the agreement despite those facilities getting the promise of future employment. About 1,100 of 1,400 workers in Romulus voted, and slightly more than half said no. At the Wentzville plant, the largest local to reject the contract, 69 percent of workers voted no.[26] Al Benchich, president of UAW Local 909 in Warren, Ohio, voiced his displeasure with the agreement and probably expressed a great deal of rank-and-file sentiment in an open letter to UAW members. He wrote, "The most chilling part of the tentative agreement is the two-tier wage and benefit provisions for new hires. It is such a tremendous step backwards for our union that I find it impossible to endorse the contract on this issue alone."[27]

But most UAW local leaders supported the agreement. UAW Local 602 President Doug Rademacher wrote in a newsletter to workers in the Lansing assembly plant, "Some may have noticed GM's stock took a huge leap the instant word got out that the union had signed off health care benefits for future and current retirees that will be funded by the new trust for retirees."[28] In the end, GM's largest local of 3,500 workers approved the deal by a 61 percent margin. According to several local union leaders and members, what sold the deal were contract provisions that permanently hired thousands of temporary workers and supposed commitments that GM made to keep plants open.[29]

But within two weeks after ratification, more than 1,000 workers at the Lansing Delta Township assembly plant received layoff notices. In total, including workers at other plants, more than 2,500 GM employees received pink slips. At the same time, the automaker and the UAW also agreed to rescind a contract provision that would have made the Delta temporary workers permanent GM employees. At a union meeting called to discuss the layoffs and contract changes, one temporary worker claimed people like him had been tricked into ratifying the contract because it contained promises of becoming permanent GM employees. He said, "There are a lot of people in here who left very good-paying jobs they had for a long time under the impression they were going to be permanent employees at General Motors." His remarks received a round of applause.[30]

Harley Shaiken described the deal as a landmark moment for the U.S. economy, as defining for this era as the wealth-sharing contracts won by the UAW in the 1950s were for an earlier generation. Shaiken suggested that the agreement formed the basis for a twenty-first century social contract that made General Motors more competitive and, at the same time, saved middle-class jobs. He elaborated by saying, "In the context of the pressure of globalization and the stumbling of the domestic industry, that's not a small feat. That proves relevance for unions under these circumstances, rather than a hint of their demise."[31] Other labor analysts disagreed. Herman Benson, secretary-treasurer of the Association for Union Democracy in Brooklyn, New York, said, "The fact that the UAW with all its power is really compelled to make this compromise on health benefits is a dramatic illustration of the inability of the labor movement to uphold the standard of the middle-class working class. That's the big lesson."[32]

Infuriated by the agreement's terms, one current GM employee and one retiree challenged a key aspect of a plan to allow the UAW to take over responsibility for retiree health care. In a letter to the U.S. Securities and Exchange Commission's director of enforcement, they questioned the legal right of the union to use a $4.4 billion GM convertible note to partly fund the UAW-controlled VEBA. Written and sent on behalf of the employee and retiree by Stephen Diamond, a law professor at Santa Clara University in California, the letter stated that GM had not disclosed enough details about its plans for the note and should have released a formal prospectus. Diamond added that the trust could be at risk if GM filed for bankruptcy and that the details "fell dramatically short of the standards."[33] Another GM worker soon to be covered by the new VEBA also expressed doubts. "I'm not fond of the VEBA, especially if it's tied to equities," said fifty-four-year-old Marty Shawl of Bay City, Michigan, an employee at GM's power train facility. Instead, Shawl said, "Unions should focus on organizing and representing workers, not managing portfolios and health care systems."[34]

The Chrysler Case

Like the GM contract, the Chrysler agreement, which covered around 49,000 workers, established a two-tier wage and benefit system to ensure a rapid transformation from a highly paid industrial workforce to a low-wage "flexible" workforce. At the same time, the agreement also relieved the company of legal obligations to pay retiree health benefits through the establishment of a multibillion-dollar health care trust controlled by the UAW officialdom. From the beginning of the contract talks, private equity firm Cerberus Capital Management LP, which bought the automaker from DaimlerChrysler for $7.4 billion in August 2007, made it clear it would accept nothing less than a "transformational" contract.[35]

For its part, the UAW officialdom ordered a six-hour strike to vent in a harmless manner the mood of concern and anger among rank-and-file workers over the unprecedented concessions contained in the contract, according to Tim Fleenary, a twenty-year veteran at Chrysler's Trenton, New Jersey, engine plant. He believed that both the Chrysler and the GM strike were a way for union officials to save face as they gave more concessions. "It's back to business as usual. And business as usual is the steady and slow decline of the American middle class," said Fleenary.[36]

As the rank and file prepared for the ratification process, the false promises made to GM workers by the UAW about job security weighed on the minds of many Chrysler workers. Dean DeMarco, a worker at Chrysler's Trenton Engine manufacturing facility, said the GM job cuts caused him to think twice about voting in favor of the tentative agreement. "If it could happen to them, you know it could happen to us," said DeMarco. Nearly 50 percent of those casting ballots at his plant voted no.[37] Commenting on the layoffs of 2,000 workers at GM plants, a *Detroit Free Press* writer explained, "GM's decision to announce layoffs so shortly after striking a landmark, money-saving labor agreement with the UAW is a stark reminder that no job is guaranteed anymore in the volatile U.S. auto industry."[38] Mike Crawford, who works at the Hamtramck plant where 767 workers received pink slips, 180 of whom were temporaries who had just received full-time status and wages under the contract, said, "A lot of us are skeptical about how all this went down. A lot of temps and people who voted for this contract did it on the basis that their kids and families would have jobs. Then, as soon as we ratify the contract, they put them on the streets."[39]

In the beginning of the ratification process, the UAW made no hard claims about job security. The agreement stipulated that at least seven facilities, including plants in Delaware, Detroit, Indiana, and Missouri, would likely close during the life of the four-year contract. Chrysler made no commitment to continue operating any of its twenty-six factories, including assembly plants in Sterling Heights, Michigan, and Belvidere, Illinois, after the 2011 contract expiration. Investments in any surviving facilities were contingent on new modern operating agreements (MOA) negotiated at the local level to impose speedup, forced overtime, and other flexible work rules. An MOA would also determine the use of outsourcing and temporary workers. The deal ended company-paid medical benefits for retired workers, and, like the GM agreement, it established a VEBA, making benefits subject to the gyrations of the stock market and the pressure of big investors to make ever-deeper cuts.[40]

With a large contingent of dissenters jeopardizing ratification of the tentative deal, UAW leaders intensified their push for passage. The efforts included recruiting UAW retirees to help make their case at informational meetings and sending e-mail and memos to workers and visits to factories by top leaders. Opponents of the deal scored early victories, with four large assembly plants rejecting the deal. The two-tier wage and benefit system for new hires to noncore jobs (those not directly tied to the manufacture of vehicles or parts) and the lack of product commitments at Chrysler plants were some of the biggest complaints about the pact.[41]

In addition to noncore workers, the Chrysler contract introduced a new category of noncore facilities, factories and divisions where the entire workforce is paid half the wages and reduced benefits, once veteran workers either retire or are bought out. These facilities are the Toledo, Ohio, Machining Plant, which employs 1,530 workers; the Detroit Axle Plant, until it is closed; and a new axle plant in Marysville, Michigan, which will replace the Detroit operation and is expected to employ 900 workers. In addition, 500 truck drivers and warehouse workers in Chrysler's transportation division will be replaced with low-wage workers, as well as more than 2,700 UAW members employed at the company's twenty-four Mopar parts distribution centers (PDCs), which distribute and sell replacement parts and accessories to Chrysler dealerships. What troubled some workers, however, was that a contract provision allowed the union and the company to expand the number of workers defined as noncore in the future.[42]

Dennis Kirkpatrick, a Detroit native and former worker at Chrysler's engine plant in Trenton, New Jersey, who had recently relocated to the Belvidere, Illinois, assembly plant, said he planned to vote no because of the two-tier system and, in particular, the vagueness in contract language surrounding its application, which UAW leaders asserted would be determined on a facility-by-facility basis. The two-tier wage system would split the union, he said. "There are too many holes in this contract. The union has always fought for the future; now they are doing the opposite," said Kirkpatrick.[43]

Thelma Lutz, a worker at the Warren, Michigan, stamping plant, expressed similar concerns. "The contract is incomplete; you wouldn't sign a contract for a new roof with this few details."[44] Her main concern was which jobs at her plant would be designated as noncore. Lutz said, "Our leadership has pulled a dirty trick. They should have written those details into the contract."[45] Tamika Floyd, a worker at the Warren Truck Plant, said the deal was fair, considering the state of the economy. Although voting yes for the deal, she added, "I'm stressed about it, it's kind of scary."[46] After attending a meeting in which local leaders explained the possible consequences for rejection of the deal, Floyd said that she feared Chrysler would cut workers if the deal were not passed. "People can't afford to be out of work," she explained.[47] Local 140 President Melvin Thompson concurred: "People are voting to protect their jobs today."[48] Ernest Milo, a worker at the Detroit axle plant said shortly after voting yes for the contract, "We are just trying to hold on to our jobs."[49]

The UAW officialdom put enormous pressure on local leaders to sell the contract. In a letter to local leaders, the union's vice president and director of the Chrysler division, General Holiefield, called for "all appointed union representatives" to "stand in solidarity in support of this tentative agreement."[50] Wrote Holiefield, "With teamwork in the leadership and solidarity in the ranks, we will prevail and our members will be best served."[51] In light of the unexpected fierce opposition, Holiefield told union Local 1700 leaders that Chrysler's Sterling Heights, Michigan, assembly plant would be guaranteed production until 2016 under a previously undisclosed secret understanding between the union and the privately held automaker. When asked about Holiefield's remarks, a Chrysler spokeswoman declined to comment.[52]

Even as Holiefield, Gettelfinger, and other high-ranking UAW officials fanned out to the shop floor of several plants, workers still continued to voice their opposition to the deal. Aaron Devers, a worker at the Sterling Heights assembly plant, explained, "They are saying it's a good contract and it's the best they can get. But everybody thinks it's a bad deal. People are afraid of it."[53] Devers had questions about the new wage system, zeroing in on fuzzy contract language about noncore workers. "There are 3,000 people in this plant. Almost half the jobs are non-core, maintenance, material handling, underbody in the body shop, paint shop, inspection, people who drive cars off the line," Devers said. "Non-core is an open window," he added. "We don't know where it closes." Devers planned to vote no and did not fear the possibility of Cerberus taking a hard line if rejection meant a new round of negotiations. "This contract is a hard line," he said.[54] Warren, Michigan, truck plant worker Nina Hodge agreed. Hodge stated, "It's a horrible contract. They tell us they are going to lower wages for non-core jobs, but they won't even tell us which jobs are non-core."[55] On the other side was Debra Hillery, a worker at the same plant. She offered, "We have to help ourselves, but we also have to help Chrysler. My primary concern is that will there be a Chrysler 10 years from now."[56]

As the vote came to a close, criticism about the lack of independent oversight of the referendums by the union emerged. And this was not the first time the UAW faced these kinds of questions. After Ford workers in 2005 narrowly approved concessions, several UAW members also complained about the process. Ellis Boal, a labor lawyer who represented union members before the union's Public Review Board, said the UAW's constitution offers little guidance for how contract ratification votes should be held. Boal explained that the review board is the avenue for appeal when he said, "The curious thing about the UAW is that there are not any detailed provisions in the constitution or any of their books about how to do ratification, whereas there are very detailed provisions about how to do an election of officers." Boal further noted that nothing in the constitution requires the voting to be done in secret. And the lack of precise detail means locals have great latitude in holding the vote.[57]

Despite stiff opposition and concern about the lack of oversight in the voting process, 56 percent of production workers and 51 percent of skilled trade workers approved the agreement. Slightly more than 94 percent of office and clerical workers approved the pact, and 79 percent of UAW-represented Chrysler engineers voted for the contract that covers about 45,000 active workers and more than 55,000 Chrysler retirees and 23,000 surviving spouses.[58] Chrysler CEO Robert Nardelli praised the new two-tier wage system for hourly workers as "revolutionary" and called the labor contract "a major step forward for us."[59] Nardelli added that he was not concerned by the level of opposition expressed by workers and that he was "absolutely" confident that Chrysler was on track to turn itself around and that widely offered stock options would allow many top officials to benefit financially. Nardelli explained, "We're talking about hundreds of individuals that will participate with our success as we go forward. And we will be successful."[60]

Two days after Nardelli's statements, when Chrysler announced the slashing of 12,000 jobs, some of the hundreds of workers who would not be benefiting from the company "going forward" expressed a different view, one of frustration and betrayal. "We gave them a lower wage structure," said Mark Mitchell, who worked at Chrysler's Sterling Heights assembly plant. "They should be moving work here from foreign plants, not laying us off."[61] Calvin Smith, another Sterling Heights worker, would not have voted for the new UAW contract had he known what was coming. Smith stated, "I don't like that we signed a contract, and then they come out with layoffs immediately. Many of us wouldn't have signed that contract."[62] Lydia Johnson, a line worker at Chrysler's Sterling Heights assembly, said, "I supported that contract and would have voted 'no' if I knew half the workers here would be laid off. It's sad."[63]

The Ford Case

When the UAW reached its tentative agreement with Ford, the layoffs following the ratification votes at GM and Chrysler put a damper on company and union claims that the new pact would guarantee investment in plants and preserve jobs. Al Figlan, a skilled tradesman at Ford's Van Dyke transmission plant in Sterling Heights, reflected some of the sentiment among the rank and file when he said, "You get promises of job security and it turns out they don't mean much. You bet a lot of us are paying attention to that."[64] One local UAW president representing Ford workers said the Chrysler and GM job cuts made his members uneasy. Garry Spencer, a UAW Local 1250 official in Brook Park, Illinois, said, "There's a lot of apprehension in general because we've waited so long, and we just want something that's fair." He added, "We have faith in our leadership, and we know they are fighting for us, but given the state of the industry, it's a tough balance."[65]

Because the Chrysler job cuts were in addition to a plan announced in February 2007 that would eliminate 13,000 North American positions and Ford also was in the midst of a sweeping restructuring plan that included closing sixteen factories by 2012, the agreement worried some workers like Lolinda Bellamy, a temporary worker at Ford's Dearborn truck plant, where she already makes a lower wage than permanent hires. She said, "I really want this job, but we already had cutbacks here. It's hard to understand why they keep asking for more sacrifices."[66]

But more sacrifices were in order for Ford workers. Unlike the GM and Chrysler deals, Ford's contract did not define hourly jobs as "core" assembly-line jobs and "noncore" manufacturing jobs, such as materials handling, to justify permanently lower wages for new hires. The Ford deal, like the GM and Chrysler pacts, also opened the door for another round of buyouts so that new hires would come in under the more favorable terms to replace older UAW workers earning compensation that the company no longer considered competitive. In all, Ford seeks to buy out an additional 10,000 to 14,000 people through 2010, on top of a previous effort to reduce hourly workers by 25,000 to 30,000 through buyouts and attrition.[67]

According to the agreement, up to 20 percent of Ford's UAW-represented workforce can be new hires working at lower wages. Their total hourly compensation, including benefits, range from $26 to $31 per hour, a savings of between $51 and $56 per hour compared with current workers.[68] Unknown to Ford workers during the ratification process, however, was the fact that Ford revealed that its contract allows it to raise the 20 percent cap by in-sourcing jobs currently outsourced to suppliers. Jobs brought back into Ford factories (in-sourced) will be filled by lower-wage workers. Ford and the UAW had already agreed to bring 1,500 outsourced jobs back into Ford and were in discussions concerning another 1,700. In addition, more could be added by mutual agreement. None of those 3,200 positions would count toward Ford's cap on second-tier workers. Also not revealed to union members during the voting process was that the UAW agreed that Ford could staff two former Visteon Corporation plants, Rawsonville and Sterling Heights, Michigan, entirely with lower-wage workers, and those 2,200 jobs would not count toward Ford's cap.[69]

The Ford pact also went further than GM's agreement by allowing the automaker to assume a lower rate of health care inflation to calculate its total liability for future retiree benefits. By assuming 6 percent inflation in health care costs, compared with GM's 9 percent, Ford could deposit less money into the union VEBA. In effect, the UAW allowed Ford to fund some $23 billion in retiree health care obligations for 46 cents on the dollar, compared with 68 cents on the dollar to fund about $47 billion in obligations at GM.[70] Part of Ford's contribution to the VEBA was in the form of a $3 billion secured note in existing company stock and a $3.3 billion convertible note, good for the purchase of company shares in the future. Like GM and Chrysler, all new hires at Ford will receive cash from the company to put into 401(k) retirement plans instead of paying traditional pensions and postretirement health care benefits. In another departure from the GM pattern, bargainers also agreed to stiffer rules for the UAW-Ford jobs bank, which pays idled workers a full salary. Workers are now limited to one year in the jobs bank and are given one opportunity to take a new job and relocate.[71]

In addition, plants that Ford pledged to remain open are subject to competitive operating agreements to ramp up productivity and rip up existing job descriptions, giving management a more "flexible" labor force. The automaker also reduced the number of skilled trade classifications from 350 to 22 and now can use assembly workers to perform most minor maintenance tasks. Ford is also allowed to outsource as many as 1,000 janitorial positions. There are no baseline wage increases for the life of the contract, and any hike in wages is linked to higher productivity. Ford also negotiated tougher rules on absenteeism and eliminated requirements for minimum employment levels at U.S. factories. Ford abandoned its previous promise to build a new, low-cost manufacturing facility in North America, while the automaker retained the ability to idle plants if demand for Ford's cars and trucks drops, discrediting company and union claims about job security.[72] Few of these details appeared in the twenty-eight-page booklet "UAW Ford Bargainers Preserve Jobs, Protect Wages and Benefits," passed out to Ford workers for the ratification vote.[73]

The lack of these details combined with other factors led some workers to voice opposition to the deal. Ken Poole, a worker at the Michigan Truck Plant in Wayne was particularly upset at the more than $28 million Ford CEO Alan Mulally made in 2006 during his first four months at Ford, a figure that included the CEO's signing bonus. He stated, "I have a problem with someone making that much money telling me I've got to give something up."[74] Junior Chrislip, a Dearborn truck worker at the Ford Rouge complex in Dearborn, Michigan, had harsh words for Ford and the UAW. Chrislip said, "I'm voting no. I just don't believe in the two-tier wage. That's selling out of union principles. I don't believe half the stuff in the contract. The job guarantees? Ask the Chrysler and GM workers what they think of job guarantees in their contract. At least in my work area, a lot of people are talking about voting no."[75]

Chrislip, however, believed the contract would pass. "I have no doubt the union and the company will do what it has to do to push this thing through," he said.[76] Chrislip's prediction was accurate. In the end, 81 percent of production workers and 71 percent of skilled-trades workers voted to approve the contract, which covers about 54,000 active workers along with some 98,000 retirees and 28,000 surviving spouses. Samuel Stephens, president of UAW Local 882 in Atlanta, probably summed up the Ford vote the best when he said, "Given the state of the industry, I'm thinking we did the best we could. A lot of our members have been in tune with what GM and Chrysler passed, so, they know what to expect. We know we have to start making profits again in North America and from this we can say we are really doing our part."[77]

The CAW Reacts: Seek a Closer Partnership with Management

When some auto analysts began to digest the significance of the Big Three settlements with the UAW, they estimated that the Big Three had created about a $25–dollar per hour cost advantage to build vehicles in the United States instead of Canada.[78] The big reduction in health care costs south of the border and a strengthening Canadian dollar that is almost at par with the greenback has effectively wiped out Canada's longtime advantage for investment. Accordingly, enormous pressure is now on the CAW to match cost cuts contained in the U.S. contracts, or Canadian operations could become uncompetitive. And although CAW President Buzz Hargrove initially reacted to the UAW settlements by saying that provisions in the deals, such as a two-tier wage system, would be nonstarters in Canadian bargaining in 2008, his posture soon shifted quickly and rather dramatically.[79]

First, in principle, the CAW never had any objection to a two-tier wage system, since it already had accepted it at some manufacturing plants in recent years, including at the huge Navistar truck plant in Chatham, Ontario, in order to keep that facility open. In March 2007, at the Chrysler plant in Brampton, Ontario, Hargrove made it clear to the membership that they had to vote to accept $5,000 in annual givebacks through the elimination of shift premiums, the intensification of work practices, and the contracting out of union janitorial jobs or accept the consequences.

Should they reject the concessions, Hargrove said that Chrysler would move auto production out of Brampton. The union's concessionary mood took an even more radical turn on October 15, 2007, when Hargrove and Frank Stronach, notorious antiunion owner of auto parts giant Magna International, signed a "Framework of Fairness" agreement. At the heart of the deal was Stronach inviting the CAW to organize his company's plants in return for the union giving an indefinite no-strike pledge and putting in place a complex process called a concern resolution subcommittee replacing the traditional union grievance procedure that deals with discipline and other nonwage disputes. Annual wage increases would depend on the performance of a plant, competitive considerations, and a manufacturing wage index.

In so doing, both Stronach and Hargrove defended their actions in the name of defending Canada's auto industry and made it clear that they sought an employer-union common front against the increasing threats to company profits and the union's dues base from Asian imports as well as from other countries in North America. The downsizing of the North American auto industry in the face of globalized production has, said Hargrove, "led all of us to say why would we waste our efforts in fighting one another over whether there's going to be a union in a particular division of Magna when it makes more sense to sit down and have a relationship that's non-traditional, that's non-adversarial in nature."[80]

Essentially, the deal, subject to a majority vote by employees before it is operational, grafts the CAW collaborationist approach onto a paternalistic corporate culture that has included profit-sharing schemes, company-run grievance hotlines, and employee charters designed to promote an "entrepreneurial spirit" and dampen collective consciousness. That Magna culture has helped create a global powerhouse that now is one of the world's largest auto parts companies generating revenue of U.S. $24.2 billion annually while employing 19,000 workers in Canada and 18,000 in the United States at seventy-two sites. Stronach said that he hopes a similar framework could soon be established with the UAW.

A deal with the UAW would help Stronach fulfill his longtime goal of building vehicles on contract for the Detroit Big Three in North America, because it would mean that any assembly jobs being outsourced by Chrysler LLC, Ford Motor Company, and General Motors would now be shifted to a unionized company. In the past, the UAW had consistently shot down such mooted initiatives as a bid to outsource to nonunion employers. Hargrove added that he would make a similar arrangement available to General Motors or other automakers that wanted to build a new Greenfield plant in Canada and provide jobs.[81]

The proposed CAW deal with Magna provoked strong rank-and-file and leadership opposition. "This is a travesty," said Gerry Michaud, retired president of CAW Local 199 in St. Catharines, Ontario. "It makes me sick to my stomach."[82] "We [the CAW] must be on another planet with this Magna deal," added Keith Osborne, chairperson for Local 222 at GM in Oshawa, Ontario. "This is the first time in my life on an emotional level, I feel ashamed of my union," said Gord Wilson, a retired CAW director of education. "What my union now needs more than new members at Magna is new leaders that haven't forgotten union principles."[83] Sam Gindin, former Hargrove executive assistant, said the CAW has "embraced" a Magna model of labor relations that emphasizes "controlled democracy" among workers. "It also accepts the language of 'we're all in this together' even while Magna pays wages that have undercut the rates won in CAW collective agreements with other corporations while Stronach has, over the past three years, paid himself a total cumulative salary of over $100 million."[84]

Other CAW leaders said privately that the union was simply trading away the workers' right to strike and shop-floor democracy for a monthly "dues grab."[85] But former CAW President Bob White applauded the deal, saying that the union must face "new realities" and noting that nowadays, "work stoppages are almost ineffective because of economic circumstances."[86] For their part, the Magna workers saw little benefit in paying as much as $75 per month in union dues simply to fund an extra layer of supervision to drive up productivity. For years, Magna told workers that the company's traditional human resources policies made the union unnecessary.[87] Additionally, Magna workers are aware the wage rates at the plants in which they work do not significantly differ from those in plants organized by the CAW and are even higher in some cases.[88] As the co-CEO of Magna, Donald Walker, noted, "When our shareholders examine the deal, they're going to see that it doesn't make us less competitive."[89] He added, "The fact that there will be no strikes at Magna plants will be looked on favourably by customers."[90]

The recent developments in the auto parts industry in Canada and the historic concessions contracts forced on American workers by Detroit's Big Three carmakers laid the groundwork for concessions in the 2008 contract negotiations. Mark Nantais, the president of the Canadian Vehicle Manufacturer's Association that represents the Canadian arms of the Detroit Big Three, set the agenda and theme for the talks in testimony before members of Parliament (MPs) on the House of Commons finance committee in Ottawa. "In the not-too-distant past, Canada had a competitive advantage within North America to help attract new investment," Nantais told key parliamentary committee MPs probing the impact of the strengthened Canadian dollar as they contemplated the 2008 federal budget.[91] In his testimony, Nantais also noted that Canada's cost advantage in recent years has been the lower value of the Canadian dollar compared with its U.S. counterpart, as well as lower labor and health care expenses.

Nantais then began to explain that labor costs of U.S. autoworkers are expected to fall from their current rate of $75 per hour to around $50 when the terms of the UAW agreement with the Big Three kick in. With Canadian labor costs currently running at around $70 per hour, Nantais concluded his testimony by saying, "Canada had a competitive advantage within North America to help attract new investment. Today, Canada is the highest-cost jurisdiction globally for many auto manufacturers to operate. This reality leaves Canada at a competitive disadvantage at attracting the ongoing investments needed to remain globally competitive."[92] Finally, Nantais pleaded with MPs to offload employment insurance payroll levies to the workforce, extend a temporary accelerated write-off rate for new equipment, and gain a refundable investment tax credit for new machinery to keep the Big Three making cars in Canada.[93]

Ford Canada CEO Bill Osborne joined the chorus in seeking government relief. He threatened that if the government removed the 6.1 percent tariff on Korean cars and granted other concessions to Korea when it finalizes a free-trade pact with that country, Ford will "have to evaluate our competitive position in any jurisdiction where we don't believe we've gotten reasonable and fair policies."[94] In evaluating Ford's competitive position, Osborne established that the theme of the 2008 talks with the CAW would be the union's willingness to grant concessions. All future labor negotiations in the North American auto sector are going to be based on cost cuts similar to those contained in the Big Three-UAW agreements. "This is a brutal business," Osborne said.[95]

The CAW corporatist deal struck with notorious antiunion auto parts boss Frank Stronach of Magna International paved the way for the early opening of the CAW-Big Three contracts and the concessions the negotiations produced. The so-called Framework of Fairness, based on a permanent no-strike pledge and the creation of a shop-floor regime that renounces the traditional union grievance procedure, confirmed Osborne's "brutal business" remark. The CAW-Magna deal also constituted a thematic starting point for the 2008 contract negotiations between the union and the Big Three.

In April 2008, CAW President Hargrove secretly approached the Big Three to propose negotiated settlements for new three-year contracts months before the mid-September contract deadlines and the traditional opening of the bargaining season. In the case of Ford, the union leadership began secret talks with the company months before the CAW assembled its collective bargaining conference. The stated purpose of the conference is for the union to establish bargaining priorities. By the end of month, however, Hargrove and his lieutenants had worked out a deal with Ford that contained a package of concessions similar to what had been agreed upon in 2007 by the UAW and the automaker.

The new agreement froze current Ford workers' wages for the life of the three-year contract. It also cut forty hours of vacation pay per year, tightened caps for long-term medical care, increased employee co-payments on prescription drugs, reduced pension benefits, and froze COLA pay for sixteen months beginning with the ratification of the new contract. The agreement also introduced a two-tier wage system. New hires start at 70 percent of the wages earned by current workers and receive reduced benefits. The Ford agreement also committed the parties to establish a prefunded, off-balance-sheet Retiree Health Benefit Fund similar to the VEBA created in the United States. In making the concessions, the CAW reacted to pressures associated with the 2007 UAW-Ford contract. That deal, according to the Ann Arbor, Michigan, Center for Automotive Research, gave more than a $20–per-hour labor cost advantage to the UAW over the CAW.[96]

After giving membership just a few days to consider the agreement, the CAW leadership called for a vote. In turn, Ford Canada workers gave the

union the lowest margin in the history of Big Three master or national contracts. Overall, the contract passed with just 67 percent voting in favor. At
Ford's flagship assembly plant in Oakville, Ontario, almost 60 percent of
production workers voted no on the contract. And it marked the first time
ever that a CAW local at a Big Three plant rejected an agreement recommended for ratification by the union leadership.

On Thursday, May 15, 2008, the CAW reached early tentative agreements
with GM and Chrysler. Hoping to ratify the new contracts that fit the Ford
pattern, the union allowed workers only forty-eight hours to consider the
contract before voting. One reason for the rush to ratification was that the
CAW-GM agreement accepted the imminent closure of GM's Windsor transmission plant in exchange for supposed job guarantees at other GM facilities.
Like the Big Three agreements with the UAW in the United States, CAW
contract provisions with GM on job guarantees were contingent on market
conditions. The GM agreement covered 12,955 CAW members, while the
union-Chrysler deal involved 9,600 employees. CAW members at Chrysler's
three Ontario-based plants voted 87 percent in favor of the deal, while GM
workers voted 84 percent in favor of its new agreement.[97]

At the ratification meetings for the GM contract, Hargrove claimed that
concessions had saved jobs at the Oshawa complex, especially at the truck
plant that already had been slated for a one-shift reduction. Hargrove told
the press that the agreement would "save GM 300 million dollars over the
next three years."[98] Three weeks later, GM announced the truck plant closure,
citing the standard "market conditions" clause within the collective agreement. In announcing the shuttering of the plant, GM claimed that market
conditions had changed. At the same time, GM decided it would continue
the production of pickup trucks in its Mexico and U.S. facilities, where it
claimed production costs were lower. Outraged, CAW Local 222 blockaded
GM offices and demanded that GM rescind its decision to close the plant.
On July 28, 2008, the CAW ended its blockade of GM in exchange for the
company's offer to provide more cash to buy out employees and promises to
assemble two new models of automobiles in other Ontario plants.[99]

The plant closings and new concessionary contracts occurred in the context of increasing pressure by auto executives on workers to accept lower
wages in order to save jobs in the face of international competitiveness. In
May 2008, Frank Stronach remarked that wages for autoworkers were still
too high and that "there's still a bit of a damn-you attitude on behalf of labor."
Stronach warned that the unions have to change because otherwise there will
not be an industry.[100] Similar statements were made by Dick Dauch, the CEO

of American Axle and Manufacturing, during a 2008 strike by 3,600 UAW members that ended with a contract that cut workers' pay by 50 percent and drastically reduced their benefits. Dauch boasted, "We have the flexibility to source all of our business to other locations around the world, and we have the right to do so."[101] Dauch's comments followed an announcement by the company a week earlier that it had moved some axle production for GM's large SUVs to its plant in Mexico.[102]

In Mexico, wages in the auto sector have been pushed down even further as a result of union concessions in the United States and Canada. Unlike in Canada and the United States, where a single national union represents most autoworkers, in Mexico unions are deeply split and may represent workers at only one manufacturer or even at a single plant. In this system of decentralized bargaining, pressures on unions to make concessions are much more intense. For example, promises made by Mexican auto union leadership to cut wages and benefits were crucial in persuading Ford to direct many of the 4,500 new jobs involved in building Fiestas to the Ford plant in Cuautitlán, on the outskirts of Mexico City. Union leaders agreed to cut wages for new hires to about half of the current wage of U.S. $4.50 per hour.[103]

When asked why the union made the concessions, Ford Cuautitlán union leader Juan José Sosa Arreola explained, "We need to be more competitive." Ford company spokeswoman Alejandra Acevedo acknowledged that to win the jobs, the plant had to compete against other Ford facilities worldwide. "It makes business sense that labor costs are much lower here, and also it's much cheaper here to grow the local supplier network," said Acevedo. She said further that Mexico's free-trade deals help slash the cost of importing parts and exporting cars.[104]

When General Motors announced in June 2008 that it would stop using relatively high-wage workers to assemble slow-selling pickups at its Toluca, Mexico, plant, the union offered to work for less to keep the plant alive. "I think we are going to have to sacrifice something in order to continue to be competitive," said Edgar Arroyo, union official at the Toluca plant, where he estimated some workers earn about U.S. $6 per hour, an extremely high rate by Mexican auto industry standards. At Volkswagen's plant in Puebla, union spokesman Arturo Monter said workers agreed to cut starting wages to U.S. $1.50 per hour from U.S. $1.95 a few years ago. Monter added that those lower labor costs helped workers at the Mexican factory win a contract for an as-yet-unnamed Volkswagen model, known at the plant only as "Project Zero," that the automaker had been considering building in the United States.[105]

These labor costs allow Mexico to stay competitive with China, where an average worker at a foreign-owned factory or joint venture can make U.S. $2 to U.S. $6 per hour. Since NAFTA, the gap in overall manufacturing wages between Mexico and the United States has widened. As a result, foreign investment in Mexico's auto industry is soaring, averaging about U.S. $2 billion per year since the 1990s. Auto exports grew by almost 68 percent between 2004 and 2007 to 1.6 million units. Mexico's abundant, youthful workforce is still drawn to auto plants despite the low wages, union leaders say, because the firms offer stable employment, a rarity in Mexico's twenty-first-century world of work.[106]

The concessions given to Ford by the union at Cuautitlán are especially significant given the fact their struggles in the 1980s and 1990s were a rallying point for autoworker unity across North America. The Ford Cuautitlán workers' movement in those years struggled for higher wages, better working conditions, and union democracy. More specifically, the Cuautitlán workers resisted the government's imposition of the Confederación de Trabajadores de México/Confederation of Mexican Workers (CTM) National Ford Workers' Union as their bargaining representative. The CTM affiliate consistently negotiated agreements that provided Ford with flexible job categories, "just-in-time" production policies, work teams, and other provisions.[107]

In doing so, the CTM sought to advance Mexico's neoliberal and export-led development policies that depended on strict labor control, low wages, and working-class fragmentation. The Cuautitlán democratic labor movement resisted these measures on several occasions by occupying plants, battling Mexican police, and facing down CTM thugs who seriously injured dozens of autoworkers while killing one. Moreover, these struggles led to the development of a broader movement of auto union solidarity inside Mexico (the Ford Workers' Democratic Movement, or FWDM) that eventually established cross-border labor linkages with U.S. and Canadian unions like UAW Local 879 in St. Paul, Minnesota. UAW Local 879 and the FWDM even signed a formal solidarity agreement that called for worker exchanges and information sharing on wages, working conditions, and Ford company policies. St. Paul Local 879 also provided partial funding of one full-time FWDM organizer at the local level.[108]

Because this type of solidarity seriously threatened the CTM's dominance, Mexico's stable investment climate, and Ford's competitive position in the global economy, the Mexican government crushed the FWDM through a combination of violence and legal chicanery designed to permanently entrench union leaders like Juan José Sosa Arreola who accept cuts in wages and benefits for autoworkers in the name of making Ford "competitive."

These events and other recent developments in the labor relations systems of the North American auto industry reveal a deepening of the fundamental contradictions between the forces of production expanding on a global scale and the social relations that guide their application. Still carried out according to the dictates of the market and the drive by privately owned corporations to earn a profit, auto production in North America is increasingly global in character, and the results of these processes are placing enormous pressure on workers and trade unions to adapt to these realities.

The auto unions in the NAFTA countries must now either deliver workers to the Big Three who are paid and worked on a scale that Ford CEO Alan Mulally calls competitive with the Asian market or face the possibility of extinction themselves. The new four-year labor agreements between the UAW and Detroit's Big Three automakers saved the union from extinction and, at the same time, built the organization into a corporate entity through control of VEBA trust funds. This capped a thirty-year corporatist strategy of collaborating with management to eliminate jobs, cut wages, and ratchet up worker productivity. During this time, the UAW officialdom transformed itself into an upper-middle-class social layer that became insulated from the negative consequences of its policies through the building of various investment and business schemes with management.

In general, the response of the auto unions in Canada to the globalization of production has mirrored that of their U.S. counterparts. In the wake of the massive concessions contracts signed by the UAW with GM, Chrysler, and Ford in the United States, the CAW entered into early negotiations that resulted in layoffs and concessions. The rapid narrowing of the labor cost differential produced an enormous crisis for the CAW officialdom. The UAW concession contracts trumped the traditional nationalist orientation of the CAW through the off-loading of health care liabilities from the books of the automakers.

The UAW model of collaboration has now been ruthlessly applied to the CAW as the union seeks to establish ever-closer relations with employers. Reflected first in the bargain struck with auto parts manufacturing giant Magna, it became more apparent in the last negotiating round with the Big Three that resulted in concessions on pay, benefits, and working conditions. As in the United States, the concessions offered no guarantee of future employment as both unions claimed. In 2007, the ranks of the UAW declined by more than 73,538, or nearly 14 percent. The UAW counted 464,910 members at the end of 2007, less than a third of its peak of 1.5 million in the 1970s and the smallest since the union began organizing workers in the years preceding World

War II. Despite the membership decline, the union's revenues rose 8 percent, to $327.6 million, in 2007 through the expansion of jointness programs with the companies.[109] In Mexico, auto unions responded to these developments by agreeing to cuts in wages and benefits in a race to the bottom to compete for jobs.

As the North American auto industry has come under intense pressure through the globalization of motor vehicle production, the trade union apparatuses are seeking to protect their privileges and offset the decline in their union dues base by forging new corporatist relations with the companies. Meanwhile, workers are trapped inside these organizations and have their paychecks docked to pay union dues to an officialdom that now has diametrically opposed interests. The downward trend in worker wages, benefits, and conditions will likely continue. In order to change their situation, workers must reject the failed nationalist orientation strategies of the auto unions, form their own organizations, and seek alliances with workers across borders. Gains in worker productivity and innovation must be utilized for achieving a higher standard of living for the citizens of the North American territories and not solely for the profits of corporations and their ancillaries in the world of finance.

Conclusion

In many ways, NAFTA explains much about the history of world capitalism. As an economic system that constantly seeks to push the productive forces to develop on a global scale, capitalism inevitably creates conflicts among nation-states in which the private property and the regulatory rules for accumulating wealth are legally rooted. In certain historical periods, this contradiction has been regulated and contained through the organization of the world economy under the hegemony of a single great power. Such was the case in the immediate decades following World War II when the United States exercised and managed its economic hegemony around the world through the Bretton Woods institutions. In this period, profits reached record levels and workers in North America made economic gains through bargaining in the workplace and by pressuring their respective national governments to enact reforms that also helped raise living standards.

But the oil shocks, stagflation, and the falling rate of profit that began in the 1970s put pressure on this arrangement. Although these developments affected all three countries in North America, their greatest impact was on Mexico and the United States. Forced to abandon its fifty-year-old development policy rooted in the goals of the 1910 revolution and the national market, Mexico began pursuing an economic strategy that promoted the nation as a haven for low-wage manufacturing. More important, Japan and Europe reemerged as major capitalist rivals to the United States. The competitive pressures that built up in the global economy as a result weakened the once-dominant economic position of the United States. When protectionist measures enacted by the United States in the 1980s failed to reverse this turn of events and American efforts to rewrite the global rules of trade encountered resistance from rival nation-states, the United States then sought to restore its economic supremacy through the negotiation of trade agreements with individual countries.

In 1994 when the United States, Canada, and Mexico entered into NAFTA, the elites of all three countries firmly believed that the agreement would generate renewed economic growth and restore profitability within their respective national economies. Canada and Mexico looked to ride the coattails of the United States, a country that had achieved its economic might through the building of its industrial base by securing access to the resources and the labor of its North American neighbors. While NAFTA positioned the United States to shore up this traditional dominance, at the same time it presented the United States an opportunity to gain significant economic leverage against rival nation-states. As the template for organizing and regulating capitalism on a regional level, it was hoped that NAFTA would aid the United States in its bid to restore economic hegemony worldwide.

The NAFTA template, however, placed strong emphasis on the integration of national economies, a factor that departed significantly from the model the United States had organized to manage the postwar economic boom. The "golden years" of postwar capitalism managed and regulated by institutions like the GATT had been based on the steady growth of economies geared toward national markets. Because the profits of corporations resulted mostly from production carried out within the boundaries of nation-states, workers and unions exercised leverage to bargain for wages and benefits from employers while pressuring governments for reforms.

By comparison, NAFTA had been established in a new period of world capitalism, one that increasingly emphasizes the international market. Beginning in the 1970s, when stagflation slowed economic growth around the world, manufacturing firms everywhere began developing and introducing methods to cut production costs. In an effort to restore profitability, firms invested in new technologies that included advances in transportation, telecommunications, and computers. This allowed manufacturers to disaggregate formerly unified production processes within national borders and spread them around the globe in search of cheap labor, lower taxes, and other factors that reduced production costs.

In North America, this process began in 1965 when United States–based corporations started transferring assembly manufacturing to locations along the Mexican side of the international border. By the 1980s, this development had gained momentum, and by the early 1990s the search for cheap labor and lower production costs in North American manufacturing was in full swing. By 1994, the year NAFTA went into effect, the offshoring of manufacturing to Mexican factories called maquiladoras had become an established trend. By 2000, thousands of maquiladoras operated in Mexico, employing nearly one million workers. Helping advance this trend was the progressive dismantling of financial regulation that had characterized the period of the postwar economic boom. Unlike the Bretton Woods years when capital remained homespun and the dollar reigned as the world's preeminent currency, the era of globalized production paralleled the freeing up of capital everywhere. The relative economic decline of the United States forced American leaders to allow the dollar to float against other currencies, giving investors and fund managers more flexibility to scour global markets in search of new ways to appropriate profits by purely monetary means.

This new regime of capital accumulation based on the freer flow of money placed enormous pressure on manufacturing and other firms to lower costs. Firms unable to reduce their costs found capital more expensive, were subject to takeover, and faced the prospect of going out of business altogether. These new realities put downward pressure on wages and generated an employer movement to drive up labor productivity everywhere. Although rank-and-file workers in the NAFTA countries initially resisted these measures by carrying out strikes, the union officialdom's response rapidly evolved into an outlook that largely accommodated employer demands.

While seeking to harness rank-and-file militancy, unions began pursuing partnerships with transnational corporations by declaring their willingness to discipline their members and adhere to "free market" principles. Marching in lockstep with capital by providing business a workforce earning less pay under constantly worsening conditions, the labor officialdom claimed that concessions by workers were necessary to save jobs and keep them within the national borders of the countries in which the unions were based. Because business faced cost structures that were now determined internationally rather than by national markets, union leaders deemed it necessary to deliver a workforce to employers that was more in sync with the requirements of the new international division of labor.

Globalization had changed everything, the labor officialdom claimed. For workers, there was no alternative strategy but to compete against those in other countries by sacrificing the hard-won gains of earlier periods. The only way to attract business investment and save jobs, the labor officialdom declared, was to abandon the strike, give back wages and benefits, and allow employers to dictate conditions on the shop floor.

But these strategies designed to defend "American," "Canadian," and "Mexican" jobs have failed miserably. Especially in the United States and Canada, instead of saving jobs, the result of this nationalist strategy has been the shutdown of one factory after another. Millions of jobs have been destroyed and union membership has declined in the process. In spite of the sweeping concessions to employers that unions have extracted from their membership, transnational corporations continue to shift production elsewhere, seeking ever-lower labor costs. In Mexico, where many manufacturing firms had moved production to take advantage of lower costs, unions bargain for lower wages with employers because many of those same jobs have left for China and other countries where labor costs are even lower.

Nowhere has the union strategy of partnership and concessionary bargaining been more apparent than in the auto industry, North America's most integrated industry. This strategy has been highlighted most in the United States, where struggles by union members in the 1950s and 1960s established the first employer-paid pensions and medical benefits for industrial workers. Beginning with the Chrysler bailout of the late 1970s, autoworkers have suffered one rollback after another while the UAW and other unions have joined management in partnership, ripping up the gains of the past and helping impose the demands of the Detroit automakers. In 2007, the union partnership strategy and givebacks in wages, benefits, and conditions reached new heights when the UAW negotiated agreements with GM, Ford, and Chrysler.

The concessions extracted from workers by the UAW in these agreements included massive layoffs, plant closings, and the downgrading of jobs that remained. All agreements included two-tier wage systems and provisions to replace many higher-paid workers with lower-paid new hires and temporary employees. While paying membership dues that contribute to the bloating of the UAW treasury, new workers are forced to endure sweatshop conditions and lack the slightest job protection and benefits. In the process of accommodating the demands of employers for a new type of worker, one that earns lower wages and receives fewer benefits while laboring in sweatshop conditions, the UAW has acquired large shares of corporate stock in exchange for accepting complete responsibility of managing and funding retiree health care through a multibillion-dollar fund called VEBA.

Ownership of company shares and the management of VEBA give the UAW a direct stake in driving down labor costs by imposing production speedups and wage cuts on its own members in order to boost the value of company stock that it now owns. This new role of the union openly conflicts with its duty to represent UAW members who are constantly pressured to accept downsizing and the downgrading of work to comply with corporate efforts to maintain global competitiveness.

This "race to the bottom" spearheaded by the UAW in the United States has had a whipsaw effect on the Canadian and Mexican auto unions. In an effort to underbid the UAW and keep jobs within their respective national borders, the CAW and the Mexican auto unions also seek out partnerships with the auto companies while they look for ways to extract even greater concessions from their members in order that the auto companies remain globally competitive. Mexican auto unions, for example, openly boast that recent wage concessions on the heels of the UAW concessions in the United States are keeping their members competitive with workers in China, thus keeping jobs inside Mexico.

Initiated more than thirty years ago, the shutting down of factories, the downsizing of workforces, and the downgrading of work have accelerated in the NAFTA years, and this has occurred not only in the auto industry but in a myriad of other industries as well. At the same time, NAFTA rules have increasingly thrown open national boundaries while removing all restrictions on the acquisition of new sources of labor, raw materials, and outlets for investment. In Mexico, the home of most migrant workers living and working in the United States, NAFTA has paralleled the devastation of national industries, the destruction of jobs, the growth of the informal economy, and worsening conditions of employment. Wholesale violations of workers' rights accompanied by a catastrophic decline in living standards are now dominant tends in Mexico.

As illustrated by the example of the auto industry, unions that once worked in tandem with the Mexican government to extract concessions from foreign companies now collaborate with the state to provide the transnationals a workforce earning poverty-level wages, receiving few or no benefits, and experiencing a steady erosion of working conditions. This union-government collaboration includes the relentless pursuit of an effective environment of deunionization through the imposition of protection contracts that deny workers' rights such as freedom of association and collective bargaining while maintaining the privileged position and the perks of compliant labor leaders. Meanwhile, the transnational corporations and the Mexican state push for changes to the nation's labor laws in an effort to make the country an even more attractive low-wage haven for the exploitation of a controlled workforce. These conditions confronting Mexican workers that have been documented through the NAALC complaint process also have forced many

Mexican workers to migrate northward, despite the recent sharp economic downturn in the United States.

The growth of the Mexican migrant workforce inside the United States also reflects dramatic changes in American labor markets. The social composition of the American working class is undergoing a radical transformation resulting from globalization and free trade. Since the 1970s, the ranks of the working class in the United States have been vastly expanded, under conditions in which substantial layers of what were once considered part of the American middle class are driven down into the ranks of the working poor. In the process, these workers are increasingly deprived of stable employment, pensions, company-paid health care, and other basic social amenities. In the NAFTA years, these adverse developments for labor in the United States have advanced to the point where they are now well-established trends. Moreover, these trends undergird an ongoing process of social and economic polarization that is increasing at an alarming rate. This is reflected in part by record-high company executive pay and an ever-widening income gap between the wealthy elite and broad layers of the population for whom living standards have either stagnated or declined.

Although NAFTA has accelerated the growth of these adverse trends for labor, at the same time it also provides potential for the struggle between the working class and capital to expand in scope and grow in intensity. The commonality of many workers' struggles emerging from these conditions across borders, such as those against downsizing, falling living standards, and attacks on social benefits, is creating historic opportunities for the realization of working-class unity on a continental level. The fact that most complaints filed under the NAALC process have included the participation of unions, worker advocacy groups, and other labor organizations from the three NAFTA countries is testimony to the potential for the further development of cross-border labor unity.

But forging working-class unity in North America also presents great challenges. In all of North America, unions have overseen a continuous erosion of workers' living standards in the midst of record-breaking corporate profits on Wall Street. While unions in the United States, Canada, and Mexico pursue partnerships with employers under these conditions and claim that the creation of a favorable business climate is the only way for workers to secure gainful employment, they also oppose the independent organization of the working class. Unions across North America constantly seek to channel discontent into the established political parties and push for national solutions to problems that are international in scope.

The unions are continuing to carry out this strategy even while NAFTA and North American integration have exposed it as ineffective and self-defeating. The integration resulting from NAFTA has greatly reduced the relevance of national borders, a factor reflected in the convergence of Mexican and U.S. labor markets. Given the close integration of the U.S. and Mexican economies, instead of pursuing strategies based on nationalism and chauvinism, everything must be done to unite the struggles of American and Mexican workers and establish the firmest possible bonds of active solidarity, mutual support, and coordinated action. For example, will supporting Teamster efforts to keep Mexican truck drivers off U.S. highways and the SEIU backing for guest worker programs help or hinder such unity? Will advocating for protectionism to save "American" jobs and will partnering with giant corporations like GM, Ford, Caterpillar, and others advance worker unity in North America?

No! Building a workers' movement in North America first requires rejection of the unions' failed nationalist and chauvinist strategies. Moreover, any genuine struggle waged by workers against these conditions is inconceivable outside of an implacable defense of workers' rights, and especially those of migrants living and working in the United States. Because capital and goods can cross borders without restrictions, any genuine movement of the working classes of North America must begin with the premise that workers have the right to freely cross borders and secure jobs with full protection and benefits. Labor must reject all attempts by the transnationals and the region's governing elites to divide them, whether inside the boundaries of nation-states or across national borders.

Accordingly, workers in North America need to organize themselves independently of the trade unions and their nationalist strategies around principles of international unity. In doing so, they must fight against the promotion of partnership with employers that pits workers against one another based on nationality. Conscious elements of the working class must recognize that any political perspective based on nationalist rather than internationalist foundations inevitably expresses the class interests of the region's economic elites and not those of working people.

In practice, this means coming to grips with the fact that the conditions faced by Mexican workers are the same that also confront workers in the United States and Canada. Those common conditions are the product of one globally integrated capitalist system, not merely the expression of one nation's economy. Understanding this reality rejects the tired tactics of pursuing bits of pressure and reforms at the national level and recognizes that such activity will not halt the assault on wages and conditions of North American workers by the transnational corporations.

Finally, any workers' movement that emerges from these struggles can and should not limit itself to the protection of workers' rights such as the right to organize unions, strike, and bargain collectively. Rather, the struggle for workers' rights must move out of the narrow economic realm in which it now is exclusively based. The working class must recognize that any lasting solution to the problems of declining wages, worsening conditions, and erosion of workers' rights is, in the final analysis, also a political struggle. It is essential that labor in North America organizes itself through a combined political and economic struggle independent of both the established, elite-dominated party system and a union officialdom that continues adhering to strategies that are increasingly self-serving. Only then can the "race to the bottom" in which workers in North America are now trapped ever be halted and reversed.

Notes

Introduction

1. Matilde Pérez U., Carolina Gómez, and Gabriel León Zaragoza, "Se agotan tiempos para el diálogo: campesinos," *La Jornada*, February 1, 2008.

2. Claudia Herrera Beltrán and David Brooks, "Rechazo al TLCAN, al llegar Calderón a barrio de Chicago" *La Jornada*, February 13, 2008.

3. James Parks, "On Capitol Hill, Mexican Miners Tell of Police Violence to Break Strike," AFL-CIO Blog, February 13, 2008, http://blog.aflcio.org/2008/02/13/on-capitol-hill-mexican-miners-describe-police-violence-to-break-their-strike/ (accessed May 31, 2008).

4. Peter Marsh, "China to Overtake US as Largest Manufacturer," *Financial Times*, August 10, 2008.

5. Larry Rohter, "Bush Faces Tough Time in South America," *New York Times*, November 5, 2005.

6. United Nations, *United Nations Investment Report* (New York: United Nations, 1992), 256.

7. Douglas A. Irwin, *Free Trade Under Fire*, 2nd ed. (Princeton, NJ: Princeton University Press, 2005), 5–21.

8. United Nations Council on Trade and Development, *World Investment Report 2006: FDI from Developing and Transition Economies—Implications for Development* (New York: United Nations, 2006), 10.

9. Ibid.

10. Ibid.

11. This process is extensively discussed in Alan Tonelson, *The Race to the Bottom: Why a Worldwide Worker Surplus and Uncontrolled Free Trade are Sinking American Living Standards* (Boulder, CO: Westview Press, 2002).

12. Several studies on globalization advance this thesis. Examples include Goran Therborn, "Introduction from the Universal to the Global," *International Sociology* 15, no. 2 (June 2000): 149–50; Jacques B. Gelinas, *Juggernaut Politics: Understanding Predatory Globalization* (London: Zed Books, 2003); Ronaldo Munck, *Labour and Globalisation: The New "Great Transformation"* (London: Zed Books, 2002).

13. Joseph Stiglitz, *Globalization and Its Discontents* (New York: W.W. Norton, 2002), 9.

14. Jeff Faux, *The Global Class War: How America's Bipartisan Elite Lost Our Future—and What It Will Take to Win It Back* (Hoboken, NJ: John Wiley and Sons, 2006), 4–11.

Chapter 1: Labor and Global Capitalism in North America, 1850–1970

1. Niall Ferguson, *Empire: The Rise and Demise of the British World Order* (New York: Basic Books, 2004).

2. C. Vann Woodward, *Reunion and Reaction* (New York: Anchor Books, 1956).

3. Ruth Schwartz Cowan, *Social History of American Technology* (New York: Oxford University Press, 1997), 11–16.

4. Ferguson, *Empire*.

5. David Montgomery, *The Fall of the House of Labor: The Workplace, the State, and American Labor Activism, 1865–1925* (Cambridge: Cambridge University Press, 1987), 214.

6. David Montgomery, "Workers' Movements in the United States Confront Imperialism: The Progressive Era Experience," *Journal of Gilded Age and Progressive Era* 7, no. 1 (January 2008): 13.

7. Errol Black and Jim Silver, *Building a Better World: An Introduction to Trade Unionism in Canada* (Halifax, NS: Fernwood, 2001), 88–93.

8. Ibid.

9. Stephen Clarkson, *Uncle Sam and Us: Globalization, Neoconservatism, and the Canadian State* (Toronto: University of Toronto Press, 2002), 18–22.

10. Black and Silver, *Building a Better World*, 89–90.

11. Gilbert G. González and Raúl A. Fernández, *A Century of Chicano History: Empire, Nations and Migration* (New York: Routledge, 2003), 29–60.

12. David Montgomery, "Labor in the Industrial Era," in Robert B. Morris, ed., *The U.S. Department of Labor Bicentennial History of The American Worker* (Washington, DC: U.S. Government Printing Office, 1976), 116–17.

13. A seminal history of the Knights of Labor is Leon Fink, *Workingmen's Democracy: The Knights of Labor and American Politics* (Urbana: University of Illinois Press, 1985).

14. David Brian Robertson, *Capital, Labor, and State: The Battle for American Labor Markets from the Civil War to the New Deal* (New York: Rowman and Littlefield, 2000), 83.

15. Philip Taft, "Workers of a New Century," in Robert B. Morris, ed., *The U.S. Department of Labor Bicentennial History of the American Worker* (Washington, DC: U.S. Government Printing Office, 1976), 153.

16. Melvyn Dubofsky, *We Shall Be All: A History of the Industrial Workers of the World* (Chicago: Quadrangle Books, 1969).

17. Black and Silver, *Building a Better World*, 95.

18. Ibid., 94–95.

19. Montgomery, "Workers' Movements Confront Imperialism," 18.

20. Black and Silver, *Building a Better World*, 99.

21. Craig Heron, *The Canadian Labor Movement: A Short History* (Toronto: James Lorimer, 1989), 47.

22. John Mason Hart, *Empire and Revolution: The Americans in Mexico Since the Civil War* (Berkeley and Los Angeles: University of California Press, 2004).

23. Gilbert G. González and Raúl A. Fernández, *A Century of Chicano History: Empire, Nations, and Migration* (New York: Routledge, 2003), 37; Josefina Zoraida Vázquez and Lorenzo Meyer, *The United States and Mexico* (Chicago: University of Chicago Press, 1985), 92–100.

24. Donald C. Hodges and Ross Gandy, *Mexico: The End of the Revolution* (Westport, CT: Praeger Books), 15.

25. Ibid.

26. Emilio Zamora, *The World of the Mexican Worker in Texas* (College Station: Texas A & M Press, 1993), 17.

27. James D. Cockroft, *Intellectual Precursors of the Mexican Revolution 1900–1913* (Austin: University of Texas Press, 1968).

28. This interpretation has been advanced by many scholars, including Ramón Eduardo Ruiz, *Labor and the Ambivalent Revolutionaries, 1911–1923* (Baltimore, MD: Johns Hopkins University Press, 1976).

29. Ibid.

30. For a recent interpretation of Zapata's rural rebellion in the 1910 Mexican Revolution, see Paul Hart, *Bitter Harvest: The Social Transformation of Morelos, Mexico, and the Origins of the Zapatista Revolution, 1840–1910* (Albuquerque: University of New Mexico Press, 2006).

31. John M. Hart, "The Urban Working Class and the Mexican Revolution: The Case of the Casa del Obrero Mundial," *Hispanic American Historical Review* 58 (February 1978): 18–19.

32. Norman Caulfield, *Mexican Workers and the State: From the Porfiriato to NAFTA* (Fort Worth: Texas Christian University Press, 1998), 11–30.

33. Ibid.

34. Friedrich Katz, *Secret War in Mexico: Europe, the United States, and the Mexican Revolution* (Chicago: University of Chicago Press, 1981).

35. For an extensive analysis of these periods and the economic and political processes that were associated with them, see Ernest Mandel, *Long Waves of Capitalist*

Development (Cambridge: Cambridge University Press, 1980); Ernest Mandel, *Late Capitalism* (London: Verso Books, 1978).

36. John Mason Hart, *Revolutionary Mexico: The Coming and the Process of the Mexican Revolution* (Berkeley and Los Angeles: University of California Press, 1987).

37. Katz, *Secret War in Mexico*; Adolfo Gilly, *The Mexican Revolution: A People's History* (New York: New Press, 2006).

38. Hart, *Revolutionary Mexico*.

39. Gregg Andrews, *Shoulder to Shoulder? The AFL, the United States and the Mexican Revolution, 1910–1924* (Berkeley and Los Angeles: University of California Press, 1991).

40. Caulfield, *Mexican Workers and the State*, 25.

41. Montgomery, "Workers' Movements Confront Imperialism," 10.

42. Dana Frank, *Buy American: The Untold Story of Economic Nationalism* (Boston: Beacon Press, 1999), 47–55.

43. Richard Ulrich Miller, "American Railroad Unions and the National Railways of Mexico: An Exercise in Nineteenth-Century Proletarian Manifest Destiny," *Labor History* 15 (Spring 1974): 239–60; Lorena Parlee, "The Impact of United States Railroad Unions on Organized Labor and Government Policy in Mexico (1880–1911)," *Hispanic American Historical Review* 64 (August 1984): 443–75.

44. Montgomery, "Workers' Movements Confront Imperialism," 34–36.

45. Paul Buhle, *Taking Care of Business: Samuel Gompers, George Meany, Lane Kirkland, and the Tragedy of American Labor* (New York: Monthly Review Press, 1999), 78.

46. Taft, "Workers of a New Century," 171.

47. Norman Caulfield, "Wobblies and Mexican Workers in Mining and Petroleum, 1905–1924," *International Review of Social History* 40 (1995): 51–76.

48. Taft, "Workers of a New Century," 172.

49. Caulfield, *Mexican Workers and the State*, 36.

50. Craig Heron, *The Workers' Revolt in Canada: 1917–1925* (Toronto: University of Toronto Press, 1998), 269.

51. Andrews, *Shoulder to Shoulder?*, 192–95.

52. Ibid., 85–86.

53. David Walker, "Porfirian Labor Politics: Working Class Organization in Mexico City under Porfirio Díaz," *The Americas* 37 (January 1981): 257–89; Hart, *Revolutionary Mexico*, 61–62.

54. Caulfield, *Mexican Workers and the State*, 41–50.

55. Caulfield, "Wobblies and Mexican Workers," 51–76.

56. Presidencia de la República, *50 Años de la Revolución Mexicana en Cifras* (Mexico, DF: Nacional Financiera, 1963), 34.

57. Jeffrey Bortz and Marcos Aguila, "Earning a Living: A History of Real Wage Studies in Twentieth-Century Mexico," *Latin American Research Review* 41, no. 2 (2006): 120.

58. Andrews, *Shoulder to Shoulder?*, 4.

59. Ibid.

60. Rick Szostak, *Technological Innovation and the Great Depression* (Boulder, CO: Westview Press, 1995), 13, 103.

61. Richard Tardanico, "Revolutionary Mexico and the World Economy: The 1920s in Theoretical Perspective," *Theory and Society* 13, no. 6 (November 1984): 757–72.

62. "1921–1939: Between Two Wars," *Canada and the World: A History of Canadian Foreign Policy,* Foreign Affairs and International Trade Canada, June 8, 2007, http://www.international.gc.ca/history-histoire/world-monde/1921–1939.aspx?lang=eng (accessed June 23, 2008).

63. Ibid.

64. Vázquez and Meyer, *The United States and Mexico,* 152.

65. "Workers and the State," *Canadian Workers in History: An Interpretation: 1600–1975,* Parks Canada, May 19, 2006, http://www.pc.gc.ca/culture/proj/tch-cwh/page7_e.asp (accessed June 27, 2008).

66. Taft, "Workers of a New Century," 174.

67. Montgomery, *The Fall of the House of Labor,* 348–50.

68. Taft, "Workers of a New Century," 174.

69. United States Bureau of the Census, *Historical Statistics of the United States, Colonial Times to 1970,* bicentennial ed., part 2 (Washington, DC: U.S. Government Printing Office, 1975), 121–82.

70. Ibid.

71. Mary Nolan, *Visions of Modernity* (Oxford: Oxford University Press, 1994), 27–36; Charles. S. Maier, *In Search of Stability* (Cambridge: Cambridge University Press, 1987), 51; Charles Maier, "The Two Postwar Eras and the Conditions for Stability in Twentieth-Century Western Europe," *American Historical Review* 86 (April 1981): 327–52.

72. Nolan, *Visions of Modernity,* 27–36.

73. Karl Polanyi, *The Great Transformation* (Boston: Beacon Press, 2001).

74. David Milton, *The Politics of U.S. Labor: From the Great Depression to the New Deal* (New York: Monthly Review Press, 1982).

75. Robert H. Zieger, *The CIO, 1935–1955* (Chapel Hill: University of North Carolina Press, 1997), 38–68.

76. Milton, *The Politics of U.S. Labor,* 90–105.

77. Ibid., 106–13.

78. John L. Lewis, "The Rights of Labor," September 3, 1937, the Papers of John L. Lewis (1916–1961), Folder 86, Special Collections Department, University of Iowa Libraries.

79. Zieger, *The CIO,* 146.

80. Ibid.

81. Black and Silver, *Building a Better World,* 98–104.

82. Ibid.

83. Ibid., 104.

84. Ibid.

85. Ibid.

86. Joe Ashby, *Organized Labor and the Mexican Revolution under Lázaro Cárdenas* (Chapel Hill: University of North Carolina Press, 1967).

87. Kevin J. Middlebrook, *The Paradox of Revolution: Labor, the State and Authoritarianism in Mexico* (Baltimore: Johns Hopkins University Press, 1995), 72–99.

88. Vázquez and Meyer, *The United States and Mexico,* 126–52.

89. Gilbert G. González, *Mexican Consuls and Labor Organizing: Imperial Politics in the American Southwest* (Austin: University of Texas Press, 1999).

90. *United Mine Workers Journal,* September 15, 1939.

91. Ibid.

92. Caulfield, *Mexican Workers and the State,* 72.

93. Serafino Romualdi, *Presidents and Peons: Recollections of a Labor Ambassador in Latin America* (New York: Funk and Wagnalls, 1967), 72–73.

94. Ruth Adler, "La administración obrera en los Ferrocarriles Nacionales de México," *Revista Mexicana de Sociología* 50, no. 3 (1988): 97–124.

95. Presidencia de la República, *50 Años,* 34.

96. Michael Snodgrass, "New Rules for Unions: Mexico's Steelworkers Confront Privatization and the Neoliberal Challenge," *Labor* 4, no. 3 (Fall 2007): 81–103.

97. Carlos Salas and Teresa Rendón, "La distribución del ingreso," in Agustín Herrera and Lorea San Martín, eds., *México a cincuenta años de la expropiación petrolera* (Mexico, DF: UNAM, 1989), 223.

98. Commission for Labor Cooperation, *Labor Relations Law in North America* (Washington, DC: Commission for Labor Cooperation, 2000), 99.

99. Middlebrook, *The Paradox of Revolution,* 164.

100. Karl Polanyi, *The Great Transformation,* 2nd ed. (Boston: Beacon Press, 2001).

101. Charles Maier, "The Politics of Productivity," *International Organization* 31 (Autumn 1977): 607–33.

102. Robert Brenner, *The Boom and the Bubble: The U.S. in the World Economy* (London: Verso Books, 2002), 8–10.

103. James M. Boughton, "Harry Dexter White and the International Monetary Fund," *Finance and Development* 35, no. 3 (September 1998): 39–41.

104. Ibid.

105. Michael Goldfield and Bryan D. Palmer, "Canada's Workers Movement: Uneven Developments," *Labour/Le Travail* 59 (Spring 2007): 151; Vázquez and Meyer, *The United States and Mexico,* 153–82.

106. Steven A. Marglin and Juliet Schor, eds., *The Golden Age of Capitalism: Reinterpreting the Postwar Experience* (Oxford: Clarendon Press, 1990), 5.

107. Faux, *The Global Class War,* 88–89; Bruce Western, *Between Class and Market* (Princeton, NJ: Princeton University Press, 1999).

108. Jack Scott, *Yankee Unions, Go Home! How the AFL Helped the U.S. Build an Empire in Latin America* (Vancouver: New Star Books, 1978), 209.

109. Ibid.

110. Barbara S. Griffith, *The Crisis of American Labor: Operation Dixie and the Defeat of the CIO* (Philadelphia: Temple University Press, 1998).

111. For a good analysis and example of this trend within the United States and its eventual extension into Mexico, see Jefferson Cowie, *Capital Moves: RCA's 70-Year Quest for Cheap Labor* (New York: New Press, 2001).

112. Buhle, *Taking Care of Business*, 91–145.

113. Scott, *Yankee Unioins Go Home!*, 197.

114. Ibid.

115. "1945–1957: A Divided World," *Canada and the World: A History of Canadian Foreign Policy,* Foreign Affairs and International Trade Canada, June 8, 2007, http://www.international.gc.ca/department/history-histoire/canada8–en.asp#culture (accessed June 23, 2008).

116. Ibid.

117. Ibid.

118. Gregor Murray, "Unions: Membership, Structures, Actions, and Challenges," in Morley Gunderson, Allen Ponak, and Daphne G. Taras, eds., *Union-Management Relations in Canada* (Toronto: Addison Wesley Longman, 2001), 79–116.

119. Norman Caulfield, "Labor Control in the Declining Mexican Revolution," in Vincent Peloso, ed., *Work, Protest and Identity in Twentieth-Century Latin America* (Wilmington, DE: Scholarly Resources, 2003), 215–34.

120. Vázquez and Meyer, *The United States and Mexico*, 168–71.

121. Middlebrook, *The Paradox of Revolution*, 209–54.

122. Thomas F. O'Brien, *Making the Americas: The United States and Latin America from the Age of Revolutions to the Era of Globalization* (Albuquerque: University of New Mexico Press, 2007), 198.

123. Ibid., 220.

124. James D. Cockroft, *Mexico's Hope: An Encounter with Politics and History* (New York: Monthly Review Press, 1998), 165.

125. Caulfield, *Mexican Workers and the State*, 101–20.

126. Norman Caulfield, "Labor Relations in Mexico: Historical Legacies and Some Recent Trends," *Labor History* 45 (November 2004): 453.

127. Ibid.

128. Ibid.

129. Brenner, *The Boom and the Bubble*, 102.

130. David Brody, *Workers in Industrial America: Essays on the 20th Century Struggle* (New York: Oxford University Press, 1993), 224.

131. Ibid.; For a thorough account on the emergence of Japanese automobile manufacturing during the period, see James P. Womack, Daniel T. Jones, and Daniel Roos, *The Machine That Changed the World: The Story of Lean Production—Toyota's Secret*

Weapon in the Global Car Wars That Is Revolutionizing World Industry (New York: Free Press, 1990).

132. Caulfield, "Labor Relations in Mexico," 453.

133. Daniel Nelson, *Shifting Fortunes: The Rise and Decline of American Labor; from the 1820s to the Present* (Chicago: Ivan R. Dee, 1997), 155–63.

134. Goldfield and Palmer, "Canada's Workers Movement," 160.

135. Ibid.

136. Clarkson, *Uncle Sam and Us*, 310.

137. Goldfield and Palmer, "Canada's Workers Movement," 149–78.

138. Ibid.

139. Suzanne Payette, "Yesterday and Today: Union Membership," *Workplace Gazette* 5, no. 3 (Fall 2002): 96.

140. Brenner, *The Boom and the Bubble*, 16–24.

141. Ibid., 35–47.

Chapter 2: The Politics of Mexican Labor and Economic Development in Crisis

1. "En 180 años, sólo Alvaro Obregón y Portes Gil no hablaron al Congreso," *La Jornada,* September 1, 2006.

2. "Apertura de la televisión, exige AMLO; 'nos calumnian,' dice," *La Jornada,* August 27, 2006.

3. "Traslado en helicóptero, entrega del Informe y adiós, plan de Los Pinos," *La Jornada,* September 1, 2006.

4. "Avala el PRD que sus legisladores impidan a Fox rendir su Informe," *La Jornada,* September 1, 2006.

5. "Virtual estado excepción rodeo la fallada lectura," *La Jornada,* September 2, 2006.

6. Ibid.

7. "Amaga AN con solicitar retiro de registro a PRD," *La Jornada,* September 2, 2006.

8. This assessment of Fox's presidency is based on numerous data found in Vicente Fox Quesada, *Sexto Informe de Gobierno* (Mexico, DF: Congreso de México, 2006), 222–66.

9. "Evadió Abascal obligación de resolver conflicto de Oaxaca," *La Jornada,* September 1, 2006.

10. "Calderón Faces Difficult Challenges," *Wall Street Journal,* August 31, 2006.

11. U.S. Department of State, "2007 Investment Climate: Mexico," August 27, 2007, http://www.state.gov/e/eeb/ifd/2007/80727.htm (accessed September 30, 2007).

12. For a study of the history of the Mexican presidency, see Enrique Krauze, *Mexico: Biography of Power* (New York: Harper Perennial, 1998).

13. Ibid.

14. Ibid.

15. This interpretation of the Mexican Revolution and what followed is advanced in Donald C. Hodges and Ross Gandy, *Mexico, the End of the Revolution* (Westport, CT: Praeger Press, 2001).

16. Gary Gereffi, "Mexico's Industrial Development: Climbing Ahead or Falling Behind in the World Economy?," in Kevin J. Middlebrook and Eduardo Zepeda, eds., *Confronting Development: Assessing Mexico's Economic and Social Policy Challenges* (Palo Alto, CA: Stanford University Press, 2003), 198.

17. Hodges and Gandy, *Mexico.*

18. Kevin J. Middlebrook and Eduardo Zepeda, eds., *Confronting Development: Assessing Mexico's Economic and Social Policy Challenges* (Palo Alto, CA: Stanford University Press, 2003); Russell Crandall, Guadalupe Paz, and Riordan Roett, eds., *Mexico's Democracy at Work: Political and Economic Dynamics* (Boulder, CO: Lynne Rienner, 2004); Gerardo Otero, ed., *Mexico in Transition: Neoliberal Globalism, the State and Civil Society* (London: Zed Books, 2005).

19. Peter Smith, "Mexico Since 1946," in Leslie Bethell, ed., *Mexico Since Independence* (Cambridge: Cambridge University Press, 1981), 376–79.

20. Hodges and Gandy, *Mexico,* 151–87.

21. David M. Gould, "Mexico's Crisis: Looking Back to Assess the Future," *Economic Review: Second Quarter 1995* (Dallas: Federal Reserve Bank, 1995), 5.

22. Gavin Capps and Prodromos Panayiotopoulos, eds., *World Development: An Introduction* (London: Pluto Press, 2001), 45–52.

23. Jorge Carrillo and María Eugenia de la O, "Las dimensiones del trabajo en la Industria Maquiladora," in Enrique de la Garza and Carlos Salas, eds., *La situación del trabajo en México, 2003* (Mexico, DF: Plaza y Valdés, 2003), 297–99.

24. Ibid., 300–302.

25. Ibid.

26. Enrique de la Garza Toledo, "Estructura industrial y condiciones de trabajo en la manufactura," in Enrique de la Garza and Carlos Salas, eds., *La situación del trabajo en México, 2003* (Mexico, DF: Plaza y Valdés, 2003), 251–72.

27. Enrique Hernández Laos, Nora N. Garro Bordonaro, and Ignacio Llamas Huitrón, *Productividad y mercado de trabajo en México* (Mexico, DF: Plaza y Valdés, 2000), 64–65, 267; Julio Boltvinik, "Nada qué festejar," *La Jornada,* May 5, 2000.

28. Jeffrey Bortz and Marcos Aguila, "Earning a Living: A History of Real Wage Studies in Twentieth-Century Mexico," *Latin American Research Review* 41, no. 2 (June 2006): 113–38.

29. Ibid.

30. For analysis of the birth of the PRD, see Kathleen Bruhn, *Taking on Goliath: The Emergence of a New Left Party and the Struggle for Democracy in Mexico* (University Park, PA: Penn State University Press, 1997).

31. Organization for Economic Cooperation and Development, *Economic Survey*

of Mexico: 1991/1992 (Paris: Organization for Economic Cooperation and Development, 1992), 89.

32. Hodges and Gandy, *Mexico,* 132.

33. Ibid.

34. Kevin J. Middlebrook and Cirila Quintero Ramirez, "Conflict Resolution in the Mexican Labor Courts: An Examination of Local Conciliation and Arbitration Boards in Chihuahua and Tamaulipas," U.S. Department of Labor: International Bureau of Labor Affairs (ILAB), December 1996, http://www.dol.gov/ilab/media/reports/nao/conflictresolution.htm#iiia (accessed July 31, 2007).

35. George W. Grayson, *The Mexican Labor Machine: Power, Politics, and Patronage* (Washington, DC: Center for Strategic and International Studies, 1989), 2–4; Dan LaBotz, *Mask of Democracy: Labor Suppression in Mexico Today* (Boston: South End Press, 1992), 101–60.

36. Enrique de la Garza Toledo and Alfonso Bouzas, "Flexibilidad del trabajo y contratacion colectiva en México," *Revista Mexicana de Sociología* 60, no. 3 (July–September 1998): 87–122.

37. Anthony DePalma, "Mexico's Unions, Frail Now, Face Trade Pact Blows," *New York Times,* December 14, 1993.

38. Francisco Hernández Juárez and María Xelhauntzi López, *El sindicalismo en la reforma del Estado: Una Visión de la Modernización de México* (Mexico, DF: Fondo de la Cultura Económica, 1993), 121.

39. Robert E. Scott, Carlos Salas, and Bruce Campbell, "Revisiting NAFTA: Still Not Working for North America's Workers," Economic Policy Institute, September 28, 2006, http://www.epi.org/content.cfm/bp173 (accessed May 2, 2007).

40. De la Garza Toledo and Bouzas, "Flexibilidad del trabajo," 87–122.

41. Hodges and Gandy, *Mexico,* 132.

42. Ibid., 133.

43. Ibid., 134–37.

44. Enrique de la Garza Toledo, "La crisis de los modelos sindicales en México y sus opciones," in Enrique de la Garza and Salas Carlos, eds., *La Situación del trabajo en México, 2003* (Mexico, DF: Plaza y Valdés, 2003), 349–77.

45. Norman Caulfield, "Labor Relations in Mexico: Historical Legacies and Some Recent Trends," *Labor History* 45, no. 4 (November 2004): 458; Organization of Economic Cooperation and Development (OECD), *OECD Economic Surveys: México* (Paris: OECD, 1997), 89.

46. Enrique Hernández Laos, "The Growth of Real Salaries and Productivity in Mexico: A Microeconomic Approach," in Commission for Labor Cooperation, *Incomes and Productivity in North America: Papers from the 2000 Seminar* (Washington, DC: Commission for Labor Cooperation, 2000), 215–50; Secretaría del Trabajo y Previsión Social, "Convenios con bono de productividad en la jurisdicción federal, 1998–2007," April 2007, http://www.stps.gob.mx/inf_sector.htm (accessed July 31, 2007).

47. David Fairris and Edward Levine, "Declining Union Density in Mexico, 1984–2000," *Monthly Labor Review* 127, no. 9 (September 2004): 10–17.

48. Martin Dumas, "Recent Trends in Union Density," Commission for Labor Cooperation, August 2003, http://new.naalc.org/index.cfm?page=293 (accessed September 12, 2008).

49. Ibid.

50. De la Garza Toledo, "La crisis de los modelos sindicales en México," 350.

51. International Labour Organization, *Decent Work and the Informal Economy* (Geneva: International Labour Conference, 90th Session, 2002), 127.

52. Mexico Startup Services, Startup Consulting Services, 2008, http://www.mexicostartupservices.com/startup.php (accessed July 31, 2008).

53. María Xelhuantzi López, *Democracy on Hold: The Freedom of Union Association and Protection Contracts in Mexico* (Washington, DC: Communications Workers of America, 2002), 3, 71.

54. Norman Caulfield, "Work Stoppages in North America," *Commission for Labor Cooperation,* October 2003, http://www.naalc.org/english/briefs.shtml (accessed June 27, 2007).

55. For excellent analysis and discussion of the dynamics surrounding these developments, see Roderic Ai Camp, *Politics in Mexico: The Democratic Consolidation,* 5th ed. (New York: Oxford University Press, 2006).

56. Ibid.

57. For insight into the intraelite struggle in Mexico during this period and especially how the PAN and the Monterrey business model of the Mexican North captured the reigns of the federal government, see Marcela Hernández Romo, *La Cultura Empresarial en México* (Mexico, DF: Miguel Angel Porrúa, 2004); Michael J. Ard, *An Eternal Struggle: How the National Action Party Transformed Mexican Politics* (Westport, CT: Praeger Press, 2003).

58. Gerardo Albarrán de Alba, "El gobierno, mentiroso, tomó partido y rompió un acuerdo histórico con desacatos, artimañas y retractaciones: Muñoz Ledo (política mexicana)," *Proceso,* November 10, 1996.

59. Vicente Fox, *Fox a los pinos* (Barcelona: Grupo Oceano, 1999).

60. Al Giordano, "Mexico's Presidential Swindle," *New Left Review* 41 (September–October 2006): 11.

61. Hernández Laos, "The Growth of Real Salaries and Productivity in Mexico," 215–50; Secretaría del Trabajo y Previsión Social, "Convenios con bono de productividad en la jurisdiccion federal, 1998–2007," *Estadísticas Laborales,* April 2007, http://www.stps.gob.mx/inf_sector.htm (accessed July 31, 2007).

62. Secretaría del Trabajo y Previsión Social, "Contratos colectivos por central obrera," February 2008, http://www.stps.gob.mx/DGIET/web/menu_infsector.htm (accessed September 5, 2008).

63. Enrique de la Garza, "Manufacturing Neoliberalism: Industrial Relations, Trade

Union Corporatism, and Politics," in Gerardo Otero, ed., *Mexico in Transition: Neoliberal Globalism, the State, and Civil Society* (New York: Zed Books, 2004), 104–20.

64. Ibid.

65. Demetrios G. Papademetriou, John J. Audley, Sandra Polaski, and Scott Vaughan, *NAFTA's Promise and Reality: Lessons from Mexico for the Hemisphere* (Washington, DC: Carnegie International Endowment for the Peace, 2004), 24; Sandra Polaski, "The Employment Consequences of NAFTA," September 11, 2006, http://www.carnegieendowment.org/publications/index.cfm? (accessed May 1, 2007).

66. Joseph E. Stiglitz, "The Broken Promise of NAFTA," *New York Times*, January 6, 2004.

67. The World Bank Group, *Entering the 21st Century: World Development Report 1999/2000* (Washington, DC: World Bank, 2000), 239.

68. Ibid., 237.

69. Norman Caulfield, "Benefits in North America," Commission for Labor Cooperation, September 2004, http://new.naalc.org/index.cfm?page=293 (accessed September 12, 2008).

70. George W. Grayson, *Mexican Messiah: Andrés Manuel López Obrador* (University Park: Penn State University Press, 2007).

71. Carlos Torres, Daniela Morales, Antonio Aguilera, and E. Martinez, "Deja 2 muertos y más de 40 heridos desalojo de mineros en Michoacán," *La Jornada*, April 21, 2006.

72. Ginger Thompson, "Mexican Mine Disaster Brings Charges of Collusion," *New York Times*, May 6, 2006.

73. Ibid.

74. David Bacon, "Mexican Workers Want a Recount," *San Francisco Chronicle*, July 17, 2006.

75. David Bacon, "Mexican Miners' Strike for Life," *The American Prospect*, October 1, 2007, http://www.prospect.org/cs/articles?article=mexican_miners_strike_for_life (accessed September 8, 2008); Adriana Arai and Alex Emery, "Grupo Mexico Seeks to Fire 2,200 Striking Workers," *Bloomberg News*, August 10, 2007, http://www.bloomberg.com/apps/news?pid=20601086&sid=aglwKh.UVgjo&refer=news (accessed August 12, 2007).

Chapter 3: Mexican Labor and Workers' Rights under NAFTA and NAALC

1. Commission for Labor Cooperation, *North American Agreement on Labor Cooperation between the Government of the United States of America, the Government of Canada and the Government of the United Mexican States*, http://www.naalc.org/english/agreement.shtml (accessed May 8, 2007).

2. Ibid.

3. Ibid.

4. Ibid.

5. Ibid.

6. Commission for Labor Cooperation, *Labor Relations Law in North America* (Washington, DC: Commission for Labor Cooperation, 2000), 100–103.

7. Ibid.

8. Graciela Bensusán, *El Modelo Mexicano de Regulación Laboral* (Mexico, DF: FLACSO/UAM/Friederich Ebert Stiftung/Plaza y Valdés, 2000), 67.

9. Ibid.

10. Enrique de la Garza Toledo, "Reconversión industrial y cambio en el patrón de relaciones laborales en México," in Arturo Anguiano, ed., *La modernización de México* (Mexico, DF: Universidad Autónoma Metropolitana, 1990), 303–14.

11. Commission for Labor Cooperation, *Labor Relations Law*, 103.

12. Ibid.

13. Ibid.

14. U.S. Department of Labor, "Overview," Status of Submissions under the North American Agreement on Labor Cooperation (NAALC), Bureau of International Labor Affairs, September 2007, http://www.dol.gov/ilab/programs/nao/submissions. htm (accessed July 28, 2008).

15. William C. Gruben, "Was NAFTA behind Mexico's High Maquiladora Growth?" *Economic and Financial Review: Third Quarter 2001* (Dallas, TX: Federal Reserve Bank of Dallas, 2001), 11.

16. Jorge Carrillo and María Eugenia de la O, "Las dimensiones del trabajo en la Industria maquiladora de exportación en México," in Enrique de la Garza and Carlos Salas, *Situación del trabajo en México, 2003* (Mexico, DF: Plaza y Valdés), 297–321.

17. Norman Caulfield, "Labor Relations in Mexico: Historical Legacies and Some Recent Trends," *Labor History* 45, no. 4 (November 2004): 454.

18. Ibid.

19. Carrillo and de la O, "Las dimensiones del trabajo en la Industria maquiladora," 297–321.

20. Ibid.

21. Jesus Cañas, Roberto Coronado, and Robert W. Gilmer, "Maquiladora Recovery: Lessons for the Future," *Southwest Economy* 2 (March/April 2007): 5.

22. Federal Reserve Bank of Dallas, "Beyond the Border: The Giant in Mexico's Rearview Mirror," *Southwest Economy* 6 (March/April 2003): 10.

23. Kathryn Kopinak, *Desert Capitalism: What are the Maquiladoras?* (Montreal: Black Rose Books, 1996), 183.

24. U.S. Department of Labor, "U.S. NAO Submissions No. 940001 and 940002 (Honeywell and General Electric)," Status of Submissions under the North American Agreement on Labor Cooperation (NAALC), U.S. Department of Labor, International Bureau of Labor Affairs, September 2007, http://www.dol.gov/ilab/programs/nao/ status.htm#iia1 (accessed August 3, 2008).

25. U.S. Department of Labor, "NAO Submission #940003: Follow-Up Report,"

Status of Submissions under the North American Agreement on Labor Cooperation (NAALC), International Bureau of Labor Affairs, September 2007, http://www.dol .gov/ilab/media/reports/nao/940003.htm (accessed September 17, 2008).

26. Ibid.

27. U.S. Department of Labor, "U.S. NAO Submission 9602 (Maxi-Switch)," Status of Submissions under the North American Agreement on Labor Cooperation (NAALC), International Bureau of Labor Affairs, September 2007, http://www.dol .gov/ilab/programs/nao/status.htm#iia5 (accessed September 17, 2008).

28. Ibid.

29. U.S. Department of Labor, "Public Report of Review of NAO Submission No. 9701," International Bureau of Labor Affairs, September 2007, http://www.dol.gov/ ilab/media/reports/nao/pubrep9701.htm (accessed September 17, 2008).

30. Ibid.

31. U.S. Department of Labor, "Public Report of Review of NAO Submission No. 9702," International Bureau of Labor Affairs, September 2007, http://www.dol.gov/ ilab/media/reports/nao/pubrep9702.htm (accessed September 17, 2008).

32. Ibid.

33. David Bacon, *The Children of NAFTA: Labor Wars on the U.S./Mexico Border* (Berkeley and Los Angeles: University of California Press, 2004), 118.

34. U.S. Department of Labor, "U.S. NAO Submission No. 9073 (ITAPSA)," Status of Submissions under the North American Agreement on Labor Cooperation (NAALC), Bureau of International Labor Affairs, September 2007, http://www.dol. gov/ilab/programs/nao/status.htm#iia8 (accessed September 16, 2008).

35. Ibid.

36. Ibid.

37. Bacon, *The Children of NAFTA*, 208–9.

38. For an excellent account of the history of the Revolutionary National Union of Euzkadi Workers (SNRTE) and the recent struggles of Euzkadi workers, see "Ex trabajadores de Euzkadi recibirán premio en Suiza," *La Jornada*, December 18, 2005.

39. Ibid.

40. "Breve historia del sindicato de Euzkadi: El sentimiento de unidad dio vida al sindicato," Sindicato nacional revolucionario de trabajadores de la compañía Hulera, 2005, http://mx.geocities.com/snrte2002/archivos/historia.htm (accessed October 3, 2007).

41. "Cronología del movimiento de huelga del Sindicato Nacional Revolucionario de Trabajadores de Euzkadi (2001–2005)," Sindicato nacional revolucionario de trabajadores de la compañía Hulera, 2005, http://mx.geocities.com/snrte2002/ (accessed September 23, 2007).

42. Amnesty International, "Mexico: Killings and Abductions of Women in Ciudad Juarez and the City of Chihuahua—The Struggle for Justice Goes On," February 20, 2006, http://www.amnestyusa.org/women/juarez/ (accessed July 30, 2007).

43. Jesus Cañas and Robert W. Gilmer, "Spotlight: Maquiladora Data Mexican Reform Clouds View of Key Industry," *Southwest Economy* 3 (May/June 2007): 10.

44. Ibid.

45. Secretaría del Trabajo y Previsión Social, "Remuneraciones Medias en la Industria Maquiladora de Exportación por Entidad Federativa," July 31, 2007, http://www.stps.gob.mx/DGIET/web/menu_infsector.htm (accessed September 17, 2008).

46. Human Resources and Social Development Canada, "Review of Public Communication CAN 2003–1: Analysis and Findings," May 11, 2005, http://www.hrsdc.gc.ca/en/lp/spila/ialc/pcnaalc/13analysis_findings.shtml (accessed July 30, 2007); U.S. Department of Labor, "U.S. NAO Submission 2003–1 (Puebla)," Status of Submissions under the North American Agreement on Labor Cooperation (NAALC), Bureau of International Labor Affairs, September 2007, http://www.dol.gov/ilab/programs/nao/status.htm#iia16 (accessed July 30, 2007).

47. U.S. Department of Labor, "U.S. NAO Submission 2003–1 (Puebla)."

48. Ibid.

49. "UE President Hovis Letter to Secretary Chao," Maquiladora Health and Safety Network, July 24, 2002, http://mhssn.igc.org/naftal1.htm (accessed August 3, 2007).

50. U.S. Department of Labor, "U.S. NAO Public Submission US2005–01," U.S. Department of Labor, Bureau of International Labor Affairs, September 2007, http://www.dol.gov/ilab/media/reports/nao/submissions/Sub2005-01.htm (accessed September 16, 2008).

51. Ibid.

52. Ibid.

53. Ibid.

54. Ibid.

55. David Bacon, "Right to Strike Imperiled in Cananea," *The Nation*, January 25, 2008.

56. Ibid.

57. Ibid.

Chapter 4: Labor Mobility and Workers' Rights in North America

1. Randal C. Archibold, "The Immigration Debate: The Overview; Immigrants Take to U.S. Streets in Show of Strength," *New York Times*, May 2, 2006.

2. "Repudio a la política laboral de Fox, tónica durante marchas en los estados," *La Jornada*, May 2, 2006.

3. Ibid.

4. Randal C. Archibold, "Immigrant Rights Rallies Smaller than Last Year," *New York Times*, May 2, 2007.

5. Demetrios G. Papademetriou, John J. Audley, Sandra Polaski, and Scott Vaughan,

NAFTA's Promise and Reality: Lessons from Mexico for the Hemisphere (Washington, DC: Carnegie International Endowment for the Peace, 2004), 5–6.

6. Jeff Faux, *The Global Class War: How America's Bipartisan Elite Lost Our Future—and What It Will Take to Win It Back* (Hoboken, NJ: John Wiley and Sons, 2006), 30–48.

7. Lawrence Mishel, Jared Bernstein, and Sylvia Alegretto, *The State of Working America, 2006/2007* (Ithaca, NY: Cornell University Press, 2007), 109–218.

8. Two notable examples of this are found in Lou Dobbs, *War on the Middle Class: How the Government, Big Business, and Special Interest Groups Are Waging War on the American Dream and How to Fight Back* (New York: Viking Adult, 2006); Patrick J. Buchanan, *State of Emergency: The Third World Invasion and Conquest of America* (New York: Thomas Dunne Books, 2006).

9. George J. Borjas, *Heaven's Door: Immigration Policy and the American Economy* (Princeton, NJ: Princeton University Press, 2001).

10. Organisation for Economic Cooperation and Development, "Globalisation, Jobs and Wages," *OECD Policy Brief* (June 2007), 1–8.

11. Joanne Steinberg, María Elena Vicario, and the Commission for Labor Cooperation, *North American Labor Markets: A Comparative Profile* (Lanham, MD: Bernam Press, 1997); Maria Elena Vicario, Sandra Polaski, and Dalil Maschino, *North American Labor Markets: Main Changes Since NAFTA* (Washington, DC: Commission for Labor Cooperation, 2003); Commission for Labor Cooperation, *Labor Markets,* 3rd ed. (Washington, DC: Commission for Labor Cooperation, 2007).

12. Ibid.

13. Organisation for Economic Cooperation and Development, "Globalization, Jobs and Wages," 1–8.

14. Andres Solimano, "International Migration and the Global Economic Order: An Overview," Policy Research Working Paper Series No. 2720 (Washington, DC: World Bank, 2001).

15. Heather Boushey, Shawn Fremstad, Rachel Gragg, and Margy Waller, "Understanding Low-Wage Work in the United States," Center for Economic Policy and Research, March 2007, http://www.cepr.net/index.php/publications/reports/understanding-low-wage-work-in-the-united-states/ (accessed August 14, 2008).

16. "What Accounts for the Decline in Manufacturing Employment?," Congressional Budget Office, February 18, 2004, http://www.cbo.gov/ftpdoc.cfm?index=5078&type=0 (accessed July 13, 2007).

17. For an excellent overview on the history of organized labor in the United States and immigrants, see Vernon Briggs, *Immigration and American Unionism* (Ithaca, NY: ILR Press, 2001).

18. Jennifer Gordon, "Transnational Labor Citizenship," *Southern California Law Review* 80 (2007): 531–34.

19. Rick Fantasia and Kim Voss, *Hard Work: Remaking the American Labor Move-*

ment (Berkeley and Los Angeles: University of California Press, 2004); Richard W. Hurd, Lowell Turner, and Harry C. Katz, eds., *Rekindling the Movement: Labor's Quest for Relevance in the Twenty-First Century* (Ithaca, NY: ILR Press, 2001).

20. Mishel, Bernstein, and Allegretto, *The State of Working America, 2006/2007,* 183.

21. Bureau of Labor Statistics, "Union Affiliation Data, Current Population Survey-CPS, Table 1," June 21, 2007, http://www.bls.gov/cps/cpslutabs.htm (accessed July 15, 2007).

22. AFL-CIO, "March 2006 Resolution Supporting Responsible Reform of Immigration Laws," March 2006, http://www.aflcio.org/issues/civilrights/immigration/ (accessed May 4, 2007).

23. AFL-CIO, "AFL-CIO Policy on Immigration," May 2007, http://www.aflcio.org/issues/civilrights/immigration/ (accessed July 13, 2007).

24. Robin Emmott, "More Migrants Die as U.S. Tightens Border Security," Reuters, *Yahoo News,* July 12, 2007, http://news.yahoo.com/s/nm/20070712/ts_nm/mexico_usa_deaths_dc&printer=1;_ylt=Asts3M4js9kWGUPlwHP8C9Vg.3QA (accessed July 13, 2007).

25. Southern Poverty Law Center, "Close to Slavery: Guestworker Programs in the United States," March 12, 2007, http://www.splcenter.org/legal/guestreport/index.jsp (accessed May 3, 2007).

26. Krissah Williams, "Unions Split on Immigrant Workers," *Washington Post,* January 27, 2007; David Bacon, "Which Side Are You On?," *MRZINE,* February 2, 2007, http://mrzine.monthlyreview.org/bacon020207.html (accessed May 16, 2007).

27. Thomas J. Donohue and Andy Stern, "Immigration Needs Strange Bedfellows," *The Politico,* June 5, 2007, http://dyn.politico.com/printstory.cfm?uuid=F883D091–3048–5C12–00B54388C525C1F2 (accessed July 4, 2007).

28. Ibid.

29. Ibid.

30. "Hoffa Praises Senate for Blocking Mexican Truck Program," Teamsters News, Press Releases and Headline News, September 11, 2007, http://www.teamster.org/press-release.aspx?id=9428 (accessed November 12, 2007).

31. "NIOSH Program Portfolio: Transportation, Warehousing and Utilities," National Institute for Occupational Safety and Health, April 25, 2008, http://www.cdc.gov/niosh/programs/twu/risks.html (accessed August 12, 2008).

32. "Hoffa Blasts Bush Plan to Open Border to Unsafe Mexican Trucks," Teamsters, News Press Releases and Headline News, February 23, 2007, http://www.teamster.org/press-release.aspx?id=7748 (accessed November 12, 2007).

33. Randal C. Archibold, "With Immigration Bill Stalled, Advocates Push Forward," *New York Times,* June 14, 2007.

34. Randal C. Archibold and Julia Preston, "Illegal Migrants Dissect Details of Senate Bill," *New York Times,* May 20, 2007.

35. Raúl Delgado Wise, "Labor and Migration Policies under Vicente Fox: Subordination to U.S. Economic and Geopolitical Interests," in Gerardo Otero, ed., *Mexico in Transition: Neoliberal Globalism* (London: Zed Books, 2004), 138–53.

36. Jeffrey Bortz and Marcos Aguila, "Earning a Living: A History of Real Wage Studies in Twentieth-Century Mexico," *Latin American Research Review* 41, no. 2 (2006): 116.

37. Gilbert G. González and Raúl A. Fernández, *A Century of Chicano History: Empire, Nations, and Migration* (New York: Routledge, 2003), 42.

38. Rodolfo Acuña, *Occupied America: A History of Chicanos* (New York: Pearson-Longman, 2004), 158.

39. Bortz and Aguila, "Earning a Living," 115.

40. Graciela Bensusán Areis, *El modelo mexicano de regulación laboral* (Mexico, DF: Plaza y Valdés, 2000). For state government legislation, see Felipe Remolina Roqueñí, *El Artículo 123 Constitucional* (Mexico, DF: Secretaría del Trabajo y Previsión Social, 2000); Felipe Remolina Roqueñí, *Evolución de las instituciones del derecho del trabajo en México* (Mexico, DF: Secretaría del Trabajo y Previsión Social, 1976).

41. Based on author's calculations from data provided in González and Fernández, *A Century of Chicano History*, 44.

42. Ibid., 135.

43. Daniel D. Arreola, "Mexican Americans," in Jesse O. McKee, ed., *Ethnicity in Contemporary America: A Geographical Appraisal* (Dubuque, IA: Kendall/Hunt, 1985), 81.

44. Carlos Salas and Teresa Rendón, "La distribución del ingreso," in Agustín Herrera and Lorea San Martín, eds., *México a cincuenta años de la expropiación petrolera* (Mexico, DF: Universidad Nacional Autónoma de México, 1989), 223.

45. Ian Roxborough, "The Urban Working Class and the Labor Movements in Latin America," in Leslie Bethell, ed., *The Cambridge History of Latin America*, vol. 4 (Cambridge: Cambridge University Press, 1984), 233–34.

46. Daniel Levy and Gabriel Szekely, *Mexico: Paradoxes of Stability and Change* (Boulder, CO: Westview Press, 1983).

47. For a comprehensive treatment of Mexican workers and their contributions to building the American labor movement during the 1930s, see Zaragosa Vargas, *Labor Rights Are Civil Rights: Mexican American Workers in Twentieth-Century America* (Princeton, NJ: Princeton University Press, 2004).

48. Gilbert G. González, *Mexican Consuls and Labor Organizing: Imperial Politics in the American Southwest* (Austin: University of Texas Press, 1999).

49. Vargas, *Labor Rights are Civil Rights*.

50. Levy and Szekely, *Mexico: Paradoxes of Stability and Change*, 127.

51. For an excellent overview and analysis of the Bracero Program, see Gilbert González, *Guest Workers or Colonized Labor?: Mexican Labor Migration to the United States* (New York: Paradigm, 2007).

52. Delgado Wise, "Labor and Migration Policies under Vicente Fox," 141.

53. Arreola, "Mexican Americans," 81.

54. Ibid., 89.

55. For a recent study of these events, see Dan LaBotz, *Cesar Chavez and La Causa* (New York: Longman, 2005).

56. Papademetriou, Audley, Polaski, and Vaughan, *NAFTA's Promise and Reality,* 45.

57. Ibid.

58. Ibid., 48.

59. Ibid.

60. Jeffrey S. Passel and Roberto Suro, "Rise, Peak and Decline: Trends in U.S. Immigration 1992–2004," Pew Hispanic Center, Reports and Fact Sheets, September 27, 2005, http://pewhispanic.org/reports/archive/ (accessed August 6, 2007).

61. Pew Hispanic Center, "A Statistical Portrait of the Foreign-Born Population at Mid-Decade," Reports and Fact Sheets, September 18, 2006, http://pewhispanic.org/reports/foreignborn/ (accessed August 6, 2007).

62. Jeffrey S. Passel, "Growing Share of Immigrants Choosing Naturalization," Pew Hispanic Center, Reports and Fact Sheets, March 28, 2007, http://pewhispanic.org/reports/report.php?ReportID=74 (accessed May 3, 2007).

63. Papademetriou, Audley, Polaski, and Vaughan, *NAFTA's Promise and Reality,* 49.

64. Passel, "Growing Share of Immigrants Choosing Naturalization."

65. Sandra Polaski, "The Employment Consequences of NAFTA," September 11, 2006, http://www.carnegieendowment.org/publications/index.cfm? (accessed May 1, 2007).

66. Laura Juárez Sánchez, "Neoliberalismo económico y empleo," *Trabajadores en línea* 48 (May-June, 2005), La Universidad Obrera de México, http://www.uom.edu.mx/trabajadores/48laura.htm (accessed April 12, 2007).

67. Papademetriou, Audley, Polaski, and Vaughan, *NAFTA's Promise and Reality,* 24.

68. Ibid.

69. Juárez Sánchez, "Neoliberalismo económico y empleo."

70. Raúl Trejo Delarbre, *Crónica del sindicalismo en México, 1976–1988* (Mexico, DF: Siglo Veintiuno Editores, 1990), 30.

71. Joseph E. Stiglitz, "The Broken Promise of NAFTA," *New York Times,* January 6, 2004.

72. Papademetriou, Audley, Polaski, and Vaughan, *NAFTA's Promise and Reality,* 24.

73. Consejo Nacional de la Población (CONAPO), *La nueva era de las migraciones: Características de la migración internacional en México* (Mexico, DF: Conapo, 2004), 1–27.

74. "The North American Free Trade Agreement (NAFTA): Effects on Human

Rights," International Federation of Human Rights, November 5, 2006, http://www .fidh.org/article.php3?id_article=3304 (accessed April 24, 2007).

75. "Bank of Mexico Cuts 2007 GDP Growth Estimate," *International Herald Tribune,* April 30, 2007.

76. Papademetriou, Audley, Polaski, and Vaughan, *NAFTA's Promise and Reality,* 40, 46.

77. Commission for Labor Cooperation, *North American Agreement on Labor Cooperation between the Government of the United States of America, the Government of Canada and the Government of the United Mexican States,* http://www.naalc.org/ english/agreement.shtml (accessed May 8, 2007).

78. "Mexican NAO Submission 9501," Status of Submissions under the North American Agreement on Labor Cooperation (NAALC), U.S. Department of Labor, Bureau of International Labor Affairs, September 2007, http://www.dol.gov/ilab/ programs/nao/status.htm#iib1 (accessed August 14, 2008).

79. U.S. Department of Labor, "Petition on Labor Law Matters Arising in the United States," Bureau of International Labor Affairs, April 13, 2005, http://www.dol.gov/ ilab/media/reports/nao/submissions/2005-01petition.htm (accessed July 13, 2007).

80. Ibid.

81. Ibid.

82. Ibid.

83. Oxfam America, "Farmworker Victory in North Carolina," Oxfam America, September 16, 2004, http://www.oxfamamerica.org/newsandpublications/news_ updates/archive2004/news_update.2004-09-28.2490092697/?searchterm=floc (accessed July 13, 2007).

84. Ibid.

85. Ibid.

86. Leon Fink, *The Maya of Morganton* (Chapel Hill: University of North Carolina Press, 2003).

87. "Illegal Immigrants Help Unionize a Hotel but Face Deportation," *New York Times,* January 12, 2001.

88. Justine Juson, *The Intersection of Immigration Law and Labor Law: The Hoffman Plastic Case and Beyond* (Washington, DC: BNA Books, 2002).

89. "UMWA Members Ratify New BCOA Contract," *UMWA Journal,* January-February 2003, http://www.umwa.org/journal/VOL113NO1/jan1.shtml (accessed July 13, 2007).

90. Guillermo Esquivel and Anne Carroll, "Utah Miners Affirm Support for UMWA Representation at Meeting of Boss 'Union,'" *The Militant* 68, no. 34 (September 21, 2004).

91. Ibid.

92. Ruth Milkman, *L.A. Story: Immigrant Workers and the Future of the U.S. Labor Movement* (New York: Russell Sage Foundation Press, 2006).

93. United Food and Commercial Workers, "The Case against Smithfield," January

2008, http://www.ufcw.org/working_america/case_against_smithfield/case_against_smthfld.cfm (accessed May 8, 2008).

94. Dan LaBotz, "Farm Labor Organizer is Murdered in Mexico," *Labor Notes* 338 (May 2007), http://labornotes.org/node/800 (accessed September 12, 2008).

95. Faux, *The Global Class War*, 221.

Chapter 5: The Crisis of Union-Management Relations in the United States and Canada

1. Charlotte Todes, *William H. Sylvis and the National Labor Union* (New York: International, 1942), 40.

2. "New Industrial Relations," *Business Week*, May 11, 1981, 85.

3. Ibid.

4. Thomas A. Kochan, Harry C. Katz, and Robert B. McKersie, *The Transformation of American Industrial Relations* (New York: Basic Books, 1986), 227.

5. Harry C. Katz and Hoyt N. Wheeler, "Employment Relations in the United States of America," in Greg J. Bamber, Russell D. Lansbury, and Nick Wailes, eds., *International and Comparative Employment Relations: Globalisation and the Developed Market Economies*, 4th ed. (London: Sage, 2004), 67–90.

6. Morley Gunderson and Douglas Hyatt, "Union Impact on Compensation, Productivity and Management of the Organization," in Morley Gunderson, Allen Ponak, and Daphne G. Taras, eds., *Union-Management Relations in Canada* (Toronto: Addison Wesley Longman, 2001), 385–413; Paula B. Voos, "An Economic Perspective on Contemporary Trends in Collective Bargaining," in Paula B. Voos, *Contemporary Collective Bargaining in the Private Sector* (Madison, WI: Industrial Relations Research Association, 1994), 1–23.

7. Harry C. Katz and Owen Darbishire, *Converging Divergences: Worldwide Changes in Employment Systems* (Ithaca, NY: Cornell University Press, 2002).

8. John T. Dunlop, "The Bargaining Table," in Richard B. Morris, ed., *The U.S. Department of Labor Bicentennial History of the American Worker* (Washington, DC: U.S. Government Printing Office, 1976), 269–72.

9. Albert E. Schwenk, "Compensation in the 1970s," Bureau of Labor Statistics, January 30, 2003, http://www.bls.gov/opub/cwc/cm20030124ar05p1.htm (accessed August 5, 2008).

10. Barry Bluestone and Bennett Harrison, *The Deindustrialization of America: Plant Closing, Community Abandonment, and the Dismantling of Basic Industry* (New York: Basic Books, 1982).

11. Bennett Harrison and Barry Bluestone, *The Great U-Turn: Corporate Restructuring and the Polarizing of America* (New York: Basic Books, 1988).

12. Bureau of Labor Statistics, "Table 1: Work Stoppages Involving 1,000 or More Workers, 1947–2007," Economic News Release, February 13, 2008, http://www.bls.gov/news.release/wkstp.t01.htm (accessed August 16, 2008).

13. Melvyn Dubofsky and Foster Rhea Dulles, *Labor in America: A History* (Wheeling, IL: Harlan-Davidson), 386.

14. Ibid.

15. AFL-CIO Committee on the Evolution of Work, *The Future of Work: A Report by the AFL-CIO Committee on the Evolution of Work* (Washington, DC: AFL-CIO, 1983).

16. AFL-CIO Committee on the Evolution of Work, *The Changing Situation of Workers and Their Unions: A Report by the AFL-CIO Committee on the Evolution of Work* (Washington, DC: AFL-CIO, 1985).

17. Bureau of Labor Statistics, "Table 1: Work Stoppages Involving 1,000 or More Workers, 1947–2007."

18. Steven Greenhouse, "Strikes at 50-Year Low," *New York Times,* January 29, 1996.

19. John Logan, "Labor's Last Stand in National Politics? The Campaign for Striker Replacement Legislation, 1990–1994," in David Lewin and Bruce Kaufman, eds., *Advances in Industrial Relations,* vol. 13 (Oxford: JAI Press, 2004), 197–256.

20. Ibid.

21. Bureau of Labor Statistics, "Major Work Stoppages in 2002," March 11, 2003, http://www.bls.gov/news.release/History/wkstp_03112003.txt (accessed August 7, 2008).

22. Bureau of Labor Statistics, "Archived Work Stoppages," July 3, 2008, http://www.bls.gov/schedule/archives/all_nr.htm#WKSTP (accessed July 31, 2008).

23. Leo Troy, "Is the U.S. Unique in the Decline of Private Sector Unionism," *Journal of Labor Research* 11, no. 2 (Spring 1990): 135.

24. Bureau of Labor Statistics, "Table 1: Current Population Survey: Historical Data for Union Affiliation," June 21, 2007, http://stats.bls.gov/cps/cpslutabs.htm (accessed July 14, 2007).

25. Leo Troy and Neil Sheflin, *U.S. Union Sourcebook: Membership, Finances, Structure, Directory* (West Orange, NJ: Industrial Relations and Research Data, 1985).

26. Bureau of Labor Statistics, "Current Population Survey: Historical Data for Union Affiliation," June 21, 2007, http://stats.bls.gov/cps/cpslutabs.htm (accessed July 14, 2007).

27. Bureau of Labor Statistics, "Table 1: Current Population Survey: Historical Data for Union Affiliation."

28. Harry Kelber, "Unions Lost 2,704 Decertification Elections in Decade, Surrendering Former Victories," *Labor Talk,* September 23, 2007, http://www.laboreducator.org/decertelections2.htm (accessed September 24, 2007).

29. John Logan, "The Union Avoidance Industry in the United States," *British Journal of Industrial Relations* 44, no. 4 (December 2006): 651–75.

30. Joseph Khan, "Clinton Imposes Tariffs on Steel Imports That Exceed Quota," *New York Times,* February 12, 2000. For an excellent overview of union support for

protectionism, see Dana Frank, *Buy American: The Untold Story of Economic Nationalism* (Boston: Beacon Press, 1999).

31. Linda A. Bell, "The Union Wage Concessions in the 1980s: The Importance of Firm-Specific Factors," *Industrial and Labor Relations Review* 48, no. 2 (January 1995): 260.

32. Linda A. Bell, "Union Concessions in the 1980s," *Federal Reserve Bank of New York Quarterly Review* (Summer 1989): 44–58.

33. Ibid.

34. George Ruben, "Labor-Management Scene in 1986 Reflects Continuing Difficulties," *Monthly Labor Review* 10, no. 1 (January 1987): 37.

35. Peter Cappelli, "Union Gains under Concession Bargaining," in *Proceedings of the IRRA 36th Annual Meeting* (Madison, WI: Industrial Relations Research Association, 1983), 297–305.

36. Bureau of National Affairs, *Sourcebook on Collective Bargaining* (Washington, DC: BNA Books, 2002), 39.

37. Kate Bronfenbrenner, "We'll Close! Plant Closings, Plant-Closing Threats, Union Organizing and NAFTA," *Multinational Monitor* 18, no. 3 (March 1997), http://www.multinationalmonitor.org/hyper/mm0397.04.html (accessed September 19, 2008).

38. Ibid.

39. "Two-Tier Wage Provisions in Collective Agreements, 2002," *Daily Labor Report*, March 25, 2003.

40. Rex Nutting, "Profits Surge to 40–Year High," Dow Jones Market Watch, March 30, 2006, http://www.marketwatch.com/News/Story/Story.aspx?guid=%7BC4257910-8351-437A-8C00-E4CF3B782091%7D&siteid=mktw&dist (accessed June 4, 2007).

41. Louis Uchitelle, "Two-Tiers, Slipping into One," *New York Times*, February 26, 2006.

42. Ibid.

43. Ibid.

44. Ibid.

45. Ibid.

46. Jerry Hirsch, "Southern California Grocery Conflict Rooted in Previous Strike," *Los Angeles Times*, April 23, 2007.

47. Ibid.

48. John W. Budd and Brian P. McCall, "The Grocery Stores Wage Distribution: A Semi-Parametric Analysis of the Role of Retailing and Labor Market Institutions," *Industrial and Labor Relations Review* 54, no. 2a (March 2001): 484–501.

49. Research-Education-Advocacy-People, "A Review of the U.S. Grocery Store Industry," March 2006, http://www.reapinc.org/index.htm (accessed May 30, 2007).

50. Andrew Galvin, "Union Protesters Underscore Supermarket Stakes: UFCW Needs to Win Concessions from Chains to Keep Members' Support," *Orange County Register*, April 20, 2007.

51. U.S. Department of Labor, "Union Reports: Online Public Disclosure Room," September 20, 2007, http://www.dol.gov/esa/regs/compliance/olms/rrlo/lmrda.htm#1 (accessed July 30, 2008).

52. "Discounts Stimulate Sales, Helping Kroger to 36% Increase in Profit for 4th Quarter," *New York Times,* March 14, 2007.

53. "Investors Pooh-Pooh 77% Safeway Profit," *San Diego Union Tribune,* February 23, 2007.

54. United Food and Commercial Workers, "Super (Market) Profits," May 30, 2007, http://www.respectworkers.com/profits (accessed July 30, 2008).

55. Ibid.

56. "Harley-Davidson and York Union Reach Agreement," Automotive.com, February 22, 2007, http://www.automotive.com/features/90/auto-news/26673/index.html (accessed June 2, 2007).

57. Ibid.

58. "Executive PayWatch Database," AFL-CIO, March 13, 2008, http://www.aflcio.org/corporatewatch/paywatch/ceou/database.cfm?tkr=HOG&pg=1 (accessed July 30, 2008).

59. "The 2005 Labor Day List: Partnerships that Work," American Rights at Work, September 2005, http://www.americanrightsatwork.org/publications/general/the-2005-labor-day-list-partnerships-that-work-20050830–323–95.html (accessed July 30, 2008).

60. John A. Fossum, *Labor Relations,* 8th ed. (New York: McGraw-Hill, 2001), 284.

61. "Goodyear United Steelworkers 2006 Master Contract Negotiations," Goodyear Contract Negotiations Web Site, December 29, 2006, http://www.goodyearnegotiations.com/ (accessed June 28, 2007).

62. Ibid.

63. Ibid.

64. James Parks, "Goodyear Workers Keep Heat on Tire Maker," AFL-CIO Blog, November 29, 2006, http://blog.aflcio.org/2006/11/29/goodyear-workers-keep-heat-on-tire-maker/ (accessed June 28, 2007).

65. "SPEEA to Picket Boeing in Chicago over Outsourcing and a Contract Offer for Kansas," *Chicago Tribune,* March 29, 2004.

66. Leslie Wayne, "Boeing Not Afraid to Say Sold Out," *New York Times,* November 28, 2006.

67. Ken Vandruff, "Cessna Moves Jobs to Mexico," *Wichita Business Journal,* September 12, 2005.

68. International Association of Machinists, "Hawker Beechcraft Plans Mexican Assembly Plant," IAM News, June 24, 2008, http://www.goiam.org/content.cfm?cID=13330 (accessed August 31, 2008).

69. Barry T. Hirsch, "Reconsidering Union Wage Effects: Surveying New Evidence on an Old Topic," *Journal of Labor Research* 25 (Spring 2004): 245–52.

70. Danny Blanchflower and Alex Bryson, "What Effect Do Unions Have on Wages Now and Would 'What Do Unions Do?' Be Surprised?" (working paper, National Bureau of Economic Research, Working Paper 9973, September 2003), http://www .nber.org/papers/w9973 (accessed May 22, 2007).

71. Steven Greenhouse and David Leonhardt, "Real Wages Fail to Match a Rise in Productivity," *New York Times,* August 28, 2006.

72. Bureau of Labor Statistics, "Tables from Employment and Earnings, B-2: Average Hours and Earnings of Production and Nonsupervisory Workers on Private Nonfarm Payrolls by Major Industry Sector, 1964 to Date," Current Employment Statistics-CES (National), August 1, 2008, http://www.bls.gov/ces/ (accessed August 31, 2008).

73. Bureau of Labor Statistics, "Productivity Change in the Nonfarm Business Sector, 1947–2007," Productivity and Costs, May 7, 2008, http://www.bls.gov/lpc/ prodybar.htm (accessed August 31, 2008).

74. Greenhouse and Leonhardt, "Real Wages Fail to Match a Rise in Productivity."

75. International Labour Organization (ILO), "New ILO Report Says U.S. Leads the World in Labor Productivity, Some Regions Are Catching Up, Most Lag Behind," Archived Press Releases, September 2, 2007, http://www.ilo.org/global/About_the_ILO/ Media_and_public_information/Press_releases/lang—en/WCMS_083976/index.htm (accessed October 12, 2007).

76. Demetrios G. Papademetriou, John J. Audley, Sandra Polaski, and Scott Vaughan, *NAFTA's Promise and Reality: Lessons from Mexico for the Hemisphere* (Washington, DC: Carnegie International Endowment for the Peace, 2004), 28.

77. Robert E. Scott, "Revisiting NAFTA: Still Not Working for North America's Workers," Economic Policy Institute, September 28, 2006, http://www.epi.org/ content.cfm/bp173#ptl (accessed May 3, 2007), 28.

78. Steven Greenhouse, "Among Dissident Union Leaders, the Backgrounds May Vary but the Vision Is the Same," *New York Times,* July 22, 2005.

79. Steven Greenhouse, "4 Major Unions Plan to Boycott A.F.L.-C.I.O. Event," *New York Times,* July 25, 2005.

80. Harry Kelber, "44 Union Heads Back Sweeney on Unity; Are Silent on Executive Council Elections," *LaborTalk,* July 15, 2005, http://www.ymlp182.com/pubarchive_ show_message.php?laboreducator+186 (accessed September 17, 2008).

81. Andy Stern, *Getting America Back on Track: A Country That Works* (New York: Free Press, 2006), 38–39.

82. Ibid., 105.

83. Ibid., 70, 105.

84. Harley Shaiken, "Unions, the Economy, and Employee Free Choice," Economic Policy Institute, Agenda for Shared Prosperity, February 22, 2007, http://www .sharedprosperity.org/bp181.html (accessed August 8, 2008).

85. Sheldon Friedman, "Why the Employee Free Choice Act Deserves Support: Response to Adams," *Labor Studies Journal* 31, no. 4 (Winter 2007): 15–22.

86. Joseph A. McCartin, "Re-Framing US Labor's Crisis: Reconsidering Structure, Strategy, and Vision," *Labour/Le Travail* 59 (Spring 2007): 133–48.

87. Susan Johnson, "Card Check or Mandatory Representation Vote? How the Type of Union Recognition Procedure Affects Union Certification Success," *Economic Journal* 12 (April 2002): 344–61.

88. Pradeep Kumar, "Industrial Relations in a New Millennium," *Workplace Gazette* 3, no. 4 (Winter 2000): 128–29.

89. Ibid.

90. Ibid.

91. Craig Heron, *The Canadian Labor Movement: A Short History* (Toronto: James Lorimer, 1989), 119.

92. Ibid., 120–27.

93. Stephen Clarkson, *Uncle Sam and Us: Globalization, Neoconservatism, and the Canadian State* (Toronto: University of Toronto Press, 2002), 25–27.

94. Errol Black and Jim Silver, *Building a Better World: An Introduction to Trade Unionism in Canada* (Halifax, NS: Fernwood, 2001), 118.

95. Bruce Campbell, Andrew Jackson, Mehrene Larudee, and Teresa Gutíerrez Haces, *Labor Market Affects Under CUFTA/NAFTA* (Geneva: International Labour Office, 1999), 1.

96. Ibid., 8–11.

97. Pradeep Kumar, Gregor Murray, and Sylvain Schetagne, "Adapting to Change: Union Priorities in the 1990s," *Workplace Gazette* 1, no. 3 (Fall 1998): 89–91.

98. Ibid.

99. Pradeep Kumar and Gregor Murray, "Union Bargaining Priorities in the New Economy: Results from the 2000 HRDC Survey on Innovation and Change in Labor Organizations in Canada," *Workplace Gazette* 4, no. 4 (Winter 2001): 44–46.

100. Ibid., 47–48.

101. Ibid., 50.

102. Morley Gunderson and Douglas Hyatt, "Canadian Public Sector Employment Relations in Transition," in Dale Belman, Morley Gunderson, and Douglas Hyatt, eds., *Public Sector Employment in a Time of Transition* (Madison, WI: Industrial Relations Research Association, 1996), 245.

103. Steven Greenhouse, "Labor Needs to Improve Conditions for Nonunion Workers, Official Warns," *New York Times,* June 23, 2008.

104. Gregor Murray, "Unions: Membership, Structures, Actions, and Challenges," in Morley Gunderson, Allen Ponak, and Daphne G. Taras, eds., *Union-Management Relations in Canada* (Toronto: Addison Wesley Longman, 2001), 79–116; Ernest Akyeampong, "Fact Sheet on Unionization," *Perspectives on Labour and Income* 13, no. 3 (2001): 46–54.

105. John Godard, "Do Labor Laws Matter? The Density Decline and Convergence Thesis Revisited," *Industrial Relations* 42, no. 3 (July 2003): 470.

106. Suzanne Payette, "Yesterday and Today: Union Membership," *Workplace Gazette* 5, no. 3 (Fall 2002): 96.

107. Akyeampong, "Fact Sheet on Unionization," 46–54.

108. Joseph B. Rose, "Competitiveness and Collective Bargaining in Canada," *Workplace Gazette* 7, no. 3 (Spring 2004): 69.

109. Suzanne Payette, "Performance-Based Pay," *Workplace Gazette* 4, no. 3 (Fall 2001): 82–83.

110. Blair Fawcett, "Selective Provisions in Major Collective Agreements: Wage Incentive Plans, 1988–1998," *Workplace Gazette* 1, no. 3 (Fall 1998): 41–44.

111. Ibid., 44.

112. Bureau of National Affairs, *Sourcebook on Collective Bargaining* (Washington, DC: Bureau of National Affairs, 2002), 35.

113. Eileen Applebaum, Thomas Bailey, Peter Berg, and Arne L. Kalleberg, *Manufacturing Advantage: Why High-Performance Work Systems Pay Off* (Ithaca, NY: Cornell University Press, 2000).

114. Bureau of National Affairs, *Sourcebook on Collective Bargaining*, 39.

115. Ibid.

116. Ibid., 35.

117. Ernest B. Akyeampong, "Increased Work Stoppages," *Perspectives on Labour and Income* 18, no. 3 (August 2006): 6–9.

118. Ibid.

119. Ibid.

120. Rachel Beardsmore, "International Comparisons of Labour Disputes in 2004," *Labour Market Trends* 114, no. 4 (April 2006): 117–28.

121. Heather Scoffield, "Canada a World Leader in Hitting the Bricks," *Globe and Mail*, April 6, 2007.

122. Ibid.

123. René Morissette, "Earnings in the Last Decade," *Perspectives on Labour and Income* 9, no. 3 (February 2008): 23.

124. René Morissette, Grant Schellenberg, and Anick Johnson, "Diverging Trends in Unionization," *Perspectives on Labour and Income* 6, no. 4 (April 2005): 7–8.

125. Tony Fang and Anil Verma, "Union Wage Premium," *Perspectives on Labour and Income* 3, no. 9 (September 2002): 13–19.

126. International Monetary Fund, *World Economic Outlook: Spillovers and Cycles in the Global Economy* (Washington, DC: International Monetary Fund, 2007), 162–80.

127. Labor officialdom's views on trade, foreign competition, and the notion of union "partnership" with employers in the United States are featured every Friday in the *Detroit News* in an opinion column called "Labor's Voices." Some examples of trade union leaders' views are Mark Gafney, "Voters Want Fair Trade, Not Free

Trade," *Detroit News,* November 17, 2006; Jeremy W. Peters, "U.A.W. President Is Nominated for a Seat on Daimler-Chrysler Board," *New York Times,* July 4, 2006.

Chapter 6: The North American Auto Industry: The Apex of Concessionary Bargaining

1. "UAW President Says His Union Must Change as Auto Industry Changes," *Washington Post,* March 31, 1999.

2. Harry C. Katz, *Shifting Gears: Changing Labor Relations in the U.S. Automobile Industry* (Cambridge, MA: MIT Press, 1985); Kevin Boyle, *The UAW and the Heyday of American Liberalism: 1945–1968* (Ithaca, NY: Cornell University Press, 1998).

3. U.S. Department of Commerce, Office of Aerospace and Automotive Industries, International Trade Administration, *The Road Ahead for the U.S. Auto Industry* (Washington, DC: U.S. Department of Commerce, 2006), 4.

4. Ibid.

5. Russell Mokhiber and Robert Weissman, "The 10 Worst Corporations of 2005," *Multnational Monitor* 11–12 (November/December 2005): 26.

6. Ibid.

7. Micheline Maynard, "G.M. to Cut 30,000 Jobs and Close Some Factories," *New York Times,* November 21, 2006.

8. Ibid.

9. Ibid.

10. David Shepardson, "UAW Loses 11% of Its Members," *Detroit News,* April 13, 2006; David Shepardson, "UAW Ranks Fall to Post-WWII Low," *Detroit News,* March 31, 2007.

11. John M. Rothgeb Jr., *U.S. Trade Policy* (Washington, DC: Congressional Quarterly Press, 2001), 168–71.

12. Maynard, "G.M. to Cut 30,000 Jobs."

13. "UAW: Expect Sacrifice," *Detroit News,* January 16, 2007.

14. Ibid.

15. Ibid.

16. Bryce G. Hoffman, "Ford Ups CEO Bonus," *Detroit News,* March 1, 2007.

17. Joe Guy Collier, "Pay Climbs for Auto Execs," *Detroit Free Press,* May 6, 2007.

18. Ibid.

19. Bryce G. Hoffman, "Mulally Honeymoon Ends, Tough Questions Begin," *Detroit News,* April 5, 2007.

20. Ibid.

21. Ibid.

22. Ibid.

23. International Labour Organization, *Global Employment Trends, 2008* (Geneva: International Labour Office, 2008), 10.

24. For the best detailed history of the beginnings of the CAW, see the personal

account of Bob White, *Hard Bargains: My Life on the Line* (Toronto: McClelland and Stewart, 1987).

25. Ronald J. Wonnacott, "Mexico and the Canada-US Auto Pact," *The World Economy* 14, no. 1 (1991): 103–12.

26. Jeffrey J. Schott, "Testimony at the Oversight Hearing on Trade Policy and the U.S. Automobile Industry," Peterson Institute for International Economics, February 17, 2006, http://www.iie.com/publications/papers/paper.cfm?ResearchID=612 (accessed November 26, 2007).

27. Canadian Auto Workers (CAW), "Manufacturing Matters," August 2007, http://www.caw.ca/campaigns&issues/ongoingcampaigns/manu-jobs/index.asp (accessed September 24, 2007).

28. Harley Shaiken, *Mexico in the Global Economy: High Technology and Work Organization in Export Industries* (San Diego, CA: Center for U.S Mexican Studies, 1990), 39.

29. J. Werner, "Mexico's Build Hits 1 Million," *Automotive News*, February 8, 1993, 104.

30. Richard Lapper, "Automobiles: NAFTA Drives Car Production," *Financial Times*, June 15, 2008.

31. "Chrysler Group to Build Engine Plant in Mexico," *Detroit News*, June 1, 2007; Michael Ellis, "GM Will Build Plant in Central Mexico," *Detroit Free Press*, April 1, 2006; Sarah A. Webster, "Reports: Ford Considering Plans to Invest $9.2B in Mexico," *Detroit Free Press*, June 15, 2006.

32. Bureau of Labor Statistics, "Hourly Compensation Costs for Production Workers in Manufacturing, 33 Countries or Areas, 22 Manufacturing Industries, 1992–2005," December 20, 2007, http://stats.bls.gov/fls/flshcindnaics.htm (accessed June 7, 2007).

33. Kevin Middlebrook, "The Politics of Industrial Restructuring: Transnational Firms Search for Flexible Production in the Mexican Automobile Industry," *Comparative Politics* 23, no. 3 (April 1991): 275–97.

34. Ibid.

35. Instituto Nacional de Estadística Geografía e Informática (INEGI), *Encuesta Nacional de Empleo, 2000* (Aguascalientes, Mexico: INEGI, 2001), 178.

36. Auto Channel, Reuters News Service, "Ford's Auto Workers Protest Decision for Mexico Plant to Build New Ford Line for U.S.," January 25, 2001, http://www.theautochannel.com/news/2005/01/21/010352.html (accessed June 16, 2007).

37. For a general discussion of the U.S. economy during these years, see Robert Brenner, *The Boom and the Bubble: The U.S. in the World Economy* (London: Verso Books, 2002).

38. For a firsthand account of the Chrysler bankruptcy, see Lee Iacocca and William Novak, *Iacocca* (New York: Bantam, 2007).

39. Ibid.

40. Katz, *Shifting Gears*, 49–72.

41. Henry Guzda, "Conventions: Constitutional Convention Marks Golden Anniversary of the UAW," *Monthly Labor Review* 109, no. 7 (October 1986): 23–25.

42. Ibid.

43. Ibid.

44. Michael Massing, "Detroit's Strange Bedfellows," *New York Times*, February 7, 1988.

45. United Auto Workers and Ford Motor Company, "UAW-Ford National Programs Center," UAW-Ford, December 2006, http://www.uawford.com/about_frameset.html (accessed June 1, 2007).

46. Richard N. Block, "Labor Relations in the Unionized Automobile Assembly Industry in the United States: 1961–2006" (paper presented at the Local Legislative Agenda for the Automotive Partnership Council for North America, Toluca, Mexico, July 19–21, 2006).

47. Ibid.

48. Louis Aguilar, "Delphi Workers Shun Pay Cuts," *Detroit News*, April 19, 2007.

49. Bill Vlasic and Sharon Terlep, "GM Workers Lose Pay for Health Care," *Detroit News*, October 21, 2005.

50. "UAW's GM Suit Seeks Court OK for Cuts," CNNMoney.com, October 19, 2005, http://money.cnn.com/2005/10/19/news/fortune500/gm_uaw_lawsuit/index.htm (accessed June 1, 2007).

51. Jeremy W. Peters, "G.M.'s Jobs Bank Looms as Major Obstacle on Road to Survival," *New York Times*, March 28, 2006.

52. Tom Krisher, "UAW Chief Warns of Changes, Slams Bush," *Washington Post*, June 13, 2006.

53. Bill Vlasic and Brett Clanton, "Delphi Demand: Brutal Cuts," *Detroit News*, October 7, 2005.

54. Ibid.

55. IUE-CWA, "Delphi Bankruptcy Updates," IUE-CWA Division News, April 10, 2006, http://www.iue-cwa.org/news/delphi-bankruptcy-updates.html?page=2 (accessed June 1, 2007).

56. Ibid.

57. Ibid.

58. UAW, "UAW Statement on Delphi Filing for Bankruptcy," UAW-Delphi Update, October 8, 2005, http://www.uaw.org/delphi/delphiupdate.cfm (accessed June 1, 2007).

59. Ibid.

60. Ibid.

61. UAW, "Wages and Labor Costs," UAW: Bargaining for America, August 14, 2003, http://www.uaw.org/barg/03/barg02.cfm (accessed June 1, 2007).

62. "Mexico: Was NAFTA Worth It? A Tale of What Free Trade Can and Cannot Do," *BusinessWeek*, December 22, 2003, http://www.businessweek.com/magazine/content/03_51/b3863008.htm (accessed September 19, 2008).

63. UAW, "UAW Statement on Delphi Filing for Bankruptcy," UAW-Delphi Update, October 8, 2005, http://www.uaw.org/delphi/delphiupdate.cfm (accessed June 1, 2007).

64. Ibid.

65. Ibid.

66. Ibid.; Brett Clanton, "American Axle Targets Labor Costs," *Detroit News*, February 1, 2006.

67. Ibid.

68. UAW, "Wages and Labor Costs," UAW: Bargaining for America, August 14, 2003, http://www.uaw.org/barg/03/barg02.cfm (accessed June 1, 2007).

69. Steve Babson, "Ambiguous Mandate: Lean Production and Labor Relations in the United States," in Huberto Juárez Núñez and Steve Babson, eds., *Confronting Change: Auto Labor and Lean Production in North America/Enfrentando el Cambio: Obreros del Automóvil y Producción Esbelta en América del Norte* (Puebla, Mexico: Autonomous University of Puebla, 1998), 43.

70. Vinnie Tong, "Delphi Bonus Plan OK'd," *Detroit News*, March 23, 2007.

71. Eric Mayne, "Visteon Execs Get Salary Hikes Despite a Sea of Red Ink," *Detroit News*, March 31, 2005.

72. "Hiring of Temporary Workers Pushes G.M. Shares Up 8%," *New York Times*, May 25, 2006.

73. Micheline Maynard and Jeremy W. Peters, "Decision Time in Detroit," *New York Times*, June 9, 2006.

74. Micheline Maynard and Jeremy Peters, "Getting Auto Workers to Leave a Golden Job," *New York Times*, March 22, 2006.

75. Ibid.

76. "UAW Votes to Beef Up Organizing Efforts, General Fund," *Detroit News*, June 13, 2006.

77. UAW, "Strikes," August 2001, http://www.uaw.org/about/works/strikes.html (accessed June 2, 2007).

78. Block, "Labor Relations in the Unionized Automobile Assembly Industry."

79. "UAW Votes to Beef Up Organizing Efforts, General Fund," *Detroit News*, June 13, 2006.

80. Keith Bradsher, "General Motors and Union Agree to End Walkout," *New York Times*, March 22, 1996.

81. Andrew Herod, "Implications of Just-in-Time Production for Union Strategy: Lessons from the 1998 General Motors-United Auto Workers Dispute," *Annals of the Association of American Geographers* 90, no. 3 (September 2000): 521–47.

82. Ibid.

83. "Has the UAW Found a Better Road?" *BusinessWeek*, July 15, 2002, http://www.businessweek.com/magazine/content/02_28/b3791006.htm (accessed September 19, 2008).

84. Ibid.

85. Sharon Terlep, "Workers: UAW Got Best Deal," *Detroit News,* June 26, 2007.

86. Tom Krisher, "UAW Workers Begin Voting on Deal with Delphi, GM," *Detroit Free Press,* June 28, 2007.

87. Sharon Terlep, "UAW Members Ratify Delphi Contract," *Detroit News,* June 28, 2007.

88. Ibid.

89. "IUE-CWA Members Ratify New 4–year Delphi Contract," *Detroit Free Press,* August 19, 2007.

90. Ibid.

91. Thomas Gnau, "Delphi Workers OK Deal That Closes Local Plant," *Dayton Daily News,* August 20, 2007.

92. Micheline Maynard, "U.A.W. Pact with Dana Signals Softer Stance," *New York Times,* July 7, 2007.

93. Bryce G. Hoffman, "UAW to Run Dana Retiree Benefits," *Detroit News,* July 7, 2007.

94. Ron Gettelfinger, "Reject Unfair Deal on Trade with Korea," *Detroit News,* April 6, 2007.

95. "Commentary: Can the UAW Stay in the Game?" *Business Week,* June 10, 2002, http://www.businessweek.com/magazine/content/02_23/b3786077.htm (accessed September 19, 2008).

96. Ibid.

97. Dana Frank, *Buy American: The Untold Story of Economic Nationalism* (Boston: Beacon Press, 1999), 131.

98. John Flesher, "UAW Chief Gettelfinger Renews Attacks on Delphi Corp," *Detroit News,* May 31, 2007.

Chapter 7: VEBA Las Vegas! Unions Play Casino Capitalism: Autoworkers Lose

1. Sharon Terlep, "New Era Begins for Big 3," *Detroit News,* November 15, 2007.

2. Sarah A. Webster, "UAW-GM Deal Cuts COLA Pay," *Detroit Free Press,* October 4, 2007.

3. David Shepardson, "UAW Loses 11% of Its Members," *Detroit News,* April 13, 2006.

4. Sharon Terlep and Louis Aguilar, "Detroit to Build GM's Car of Future," *Detroit News,* September 29, 2007.

5. Santiago Esparza, Nathan Hurst, and Eric Morath, "Workers Relieved; Impatient to Hear Terms of UAW-GM Deal," *Detroit News,* September 27, 2007.

6. Tom Walsh, "Striking Workers Want Answers," *Detroit Free Press,* September 26, 2007.

7. Esparza, Hurst, and Morath, "Workers Relieved."

8. Tom Walsh, "UAW Strikers Are Asking Why," *Detroit Free Press,* September 26, 2007.

9. "Full Text of UAW Press Release," *Detroit News*, September 24, 2007.

10. Ibid.

11. Micheline Maynard and Nick Bunkley, "GM and Union Reach Tentative Agreement," *New York Times*, September 26, 2007.

12. UAW, "Union Advantage: June 2007," *Just the Facts: Economics for Working People*, September 21, 2007, http://www.uaw.org/facts/index.cfm (accessed November 26, 2007).

13. Bill Vlasic and Sharon Terlep, "Historic Deal Shrinks Gap," *Detroit News*, September 27, 2007.

14. Bryce G. Hoffman and David Shepardson, "With Health Deal, UAW's Clout, Influence Grow," *Detroit News*, September 27, 2007.

15. Webster, "UAW-GM Deal Cuts COLA Pay."

16. Sharon Terlep, "GM Job Costs to Plummet," *Detroit News*, October 16, 2007.

17. Kate Merx, "Manufacturing Jobs, UAW at Risk with 2–Tier Wage," *Detroit Free Press*, October 4, 2007.

18. Joseph B. White, John D. Stoll, and Jeffrey McCracken, "GM Labor Deal Ushers In New Era for Auto Industry," *Wall Street Journal*, September 27, 2007.

19. Ibid.

20. Vlasic and Terlep, "Historic Deal Shrinks Gap."

21. Webster, "UAW-GM Deal Cuts COLA Pay."

22. Sharon Terlep, "GM Workers So Far Favor Contract," *Detroit News*, October 4, 2007.

23. Vlasic and Terlep, "Historic Deal Shrinks Gap."

24. Ibid.

25. Tiffany Kary, "37.6M Delphi Bonus Plan OK'd," *Detroit News*, September 28, 2007.

26. Louis Aguilar and Sharon Terlep, "GM Deal Rejected by Some Plants," *Detroit News*, October 6, 2007.

27. Bryce G. Hoffman, "Most Back UAW-GM Pact," *Detroit News*, October 10, 2007.

28. Sharon Terlep, "Shares at GM Highest Since 2004," *Detroit News*, October 13, 2007.

29. Sharon Terlep, "GM's UAW Members Approve Labor Deal," *Detroit News*, October 10, 2007.

30. Barbara Wieland, "Workers Get Short Reprieve from GM," *Lansing State Journal*, November 8, 2007.

31. John Gallagher, Jennifer Dixon, M. L. Elrick, and John Wisely, "Improved Prognosis: GM-UAW Agreement Begins New Era for Organized Labor," *Detroit Free Press*, September 30, 2007.

32. Ibid.

33. David Shepardson, "Workers Challenge GM Health Care Plan," *Detroit News*, October 10, 2007.

34. Ibid.

35. Nathan Hurst and Louis Aguilar, "Workers Happy Strike Was Short but Anxious to Hear Details," *Detroit News*, October 11, 2007.

36. Ibid.

37. Sharon Terlep, "New Deal, New Layoffs for GM," *Detroit Free Press*, October 25, 2007.

38. Ibid.

39. Ibid.

40. Louis Aguilar, "Chrysler Deal Riles UAW Ranks," *Detroit News*, October 19, 2007.

41. Ibid.

42. Ibid.

43. Eric Morath, "Chrysler Deal May Be Sealed Today," *Detroit News*, October 27, 2007.

44. Eric Morath and Louis Aguilar, "UAW-Chrysler Pact Vote Too Close to Call," *Detroit News*, October 24, 2007.

45. Ibid.

46. Ibid.

47. Ibid.

48. Ibid.

49. Eric Morath and Nathan Hurst, "More Locals Vote on the Chrysler Deal," *Detroit News*, October 20, 2007.

50. Ibid.

51. Ibid.

52. Jui Chakravorty and Kevin Krolicki, "Chrysler-UAW Deal Backed by Secret Product Pledge," *Boston Globe*, October 22, 2007.

53. Sholnn Freeman, "UAW Leaders Hit the Shop Floor to Lobby Workers on Chrysler Deal," *Washington Post*, October 24, 2007.

54. Ibid.

55. Bill Vlasic, Louis Aguilar, and Eric Morath, "Chrysler Contract Narrowly Ahead," *Detroit News*, October 23, 2007.

56. Ibid.

57. Tim Higgins, "Independent Oversight Lacking," *Detroit Free Press*, October 24, 2007.

58. Louis Aguilar, "Chrysler Workers Approve UAW Contract," *Detroit News*, October 27, 2007.

59. Nick Bunkley, "Chrysler Chief Calls Pay Pact Revolutionary," *Wall Street Journal*, October 30, 2007.

60. Ibid.

61. Bill Vlasic and Sharon Terlep, "Cerberus Shrinks Chrysler," *Detroit News*, November 2, 2007.

62. Ibid.

63. Louis Aguilar and Eric Morath, "Job Promises Don't Mean Much," *Detroit News,* November 2, 2007.

64. Ibid.

65. Ibid.

66. Ibid.

67. Mike Spector and Jeffrey McKracken, "UAW Seeks to Build Support for Ford Deal," *Wall Street Journal,* November 5, 2007.

68. Bryce G. Hoffman, "Ford Narrows Asian Labor Gap," *Detroit News,* November 16, 2007.

69. Ibid.

70. Terlep, "New Era Begins for Big 3."

71. Ibid.

72. Hoffman, "Ford Narrows Asian Labor Gap."

73. UAW, "UAW Ford Bargainers Preserve Jobs, Protect Wages and Benefits," November 2007, http://www.uaw.org/contracts/07/ford/hrly/index.php (accessed November 23, 2007).

74. Bryce G. Hoffman, "Ford Workers Fret as Issues Prolong Talks," *Detroit News,* November 2, 2007.

75. Bryce G. Hoffman and Louis Aguilar, "Key Ford Plants Approve UAW Pact," *Detroit News,* November 12, 2007.

76. Ibid.

77. Bryce G. Hoffman and Louis Aguilar, "Ford to Invest in Its Michigan Factories," *Detroit News,* November 6, 2007.

78. Tony Van Alphen, "CAW to Resist GM's Deal," *Toronto Star,* August 27, 2007.

79. Ibid.

80. Frank Stronach and Buzz Hargrove, "For the Sake of the Auto Industry, We've Put Aside Our Differences," *Globe and Mail,* October 17, 2007.

81. Greg Kennan, "Magna's Union Deal: No Strikes," *Globe and Mail,* October 16, 2007.

82. Tony Van Alphen, "Hargrove Gambles with Magna Deal," *Toronto Star,* October 20, 2007.

83. Ibid.

84. Ibid.

85. Ibid.

86. Bob White, "Unions Have to Innovate to Better Serve Workers," *Toronto Star,* October 30, 2007.

87. Greg Kennan, "CAW Rift Deepens over Magna Pact," *Globe and Mail,* October 30, 2007.

88. Ian Austen, "Canadian Industrialist Urges Workers to Join Union," *New York Times,* October 16, 2007.

89. Ibid.

90. Kennan, "Magna's Union Deal."

91. Steven Chase and Greg Keenan, "Manufacturers Seek Relief from High-Flying Loonie," *Globe and Mail,* November 21, 2007.

92. Ibid.

93. Ibid.

94. John McCrank, "Ford Canada CEO Warns of 'Unfair' Deal with South Korea," Reuters News Service, November 22, 2007, http://www.reuters.com/article/tnBasicIndustries-SP/idUSN2226992220071122 (accessed November 30, 2007).

95. John McCrank, "GM-UAW Deal Is Way of the Future," Reuters News Service, October 10, 2007, http://www.reuters.com/article/reutersEdge/idUSN1044883820071010 (accessed November 30, 2007).

96. Sharon Terlep, "CAW faces GM, Chrysler Hurdles," *Detroit News,* May 6, 2008.

97. "Canadian Auto Workers at Four GM Plants Ratify New Deal," *International Herald Tribune,* May 18, 2008.

98. Ibid.

99. Linda Nguyen, "CAW Wins New Models, Rich Buyouts in Deal with GM," *Financial Post,* July 28, 2008.

100. Nicolas Van Praet, "Cut Wages or Lose Industry, Magna Tells Automakers," *Financial Post,* May 2, 2008.

101. Tom Walsh, "Union Warned of Outsourcing," *Detroit Free Press,* March 27, 2008.

102. Jewell Gopwani, "American Axle Said to Move Work to Mexico," *Detroit Free Press,* March 20, 2008.

103. "Race to the Bottom: Mexico Lowers Wages to Snare International Auto Production," *International Herald Tribune,* June 5, 2008.

104. Ibid.

105. Ibid.

106. Ibid.

107. Ralph Armbruster, "Cross-Border Labor Organizing in the Garment and Automobile Industries: The Phillips Van-Heusen and Ford Cuautitlán Cases," *Journal of World-Systems Research* 4, no. 1 (Winter 1998): 30–33.

108. Ibid.

109. Justin Hyde, "UAW Membership Drops 14%," *Detroit Free Press,* March 25, 2008.

Index

NORMAN CAULFIELD is a history professor at Fort Hays State University in Hays, Kansas. He is the author of *Mexican Workers and the State: From Porfiriato to NAFTA*. From 2002 to 2005, he worked in the secretariat of the Commission for Labor Cooperation in Washington, DC, an organization created by the labor side agreement to NAFTA.

Workers on the Waterfront: Seamen, Longshoremen, and Unionism in the 1930s
   Bruce Nelson
German Workers in Chicago: A Documentary History of Working-Class Culture from
   1850 to World War I   *Edited by Hartmut Keil and John B. Jentz*
On the Line: Essays in the History of Auto Work   *Edited by Nelson Lichtenstein and
   Stephen Meyer III*
Labor's Flaming Youth: Telephone Operators and Worker Militancy, 1878–1923
   Stephen H. Norwood
Another Civil War: Labor, Capital, and the State in the Anthracite Regions of
   Pennsylvania, 1840–68   *Grace Palladino*
Coal, Class, and Color: Blacks in Southern West Virginia, 1915–32
   Joe William Trotter, Jr.
For Democracy, Workers, and God: Labor Song-Poems and Labor Protest, 1865–95
   Clark D. Halker
Dishing It Out: Waitresses and Their Unions in the Twentieth Century
   Dorothy Sue Cobble
The Spirit of 1848: German Immigrants, Labor Conflict, and the Coming of the Civil
   War   *Bruce Levine*
Working Women of Collar City: Gender, Class, and Community in Troy, New York,
   1864–86   *Carole Turbin*
Southern Labor and Black Civil Rights: Organizing Memphis Workers
   Michael K. Honey
Radicals of the Worst Sort: Laboring Women in Lawrence, Massachusetts, 1860–1912
   Ardis Cameron
Producers, Proletarians, and Politicians: Workers and Party Politics in Evansville and
   New Albany, Indiana, 1850–87   *Lawrence M. Lipin*
The New Left and Labor in the 1960s   *Peter B. Levy*
The Making of Western Labor Radicalism: Denver's Organized Workers, 1878–1905
   David Brundage
In Search of the Working Class: Essays in American Labor History and Political
   Culture   *Leon Fink*
Lawyers against Labor: From Individual Rights to Corporate Liberalism
   Daniel R. Ernst
"We Are All Leaders": The Alternative Unionism of the Early 1930s   *Edited by
   Staughton Lynd*
The Female Economy: The Millinery and Dressmaking Trades, 1860–1930
   Wendy Gamber
"Negro and White, Unite and Fight!": A Social History of Industrial Unionism in
   Meatpacking, 1930–90   *Roger Horowitz*
Power at Odds: The 1922 National Railroad Shopmen's Strike   *Colin J. Davis*
The Common Ground of Womanhood: Class, Gender, and Working Girls' Clubs,
   1884–1928   *Priscilla Murolo*
Marching Together: Women of the Brotherhood of Sleeping Car Porters
   Melinda Chateauvert

Down on the Killing Floor: Black and White Workers in Chicago's Packinghouses,
  1904–54   *Rick Halpern*
Labor and Urban Politics: Class Conflict and the Origins of Modern Liberalism in
  Chicago, 1864–97   *Richard Schneirov*
All That Glitters: Class, Conflict, and Community in Cripple Creek
  Elizabeth Jameson
Waterfront Workers: New Perspectives on Race and Class   *Edited by Calvin Winslow*
Labor Histories: Class, Politics, and the Working-Class Experience   *Edited by
  Eric Arnesen, Julie Greene, and Bruce Laurie*
The Pullman Strike and the Crisis of the 1890s: Essays on Labor and Politics
  Edited by Richard Schneirov, Shelton Stromquist, and Nick Salvatore
AlabamaNorth: African-American Migrants, Community, and Working-Class
  Activism in Cleveland, 1914–45   *Kimberley L. Phillips*
Imagining Internationalism in American and British Labor, 1939–49   *Victor Silverman*
William Z. Foster and the Tragedy of American Radicalism   *James R. Barrett*
Colliers across the Sea: A Comparative Study of Class Formation in Scotland and the
  American Midwest, 1830–1924   *John H. M. Laslett*
"Rights, Not Roses": Unions and the Rise of Working-Class Feminism, 1945–80
  Dennis A. Deslippe
Testing the New Deal: The General Textile Strike of 1934 in the American South
  Janet Irons
Hard Work: The Making of Labor History   *Melvyn Dubofsky*
Southern Workers and the Search for Community: Spartanburg County, South
  Carolina   *G. C. Waldrep III*
We Shall Be All: A History of the Industrial Workers of the World (abridged edition)
  Melvyn Dubofsky, ed. Joseph A. McCartin
Race, Class, and Power in the Alabama Coalfields, 1908–21   *Brian Kelly*
Duquesne and the Rise of Steel Unionism   *James D. Rose*
Anaconda: Labor, Community, and Culture in Montana's Smelter City   *Laurie Mercier*
Bridgeport's Socialist New Deal, 1915–36   *Cecelia Bucki*
Indispensable Outcasts: Hobo Workers and Community in the American Midwest,
  1880–1930   *Frank Tobias Higbie*
After the Strike: A Century of Labor Struggle at Pullman   *Susan Eleanor Hirsch*
Corruption and Reform in the Teamsters Union   *David Witwer*
Waterfront Revolts: New York and London Dockworkers, 1946–61   *Colin J. Davis*
Black Workers' Struggle for Equality in Birmingham   *Horace Huntley and
  David Montgomery*
The Tribe of Black Ulysses: African American Men in the Industrial South
  William P. Jones
City of Clerks: Office and Sales Workers in Philadelphia, 1870–1920
  Jerome P. Bjelopera
Reinventing "The People": The Progressive Movement, the Class Problem, and the
  Origins of Modern Liberalism   *Shelton Stromquist*
Radical Unionism in the Midwest, 1900–1950   *Rosemary Feurer*

The University of Illinois Press
is a founding member of the
Association of American University Presses.

Composed in 10.5/13 Adobe Minion Pro
with FF Meta display
at the University of Illinois Press
Manufactured by Cushing-Malloy, Inc.

University of Illinois Press
1325 South Oak Street
Champaign, IL 61820-6903
www.press.uillinois.edu

1801